A Turn in the South

V. S. Naipaul was born in Trinidad in 1932. He went to England on a scholarship in 1950. After four years at University College, Oxford, he began to write, and since then has followed no other profession. He has published more than twenty books of fiction and non-fiction, including *Half a Life*, *A House for Mr Biswas*, *A Bend in the River* and most recently *The Masque of Africa*, and a collection of correspondence, *Letters Between a Father and Son*. In 2001 he was awarded the Nobel Prize in Literature.

ALSO BY V. S. NAIPAUL

FICTION

The Mystic Masseur
The Suffrage of Elvira
Miguel Street
A House for Mr Biswas
Mr Stone and the Knights Companion
The Mimic Men
A Flag on the Island
In a Free State
Guerrillas
A Bend in the River
The Enigma of Arrival
A Way in the World
Half a Life
Magic Seeds
In a Free State

NON-FICTION

The Middle Passage
An Area of Darkness
The Loss of El Dorado
The Overcrowded Barracoon
India: A Wounded Civilization
The Return of Eva Perón
Among the Believers: An Islamic Journey
Finding the Centre
India: A Million Mutinies Now
Beyond Belief
Letters Between a Father and Son
The Writer and the World: Essays
Literary Occasions
A Writer's People: Ways of Looking and Feeling
The Masque of Africa

V. S. NAIPAUL

A Turn in the South

PICADOR

First published 1989 by Vintage Books, a division of Random House, Inc., New York

First published in Great Britain 2003 by Picador

This edition published 2011 by Picador
an imprint of Pan Macmillan, a division of Macmillan Publishers Limited
Pan Macmillan, 20 New Wharf Road, London N1 9RR
Basingstoke and Oxford
Associated companies throughout the world
www.panmacmillan.com

ISBN 978-0-330-52294-6

Grateful ... viously
published ...

Louisiana S... Press. Sele... from the poetry of *James Applewhite*. ...eprinted by
permission. *... Songwriter Guild of Amer...* ...thy O'Brien.
Copyright © 1987 by Pinspotter Music, Inc. Pursuant to sections 104(c) and 401(b) of the U. S.
Copyright Act, all rights administered by The Sec... Songwriters Guild of America. *Warner Chappell Music
Inc.*: Excerpt from 'Eighteen Wheels and a D... ...son. Copyright
© 1988 by Warner Tamerline Publishing Corp., Bellamie and Nice Music, Screen Gems-EMI Music.
All rights reserved. Used by permission. *Polygram International Publishing Companies*: Excerpt
from 'Good Ole Boys Like Me' by Bob McDill. Copyright © 1979 by Polygram International
Publishing, Inc. International copyright secured. All rights reserved. Used by permission.

1 3 5 7 9 8 6 4 2

A CIP catalogue record for this book is available from
the British Library.

Printed in the UK by CPI Mackays, Chatham ME5 8TD

Visit **www.picador.com** to read more about all our books
and to buy them. You will also find features, author interviews and
news of any author events, and you can sign up for e-newsletters
so that you're always first to hear about our new releases.

A Turn in the South was written in an extraordinary period of excitement in 1987. Not the excitement of a week or month, but excitement that lasted as long as the first draft was being written – about five or six months. I use the word excitement with care: when I was writing the draft I didn't like being physically separated from it. I grudged every moment when this happened; and people I wanted to meet could be puzzled by what must have looked to them as strangely bad behaviour: asking them to come, kindly strangers, and then backing off.

I have often wondered about this excitement, which I had never known before. Much of it would of course have had to do with the nature of the southern material, the extraordinary history, the extraordinary language, all so remarkably accessible, even to someone from far away, requiring only a simple journey to enter.

The book written with this afflatus didn't have an easy passage on publication. Some people thought my use of southern speech was overdone, was at times too mechanical, and made for hard reading. This was not easy for me to take, since the language was so much part of my enchantment with the material. It gradually came to me, however, that a more varied tone would have made for better writing and served the book better. A more serious criticism was of the book's poor political judgement. I wasn't aware that the book had this kind of judgement. My feeling was that the book was fair, not coming down on one racial side or the other; it took some time for me to understand the difficult truth that where the history was so bad, impartiality could come out as prejudice. If I had understood this at the beginning it would have been hard to get started on the book.

I suppose that at the end of the day the point of all this worry about the material of *A Turn in the South* has to do with the nature of writing rather than the book's politics or history. And the worry might be put like this: however beguiling the subject of a work, whatever its excitement, the writer must never fail to exercise his literary judgement.

SEEPERSAD NAIPAUL
14 April 1906
3 October 1953
In ever renewed homage

CONTENTS

A Turn in the South

Down Home:
A Landscape of Small Ruins

J IMMY WORKED in New York as a designer and lettering artist. Howard was his assistant. Jimmy, who could become depressed at times, said to Howard one day, "Howard, if I had to give up, and you couldn't get another job, what would you do?" Howard, who was from the South, said, "I would go home to my mama."

Jimmy was as struck by this as I was when Jimmy told me: that Howard had something neither Jimmy nor I had, a patch of the earth he thought of as home, absolutely his. And that was where—many months after I had heard this story—I thought I should begin this book about the South: with the home that Howard had.

Howard arranged the visit. Jimmy decided to come with us. We went on the Easter weekend; the timing was pure chance.

It was raining, had been raining in New York for two days.

At La Guardia Howard said, "I hated the place when I was young, for the continuity."

I thought he meant historical continuity, the past living on. But from other things he then said, I felt he meant only that it was a country place where little changed and little happened. I had this trouble with Howard's words sometimes; I was too ready to find in them meanings he didn't intend.

Howard was six feet tall, but slender and light of movement. He was in his late twenties or early thirties. He was very much his own

3

man. He lived alone, and he preferred not to live in Harlem. He was a serious reader of newspapers and magazines, and he had a special interest in foreign affairs. He liked to cook; and he kept himself fit by playing paddle ball on weekends. He was easy to be with, not spiky; and I put this down in part to the home he was so sure of and still close to.

Howard said, "You see how the South begins. More black people here, on the plane."

Most of the passengers were black, and they were not like an African or West Indian crowd. They were almost subdued, going home from the big city for Easter.

We landed at Greensboro. It was a big airport; and then, just a few minutes away, proof of the scale of things here, there was another airport, just as big. We got off there. There were military people in the waiting areas. It was warmer than in New York; I changed into a lighter jacket.

Soon we were on the highway.

Howard said, "Look, the dogwood and the pines. It is what you see a lot of in the South."

The dogwood was a small tree, and it was now in single-petaled white blossom. Not the dogwood of England, the water-loving red-stemmed shrub or small tree that made a bright autumn and winter show. And there were—Howard identified them for me—oaks and maples, in the freshest spring-green.

The land was flat, like the pampas of Argentina or the llanos of Venezuela. But trees bordered the fields and gave a human scale to things. We passed tobacco barns, tallish, squarish, corrugated-iron structures, where in the old days tobacco was cured. They were in decay, the corrugated iron rusted dark red, the wood weathered gray. Against the green this corrugated-iron rust was a lovely color; it gave an extra beauty to the land.

The highway looked like highways everywhere else in the United States: boards for motels and restaurants and gas stations.

Tobacco was still a crop. We saw the seedlings being mechanically planted: one black man on the tractor, two men on the trolley behind dropping earth-rooted seedlings down a shafted dibble. All this used to be done by hand, Howard said. He picked tobacco in the school holidays. The resin from the green leaf stained his hands black and was hard to clean off. I never knew about this black-staining resin from the green leaf, but it was immediately comprehensible. It was for that resin, that tar, that people smoked the cured leaf.

We had driven so fast on the highway that we were in Howard's area almost before I was ready for it. There was a small town center, a small rich white suburb attached to that town, and then outside that a black area. The differences were noticeable. But Howard, near his home now, appeared to claim both the white area and the black area.

He had been excited all morning; he was more excited now. And then, entering another little town, we were seeing the places he had known as a boy. He had cut the grass and cleaned the swimming pool and mopped the porch of that house, the Bowen house, the house of the people who still more or less owned the little town that was called Bowen. And he had done the same job for people in that other house.

That little green wooden house, now closed up, just beside the highway, had been his mother's house. He had grown up there. His mother lived in another house now; another house—bigger and newer —was home. We saw it from the highway. It was a concrete-block house set back from the road, behind some other houses: not the old, tree-embowered house I had had in my imagination. We didn't stop; we were going first to the motel, which was some way outside the town.

The main building of the motel was a loghouse. In the sandy yard there were subsidiary little barracklike room-rows below trees and behind shrubs. A black boy was hosing down the veranda floor of the loghouse. He looked timid—for the first time that morning I had a feeling of racial constraint—and he said the office was inside.

There was no apparent office. Only an empty low-ceilinged room with two or three close-set rows of little tables with red- or blue-checked tablecloths. The air conditioning had been turned off a long time before, and the air was dead and smelly.

Howard called out, and after some time a young white man in shorts, with a yellow plastic apron and a large kitchen knife, came in from the back, through two doors. He was sallow, open-mouthed, and his movements were uncoordinated. A little while later a fat old white woman with a twisted face came in through the same two doors. I felt we had been wrong to disturb them, the old woman and the young man who was really a boy.

Two rooms? Would we want two double rooms or two single rooms?

I couldn't understand the old woman's questions. But then, putting down his knife, the boy with the shorts and the yellow plastic apron half beckoned to us, and we followed him—he walked with stamping, awkward steps—out of the dining room to the sandy yard below the pine trees, and then to a low building at the edge of the yard. The ground there was damp; and the small rooms that the boy opened up, one after the other, had the dampness of the ground, with a shut-in, old smell, and with stained cheap carpets.

Better judgment was at work, however. And even while Jimmy and I were looking at the rooms with the silent boy in the yellow apron, Howard—who had not followed us—had heard from somebody in the motel (perhaps the old woman with the twisted face) that there was a more up-to-date motel in the next town, Peters. (Bowen, Peters: American places, big and small, are often named after people; and the ordinariness of the names can make some itineraries read like the muster of an army squad or a sports team.)

To Peters, then, we went, through the highway landscape. And the Peters motel was an altogether bigger affair, with a number of two-story buildings in red brick. It even advertised a swimming pool (though something had happened to the filter, and the pool was green with algae).

Howard, going up the steps ahead of us and entering the office through the two doors, turned to me and said mysteriously, with a touch of humor, "This is something for you."

And what he meant by that was that the lady in the office was Indian, unmistakably, Indian from India, though she was not in a sari, and though there was an un-Indian confidence in her voice and manner. Her speech was American—to me. It let her down only once, when she said, in her brisk, undeferential way, that coffee and things like that were not available on the "pre-mises," making the word rhyme with "vices." That was Indian; that had a flavor of India.

I heard later from Howard that in the last six years or so Indians from India had been buying the motels in the South from white people. (And this perhaps explained the big neon sign, AMERICAN OWNED, that I saw some time later on a motel in northwestern Georgia.)

So there, in the place that was home to Howard: the white folk, who might have come out of a novel; and, not far away, people from the other side of the world who were already making themselves American, according to the special idea they would have had of the word.

The motel lady's husband came into the office. He too was Indian.

He wore a short-sleeved fawn-colored velour shirt, and he had a Texas accent—or so it seemed to me. His wife had said (and he now confirmed) that he had been in the oil business, as a petroleum engineer, in Houston. He had left oil and Houston six years before; and he thought (as his wife had said earlier, though admitting that Peters, North Carolina, was a very quiet place) he had made a good decision.

HETTY'S HOUSE, Howard's new home, had been built in parts by Hetty herself, with her own hands. It was set back from the road, behind other houses in the settlement, and a drive led to it from the highway. The site had been well chosen. The house had a front portico with steps on either side, and a porch-garage at the end of the drive from the highway. At the back of the house was woodland.

The fluffy, carpeted, upholstered sitting room was welcoming. In one corner was the kitchen, with a dining or serving counter. The bedrooms and general rooms were on either side of a central corridor that ran off from the sitting room.

Hetty was a big but shapely woman. She was sixty, but her skin was still good. She wore glasses. She made a great deal of friendly noise welcoming Jimmy, whom she knew; and Howard acted out the role of the son returning home. He sat on a high stool in front of the kitchen counter, relaxed, his limbs elegantly arranged, one leg folded, one leg straight: in this house a son and now, in addition, half our host. On the wall beside the door that led to the porch-garage there were family photographs, including one of Howard in a graduation gown.

We had lunch: fried fish, collard greens, sweet potatoes with the color of boiled carrots. Four of us sat at the dining table in the dining part of the front reception room.

While we were sitting—I with my back to the front door, which opened out onto the portico with the steps on either side—there were great shouts. A party had arrived: Hetty's sister from Augusta, Dee-Anna (as I heard the name), and Dee-Anna's husband and son. Dee-Anna didn't look like Hetty. She was much bigger and more full of bulges than Hetty, and darker (Hetty was brown). She was more vivacious—acting up a little to her figure—but she had more searching eyes. She didn't have Hetty's serenity.

Dee-Anna's son seemed sloppily dressed at first, but then I saw that his outfit had been assembled with care and was absolutely for show: a

slate-blue jacket in the contemporary shapeless style, a shining, tex-
tured white shirt, tapered trousers with patches and exposed labels,
and new shoes (new from the near-white appearance of the instep).
Easter visitors; holiday dressing up.

They talked for a while about a recent big boxing match. They all
liked the winner. Howard said he was like a modern black man, smooth
and educated; the other fellow was big and strong, but rougher.

The young man with the contemporary clothes asked what I was
doing in North Carolina.

When I told him, he said, "What sort of book? Historical?"

And when Howard and I explained, Dee-Anna said, with a knitting
of her brows, "I hope you are not going to give us the gloom."

Her son—his seriousness now seeming quite separate from his
clothes—said, "We've had too much of the past." They were not interested in the past; they were interested in the present.

IT HAD not occurred to me to ask whether Hetty did a job. Howard
hadn't told me; and it was only after we had got to the house that I
gathered that she worked part-time in the café side of a convenience
store that was owned by the present head of the Bowen family. She
took Jimmy and me to meet him after lunch. She said he was a good
man.

The convenience store was only one of Mr. Bowen's interests. We
went to see him in his furniture factory. He said that he wasn't really a
Bowen. He had only married into the family, but people spoke of him
as a Bowen, and he had grown to accept the name. The first record of
the name in the town of Bowen was a few years before the Declaration
of Independence, but at that time the name of the town was Lawrence
(which suggested some kind of dispossession during or after the War
of Independence).

History, though, wasn't what Mr. Bowen wanted to talk about. He
was a big man in his early sixties, and he wanted Jimmy and me to see
the furniture he made; he wanted to talk about business in Bowen; he
wanted us to know that the little town was a go-ahead place, that,
though it had only a few thousand people, there were very many millions deposited in the local banks. He was a Bowen man through and
through; and while he gave us all the figures, walking Jimmy and me

round the furniture factory, showing us the things he or his machines did with veneers, Hetty stood aside, in her full denim skirt, with something of Howard's elegance in her posture.

Bowen—I had never heard of the name of the place until Howard had told me. And here it was everywhere, attached to every kind of local business, farm equipment and agricultural supplies, general store, video rentals, gas station, furniture, convenience store.

He was a good man, Hetty said again, after we had left Mr. Bowen and the furniture factory. She had gone to him when she wanted $5,000 for her house. He had spoken that same day to the bank, and a loan had been arranged, and all that the bank had required as security was Hetty's car and some other small thing. And Mr. Bowen was a religious man, Hetty said. He had given land for the black cemetery. She had a family plot there, with carved headstones.

We drove through suburban woodland to the cemetery. We drove up almost to the headstones. Hetty wanted us to see them, but she didn't encourage us to get out of the car. We stayed in the car and looked for a while. It was a small cemetery, not set apart by a fence or any kind of planting. Now, with all the spring growth, it was like part of the woodland.

One of the headstones was of Hetty's father. When we were back in the house she told us something about him. He was a smart man; there had always been a lot of food in the house because of him. He worked on a farm for a white man—and I was beginning to understand how necessary it was for Hetty to define people in the way she did. The white man took no interest in his farm. Hetty's father did it all for him, the selling of the produce and everything. Now the farmhouse—where Hetty's father had lived and died—had deteriorated. It was still owned by the white family, but they didn't want to sell; they wanted to keep it for the memory.

Where did this father of Hetty's come from? He had died in 1961. Had he perhaps been born around 1900? In 1894, Howard said. That was the year on the headstone in the black cemetery, on the land given by Mr. Bowen. And the story of the father was vague. He had been orphaned; he had run away from a difficult uncle and had found a job on the railroad and had then fetched up here, sharecropping for Mr. Smith, the white man, and ending successfully, being one of the first black men in the area to own a car. It was not possible to get more about this father, to push back further into time. Beyond that was vagueness, and the gloom Hetty's sister and the sister's son, and perhaps all black people, had had too much of.

Later, after a nap—Jimmy in one of the bedrooms of Hetty's house, I in another—and after tea, we went out for a drive. Hetty knew the land well; she knew who owned what. It was like a chant from her, as we drove.

"Black people there, black people there, white people there. Black people, black people, white people, black people. All this side black people, all this side white people. White people, white people, black people, white people."

Sometimes she said, "Black people used to own this land." She didn't like that—that black people had lost land because they had been slack or because of family disputes. But blacks and whites appeared here to live quite close to one another, and Hetty herself had no racial complaints. White people had been good to her, she said. But then she said that that might have been only because she liked people.

It was a landscape of small ruins. Houses and farmhouses and tobacco barns had simply been abandoned. The decay of each was individual, and they were all beautiful in the afternoon light. Some farmhouses had very wide eaves, going down low, the corrugated iron that once provided shelter now like a too-heavy weight, the corrugated-iron sheets sagging, fanning out in places.

We went to see the house, now abandoned, where Hetty's father had lived when he had sharecropped for Mr. Smith. Bush grew right up against the open house. The pecan trees, still almost bare, just a few leaves now, were tall above the house and the tobacco barns. The colors were gray (tree trunks and weathered timber) and red (rusted corrugated iron) and green and the straw-gold of reeds. As we stood there Hetty told us of the death of her father in that house; the event was still vivid to her.

Another house, even more beautiful, was where Hetty and her husband had lived for ten years. It was a farmhouse with a big green field, with forest trees bounding the distance on every side.

Home was not for Howard just his mother's house, the little green house that was now closed up, or the new concrete-block house she had moved to. Home was what we had seen. And we had seen only a part: all about these country roads, within a few miles, were houses and fields connected with various members of Howard's family. It was a richer and more complicated past than I had imagined; and physically much more beautiful. The houses I was taken to were bigger than the houses many people in Trinidad or England might have lived in.

But, still, in the past there was that point where darkness fell, the historical darkness, even here, which was home.

We went to dinner at the Seafood Bar-B-Q. It was really the only place possible. It was a roadhouse, a big dimly lit room with a silent jukebox and a few dressed-up white family groups. Beer couldn't be served. So we had the iced tea, which Howard said was very Southern. It was syrupy, the taste no doubt of the waitresses, who were white and young and friendly. One of them was very young, perhaps about twelve, and delighted to be dressed like a waitress, helping out a sister or a parent during the holiday weekend, serving goodies.

I asked Hetty what she wanted for herself and her family. Her reply was strange and moving. For her family, she said, she wished that one of her sons had been cured of his drinking. And this was strange because it was a look backwards: the son she spoke of was dead.

For herself, she said she would like, if it were possible, to get married. She didn't want to get married for the sake of getting married. She was old—she knew that—but that was why she would like to get married. She spent too much time alone; she wanted the companionship. Howard understood. But both he and Hetty didn't think it would be easy for her to find someone.

Hetty said: "Men are scarce here. There are very few men here. Go to church and count the men. The good ones have gone away. And the ones who have stayed are no good. There may be a couple of good ones on the quiet, but . . ."

What of the past, though? Had it been a reasonable sort of life? She said she had no regret for the past. Hadn't things got better for her? Hadn't things got better in the 1950s?

She said, "I hardly think even about my own past."

And Howard said, "I can hardly remember the past."

The words were like the words spoken at lunchtime by Hetty's sister.

But then Hetty said: "I didn't like the tobacco. It would make me sick at the end of one row, smell and all. When I was married we would get up early in the morning, when the dew was still on the tobacco leaves, and it didn't smell then. Even now tobacco makes me sick. When I was young I would be in a field and after two hours I would cry. That was when I was working with my father."

And behind that was the unmentionable past.

O N SATURDAY Hetty had talked with holiday excitement of the Easter Sunday sunrise service at five in the morning. She had said she might go to that. But when Jimmy and I checked out of the Peters Indian motel in the morning and went to the house for breakfast, we found Hetty there. The driving around the previous afternoon had tired her; she hadn't been able to make the sunrise service. She thought now she would go to the eleven o'clock service.

Jimmy and I thought that we would go at eleven-thirty to hear the singing and at least the beginning of the sermon, which Hetty said would start at twelve. The problem about that was Jimmy's clothes. In New York Howard had said that Bowen was a very country sort of place and that casual clothes and sneakers would be enough for whatever we might have to do. The only warm-weather clothes Jimmy had was a Banana Republic safari outfit. Hetty said it would be all right; but she would at a certain stage have to stand up in church and ask the congregation's forgiveness for his clothes.

On the television set in Hetty's sitting room there was constant religious excitement, with services from black churches and white churches, pastor and choir always stylishly dressed, each church having its own colors in clerical gowns, almost its own livery.

One preacher, with a serious, hectoring manner, broke off from the matter in hand to give a puff for a new book about the Bible and the afterlife. The book answered the questions people asked, he said. "Will we be merry in heaven?" And before I could fully savor that "merry" —merry with wine, Merry Christmas, Old King Cole was a merry old soul—the other question the book answered was spoken: "Will there be progress in heaven?" This American heaven clearly being a replication of American earth, with black and white, and North and South, and Republicans and Democrats.

Hetty, going into her room in her denim skirt, came out dressed for church in a bright-pink dress, quite overwhelming; and then she put on her flat dark-blue hat. The hat, and her glasses, gave her an executive appearance.

She drove to church. Howard had allowed his driver's license to lapse; he couldn't drive Hetty and then come back for us. We walked. The church was about a mile away. Jimmy was in his Banana Republic clothes. Howard was casually dressed and in sneakers; he wasn't going to the service. He said he didn't like going to church; it was something he had had to do too often when he was a child.

The road was wide. Cars went by one or two at a time. The grass was full of purple spring flowers; and from time to time, unexpectedly, there was black swamp (making one think of the primeval land, before the settlers came, and of the desolation the settlers must have felt sometimes).

We walked past Mr. Alexander's house. He was an old black man, formally dressed for Sunday, with a jacket and tie and hat; and he was in the bare patch of ground at the side of his house, practicing putts, or at any rate holding a golf club. The area in front of his small house was choked with ornamental garden statuary and anything that could be put in a yard as an ornament. He said his grandfather had started the collection; and then, with his own quicksilver sense of time, he said, "Two hundred years." Some of the pieces came from Jamaica in the West Indies; Mr. Alexander pronounced it "Jee-maica."

Howard said, as we walked on, "You can tell he's an oddball. Not only because of the golf club. But because he's not at church."

A car stopped on the road beside us. There were three white men inside—the race and color of people being now what was very noticeable about them. They wanted to know where the country club golf course was. Howard said he couldn't help them; he was a visitor himself. And they drove on.

The church was small and neat, in red brick, with a white spire and with the pediment of its portico resting on slender wooden columns. There were many cars in the yard at the side of the church. I said the cars made the town look rich. Howard said everybody had a car; cars meant nothing.

As we went up the steps to the portico Howard said, "They're singing." He didn't go in with us. He said—very boyish now, very much the licensed son—that he would wait outside.

A slender young brown woman welcomed Jimmy and me at the door and gave us an order of service. We sat at the back. And I remembered what Hetty had said: "Go to the church. Count the men." The men were fewer than the women. Some children were at the back, with their mothers. And everyone—as Hetty had hinted—was in his Sunday best.

The church inside was as plain and neat as it was outside. It had newish blond hardwood pews and a fawn-colored carpet. At the end of the hall, on a dais, was the choir, with a pianist on either side. The men of the choir, in the back row, were in suits; the women and girls, in the three front rows, were in gold gowns. So that it was like a local and smaller version of what we had been seeing on the television in Hetty's sitting room.

At the back of the choir, at the back of the girls in gold and the men in dark suits, was a large, oddly transparent-looking painting of the baptism of Christ: the water blue, the riverbanks green. The whiteness of Christ and the Baptist was a surprise. (As much a surprise as, the previous night, in the house of the old retired black teacher, the picture of Jesus Christ had been: a bearded figure, looking like General Custer in *Little Big Man*.) But perhaps the surprise or incongruity lay only in my eyes, the whiteness of Jesus being as much an iconographical element as the blueness of the gods in the Hindu pantheon, or the Indianness of the first Buddhist missionary, Daruma, in Japanese art.

The singing ended. It was time for "Reports, Announcements, and Recognition of Visitors." The short black man in a dark suit who announced this—not the pastor—spoke the last word in an extraordinary way, breaking the word up into syllables and then, as though to extract the last bit of flavor from the word, giving a mighty stress to the final syllable, saying something like "vee-zee-TORRS."

He spoke, and waited for declarations. One man got up and said he had come from Philadelphia; he had come back to see some of his family. Then Hetty stood up, in her flat blue hat and pink dress. She looked at us and then addressed the man in the dark suit. We were friends of her son, she said. He was outside somewhere. She explained Jimmy's tieless and jacketless appearance, and asked forgiveness for it.

We got up then, I first, Jimmy after me, and announced ourselves as the man from Philadelphia had done. A pale woman in one of the front rows turned around and said to us that she too was from New York; she welcomed us as people from New York. It was like a binding together, I thought. And when, afterwards, the man in the dark suit spoke of brothers and sisters, the words seemed to have a more than formal meaning.

The brass basin for the collection was passed up and down the pews. (The figure for the previous week's collection, a little over $350, was given in the order of service.) The pastor, a young man with a clear, educated voice, asked us to meditate on the miracle of Easter. To help us, he called on the choir.

The leader of the choir, a big woman, adjusted the microphone. And after this small, delicate gesture, there was passion. The hymn was "What About Me?" There was hand-clapping from the choir, and swaying. One man stood up in the congregation—he was in a brown suit—and he clapped and sang. A woman in white, with a white hat, got up and sang. So I began to feel the pleasures of the religious meeting: the pleasures of brotherhood, union, formality, ritual, clothes, music, all combining to create a possibility of ecstasy.

It was the formality—derived by these black people from so many sources—that was the surprise; and the idea of community.

Someone else in a suit got up and spoke to the congregation after the black man in the dark suit had spoken. "This *is* a great day," the new speaker said. "This is the day the Lord *rose*. He rose for every-body." There were constant subdued cries of "Amen!" from the con-gregation. The speaker said, "A lot of people better off than we are didn't have this privilege."

Finally the educated young pastor in his elegant gown with two red crosses spoke. "Jesus had to pray. *We* have to pray. Jesus had to cry. *We* have to cry. . . . God has been so good to us. He has given us a second chance."

Torture and tears, luck and grief: these were the motifs of this religion, this binding, this consoling union—union the unexpected, moving idea to me. And, as in Muslim countries, I understood the power a preacher might have.

As Howard said afterwards, as he and Jimmy and I were walking back to the house, "*Everything* happens in the church."

We came upon another local oddball, to use the word Howard had used on the way out: this was the drinker of the black community. We were some way from the man's house when Howard spotted him look-ing out of a window. And Howard said, "Look down. Don't talk to him. Don't see him." It was one of the ways Howard had learned, both here and in New York, of avoiding trouble: avoiding "eye contact," which, he said, provoked the mugger, the beggar, the racial fanatic, the madman, the alcoholic.

The drinking man, framed in his window, considered us as we

walked towards his house. When we passed the house I glanced at him out of the corner of my eye. Standing at his window in his undershirt, isolated in his house, he was red-eyed, spiritually and mentally far away.

I told Howard that the idea I had been given that morning of a black community with its own strict code was surprising to me.

He said, "This community, or what you see, is going to disappear in twenty or twenty-five years." Segregation had preserved the black community. But now blacks and whites, especially of the younger generation, were doing more things together. This gave point to what Hetty (grieving for a son) had said the day before about black and white boys now "drinking together." And I wasn't sure whether Howard or Hetty wholly liked the new mixing and what it foreshadowed. I didn't think that Hetty could be as serene as she was, without her community.

At lunch, when Hetty had come back from church, we talked for a little about the position of black people. We hadn't touched that subject the day before.

Black people had lived through the bad times. Now, when things should have been easier for them, there were new racial elements in the country: Mexicans and Cubans and the other foreigners. The Mexicans were soon going to be politically powerful in the country. The Asians were not just buying motels; they were going into other kinds of business as well; and they had been here only a few years. In a hospital not far away, Hetty said, there were only two *American* doctors.

And soon Howard and Hetty were reminding each other of the way things were changing. In the old days trucks would come around to pick up blacks for the fruit-picking. The trucks didn't come now: the Mexicans did the fruit-picking. And Howard said the blacks had eased themselves out of Miami. The blacks hadn't wanted the hotel jobs; they thought those jobs demeaning. So the Cubans had taken over those jobs, and the blacks wouldn't be allowed to get in there again. In ways like that the blacks had allowed the Cubans to get control of the city. Spanish was now the language of Miami.

Later, when we were going back to the airport, we saw a white congregation coming out of the other Baptist church in Bowen. It wasn't far from the black church where we had been. And it was only then that I realized that what I had been seeing was a segregated small town, with old segregated institutions.

It gave a fuller meaning to Hetty's words, her chant, as we had driven through the countryside: "All this side white people, all that side black people. Black people, black people, white people, black people. Black people, white people."

Reading the familiar land in her own way—where I saw only the colors of the spring, the purple flowers on the roadside, the sour weed, the pines and dogwood and oaks and maples, and the gray and green and dark-red colors of abandoned farmhouses and tobacco barns. Going back to the airport now, I saw the past a little more clearly. I saw a little more clearly what I had seen the day before.

And I began to see how Howard, leaving his home and going to New York, could hold himself separate both from the past and from the rage of Harlem.

I asked him why he didn't live in Harlem.

"My rhythm is different. And they pick up on that. Rhythm? It's like your energy level. How shall I put it? I'm not angry. Most people in Harlem are angry." And, trying to explain more about himself, he said, "I'm different. I felt different at the high school. It's what you think and what you feel that makes you different. I always felt different. Which leads me to believe I was born in the wrong town. Like many people."

TWO DAYS later, in New York (and just before I began my true Southern journey), I talked again with Howard, to make sure I had got certain things right.

About the presence of Asians and Cubans and Mexicans he said, "I get very pro-American when I think about that." And that pro-American attitude extended to foreign affairs, which were his special interest. So, starting from the small Southern black community of Bowen, Howard had become a conservative. He said, "I think that when you come out of a Southern Baptist background that is the groundwork of being a conservative."

I asked him about what he had said about the black community as we had walked back from the church. He had said that the community was going to disappear in twenty to twenty-five years; and he had seemed to talk neutrally about that. Was he really neutral?

He didn't commit himself. He said that there would be less unity in the community, but that good would come of the change. Making a mystical leap, he said, "Change is like death. Good things can come out of it. It's like the Civil War, when a whole way of life ended."

So at the end it turned out that his early comment, about the continuity of his home town, had had to do with history, as I had thought at the beginning. I had changed my mind because the word had then appeared to contain the idea of sameness and dullness: the same buildings, the ruins left standing in the fields, the dullness of the small-town life. He had meant that; but he had also meant the past living on. It was as though, talking to me, a stranger, he had had to find a way of talking about the unmentionable past.

1

■■■

Tuning In

IT WAS in New York that I planned my trip. One suggestion was that I should go to Tuskegee in Alabama, to have a look at the trades institute, now a university, that Booker T. Washington had founded more than a hundred years before for black people, then barely out of slavery.

Tuskegee was a name I knew. It was half mythical for me, from my memories of the Booker T. Washington book *Up from Slavery,* which I had been introduced to as a child in Trinidad. So far away: it was hard to think of this place with the strange name being there still, in the light of common day.

I was given the name of a writer who had been educated at Tuskegee, Al Murray. He was, or had been, a protégé of Ralph Ellison's, and he lived in New York. He was friendly on the telephone, interested in my project, and ready to talk on. He wanted me to come to his apartment. It was in the heart of Harlem, he said; and he thought I should see Harlem. It would be part of my preparation for the journey.

He lived on 132nd Street. He thought I should simply take the Madison Avenue bus. He made it sound feeble to do anything else, and it was my intention to take the bus; but at the last moment I faltered and waved down a taxi. In no time we were in Harlem. In no time, racing through the synchronized lights, we were in what looked like a caricature of the city lower down.

It was like a jump ahead in time, a turning of the page: upper windows blown out and blackened in walls of warm brown stone or old red brick, houses surrendered, camped in, old craft and elegance surviving in stonework (as in some pillaged ancient Roman site), some house walls enclosing only earth, awaiting excavation one day: no apparent relation between the people and the place, the mixed population of the city lower down altered, the pavement bustle gone, the people now all black, not many women about, and the men often in postures of idleness, sitting on steps or standing on street corners. In the same light of fifteen minutes before, the same weather, in what was still Fifth Avenue.

It should have stopped after a while; but it went on. At some lights a thin, expressionless boy ran to the car and said something to the driver. The driver, a fat black man, didn't reply. The lights changed; the thin-legged boy ran off again between the cars without another word. What had he wanted? The driver, from his accent a West Indian from one of the smaller islands, said, "He wanted to clean my windscreen." The driver gave a nervous laugh and—only now—turned up his window.

Not far away was the apartment building where Al Murray lived. It was one of a set of three or four tall apartment buildings that must have been built on the site of old house-rows. In Al's building—set back from the sidewalk, and with a shallow curved drive to the glass-doored entrance—there was, unexpectedly, a uniformed doorman, and a notice that visitors had to be announced.

His apartment was at the very end of a central, windowless corridor. It got warmer towards the end of the corridor; electric lights were on. When Al opened the door it was daylight again, and there was a glimpse, through the big glass window at the end of his sitting room, of the New York sky again. He was a brown man, and older than I had thought. I had expected a young man or a man in mid-career; and he had sounded young on the telephone. But Al had just turned seventy.

His sitting room was full of books and records. A moment's looking showed that the books were a serious collection of twentieth-century American writing in first or very early editions: Al had been buying, or collecting, for more than forty years. His jazz records (worn sleeves standing upright, filling many shelves) were equally valuable. Jazz was one of his passions, and he was a noted writer on the subject. Among the first things he showed me were private photographs of Louis Armstrong—a small man, unexpectedly, Picasso-size, and, again unexpectedly, a careful dresser: everything about the great man noteworthy, almost an aspect of the talent, and to Al exciting.

He was a man of enthusiasms, easy to be with, easy to listen to. His life seemed to have been a series of happy discoveries. Tuskegee—where he had studied fifty years before—had been one of those discoveries. He loved his school, and admired its founder.

He showed photographs of the place: Georgian-style brick buildings built by the students themselves eighty or ninety years before. They were the first photographs I had seen of Tuskegee, and they made me want to go there. And Booker T. Washington, as Al spoke about him, became a little more real. He was born a slave in 1856, but that was only five years before the Civil War; so (whatever his memories) he hadn't been a slave for very long. And he would have grown up in the extraordinary period just after the Civil War, when freedmen asserted themselves here and there, and some of the gifted ones did well. He would have grown up with American ideas, the big ideas of the late nineteenth century. Booker Washington, Al said, had to be seen as an American of the late nineteenth century, in his energy and in his understanding of the way capitalist America worked. He would have been at one with the very rich and powerful men he successfully appealed to.

Al Murray took down the two volumes of the Louis R. Harlan biography to show the photographs. They were moving: those long-held poses, Booker T. Washington with his family, with his dandified male secretary, all those clothes of turn-of-the-century respectability—and the great man's eyes always tired. And the Tuskegee students, men and women, doing as students the tasks so recently performed by slaves —raking hay, building brick walls—but doing those jobs now in respectable clothes, the men sometimes even in suits—clothes being important to people who, as slaves, hardly had any.

Tuskegee was on the site of an old plantation, Al Murray said. The plantation mansion had for many years remained outside the school compound; but he had heard that it had been acquired recently and was now the residence of the school's president. Change, in the American way. And it might have been said that Al Murray, with his books and records, was a demonstration in himself of that change. He had been born in Alabama in the deepest South; had gone to Tuskegee; had served in the air force and retired as a major; and had then had a second career as an academic and a writer.

It was at the end of his time with the air force that he had come to New York, to that apartment. Were his neighbors there middle-class, professional blacks? No; they were a mixed group. One neighbor, for instance, was a doorman at the midtown club of which Al was a member. "He's a doorman there. Here he's my neighbor." Al liked that. He also liked the apartment for its own sake.

But there was the setting. When he took me out to his dizzying little balcony to show me the view, the elegance that the first builders of Harlem had intended, I saw from a height the streets that at ground level had so demoralized me. I also saw the ruins of the red-brick house-row to the south. There had been a fire six years before, Al said; the brick shells had simply been allowed to stand since then. A big tree (now with spring foliage) had grown within the walls of one house without damaging the walls. The scene was a little like the war ruins preserved in parts of East Berlin as a memorial—and certain ravaged streets of Harlem did make one think of war.

But Al had lived for a long time with the burned-out houses on the next block. He seemed to have almost stopped seeing them; he saw the larger view. To the south, all Manhattan lay at our feet. If that tall building some blocks down wasn't in the way, Al said, we would have been seeing the Empire State Building from where we were. To the west was a multicolored row of buildings that a famous black artist, a friend of Al's, had made the subject of a picture. And when Al looked down at the street below he saw the two or three churches and the house of the local congressman: buildings standing for important aspects of local life.

So, with Al's help, my eye changed. And where at first I had seen only Harlem and gloom, I began on the high balcony to see the comparative order of the area where Al lived. And the splendor of the original Harlem design: grander, in the intention of the planners, than anything farther south.

But those first planners of Harlem had overbuilt. There were not enough people, in the 1890s, for the new houses of Harlem. Some businessmen had then begun to buy the houses, with the aim of renting to blacks from the South. They advertised; they tried to get the good-will and participation of Booker T. Washington, at that time the best-known black man in the United States. Washington didn't like the idea; he thought it too commercial. But Washington's secretary, Emmett Scott, one of the big three of Tuskegee (the big houses of Washington, his treasurer, and his secretary still stand side by side at Tuskegee), joined the business venture. So black Harlem began as it was to continue, in need and exploitation. And there was, ever so slightly, a Tuskegee connection.

Al Murray took me walking in the neighborhood. He asked me to notice the very wide sidewalks: it was part of the elegance of the original Harlem plan. He took me to a bookshop with books about the black cause, and posters and leaflets about local events. I bought a paperback of *The Souls of Black Folk* by Du Bois, a contemporary black critic of Washington (there was a very early edition of this book on Al's shelves); and we exchanged courtesies with the dedicated and cultured lady who ran the shop. He said, about the Harlem Hospital—the most important building in the neighborhood—that its standards were professional and that it was getting better. And then, my "disentangling" vision developing, we went to the Schomburg Center, a splendid new building devoted to black studies, with an extraordinary collection of books and documents, and with enthusiastic staff, black and white.

The Center gave researchers a stipend to work in its library. The stipendiary or scholar I met was a handsome brown woman who had traveled much and was doing work on the cultural links between Brazil and West Africa. She spoke of her work with the excitement of a discoverer. For her the black cause, or this extension of it, was like a new country.

I didn't take a taxi back. There were no taxis in the streets. Al waited a little while with me, talking of Ralph Ellison, until a bus came. And then, unwillingly, I saw again, and more slowly this time, stop by stop, what I had seen on the way out: a whole section of a great city in decay.

IT WAS in Dallas in 1984, at the Republican convention, that the idea of traveling in the American South, or Southeast, came to me. I had never been in the South before; and though Dallas was not part of the Southeast I later chose to travel in, I had a sufficiently strong sense there of a region quite distinct from New York and New England, which were essentially all that I knew of the United States.

I liked the new buildings, the shapes, the glossiness, the architectural playfulness, and the wealth that it implied. Architecture as pleasure—it was interesting to see it growing out of the drabness of the older, warehouse-style town.

It was mid-August, and hot. I liked the contrast on the downtown streets of bright light and the deep shadows of tall buildings, and the strange feel of another, more temperate climate that those shadows gave. One constantly played with contrasts like that. The tinted glass of the hotel room softened the glare of the hot sky: the true color of the sky, outside, was always a surprise. Air conditioning in hotels, cars, and the convention center made the heat, in one's passages through it, stimulating.

The heat was a revelation. It made one think of the old days. Together with the great distances, it gave another idea of the lives of the early settlers. But now the very weather of the South had been made to work the other way. The heat that should have debilitated had been turned into a source of pleasure, a sensual excitement, an attraction: a political convention could be held in Dallas in the middle of August.

On the wall at the back of the podium in the convention center the flags of the states were laid flat, in alphabetical order. The flags of the older states were distinctive; they made me think of the British-colonial flag (and the British-given colonial motto, in Latin, from Virgil) I had known as a child in Trinidad. And for the first time it occurred to me that Trinidad, a former British colony (from 1797), and an agricultural slave colony (until 1833, when slavery was abolished in the British Empire), would have had more in common with the old slave states of the Southeast than with New England or the newer European-immigrant states of the North. That should have occurred to me a long time before, but it hadn't. What I had heard as a child about the racial demeanor of the South had been too shocking. It had tainted the United States, and had made me close my mind to the South.

The convention center was very big. The eye could not take it all in at once. In that vast space the figures on the podium looked small. They could have been lost; but a big screen above them magnified their image, and scores of smaller screens all over the center repeated this living, filmed picture. It was hypnotic, that same face or gesture in close-up coming at one from so many angles. The aim might only have been communication and clarity; but no more grandiose statement could have been made about the primacy of men; nothing could have so attempted to stretch out the glory of the passing moment. And yet, almost as part of its political virtue, this convention dealt in piety and humility and heaven, and daily abased itself before God.

A famous local Baptist pastor spoke the final benediction. His church organization was prodigious; its property in downtown Dallas was said by the newspapers to be worth very many millions. His service, on the Sunday after the convention, was to a packed congregation. It was also being carried on television; and it was a full, costumed production, with music and singing. But the hellfire sermon might have come from a simpler, rougher time, when perhaps for five or six months of the year people had no escape from the heat, when travel was hard, when people lived narrowly in the communities into which they had been born, and life was given meaning only by absolute religious certainties.

I began to think of writing about the South. My first travel book—undertaken at the suggestion of Eric Williams, the first black prime minister of Trinidad—had been about some of the former slave colonies of the Caribbean and South America. I was twenty-eight then. It seemed to me fitting that my last travel book—travel on a theme—should be about the old slave states of the American Southeast.

My thoughts—in Dallas, and then in New York, when I was planning the journey—were about the race issue. I didn't know then that that issue would quickly work itself out during the journey, and that my subject would become that other South—of order and faith, and music and melancholy—which I didn't know about, but of which I had been given an intimation in Dallas.

FROM NEW YORK I went to Atlanta. I had been told that there was an old black elite there, a kind of black-American aristocracy; that there were many established black businessmen, and a number of black millionaires; and that blacks ran the city. I booked an airplane flight; in Atlanta stood in a line at the airport to hire a car; and then drove through the mighty roadworks of the city center to the hotel. And there I was, slightly astonished that the journey, so long in the planning, should begin in such a matter-of-fact way.

And, as if answering my anxiety, all the little Atlanta arrangements I had made in New York came to nothing, one after the other, and very quickly. A newspaperman had gone to another town to cover a story; a black businessman said on the telephone that he was out of touch, had lived these last twenty years out of Atlanta. And the black man whose name had been given me by a filmmaker said that almost everything I had heard about Atlanta was wrong.

The talk about a black aristocracy was exaggerated, this man said. By the standards of American wealth, blacks in Atlanta were not wealthy; in a list of the richest Atlantans, a black man might come in at number 201. Political power? "Political power without the other sort of power is meaningless."

He sipped his wine, my informant, and seemed not at all displeased to have floored me.

I actually believed what he said. I had felt that the grand new buildings of Atlanta one had seen in so many photographs had as little to do with blacks as the buildings of Nairobi, say, had to do with the financial or building skills of the Africans of Kenya. I had felt that the talk of black power and black aristocracy was a little too pat and sudden.

I wanted to see for myself, though; and I was hoping to be put in touch with people. But there was no hint from this black man of that kind of help. I might see Andrew Young, the mayor, he said; but Andrew Young probably had about two hundred interviews lined up. (So I might be number 201—a popular number.) I felt about this black man, in fact, that—sipping his wine, looking at me over the top of his glass, enjoying my discomfiture, awaiting my questions and swatting them down—I felt he was being seized more and more by a spirit of contradiction and unhelpfulness and was about to grow quite wild: that soon I would be hearing, not only that there were no moneyed blacks in Atlanta, but that there had never been anything in Georgia, no plantations, no cotton, corn, or taters, that there was only himself in the wide vessel of the black Atlanta universe.

From my room at the Ritz-Carlton, the view at night of the windows of the big Georgia Pacific building was like a big pop-art print. The windows, of equal size, were all lighted. Each level was like a filmstrip, or a strip of contact prints, of views almost the same. From my room the view changed, level by level. At the lower levels I looked down at the tops of desks and the floor of offices. At eye level I saw the desks silhouetted against the office wall. Level by level, then, the desks vanished. At the higher levels I saw only the lighted ceilings; and at the very top there was only light, a glow in the window. The offices were all empty; the men who sat in them during the day were in the suburbs somewhere. The paintings that hung on the walls of the offices of senior people were like arbitrary symbols of rank, mere rectangles at this distance, quite indistinct, even without color—the way great cities, from very high up, show as smudges below the earth's swirls.

A formal society, private lives, a formal view: an introduction was needed to every one of those rooms, and the visitor didn't know on what door to knock. Where did the news happen? Was it only a production, on the television?

BUT THEN I read in the newspaper about the affair of Forsyth County. Forsyth County was forty miles or so to the north of Atlanta. In that county in 1912 a young white girl was raped and beaten so badly that she died a few days later. A number of blacks were implicated. One was lynched; two others were tried and hanged. All the blacks of Forsyth were chased out of the county; and since then (so it was said) no blacks had been allowed to live in the county.

This last fact, about blacks not being allowed to live in Forsyth, became a public issue earlier in the year, when someone organized a "Walk for Brotherhood" in Forsyth in the middle of January, to mark the anniversaries both of the assassination of Mahatma Gandhi and the birth of Martin Luther King. This march was attacked by some local people and Ku Klux Klan groups; it made the news. A second brotherhood march a week later—after all the publicity—was a much bigger affair. Twenty thousand people went to Forsyth to march, and there were about three thousand National Guardsmen and state and local police officers to keep the peace. There were protests nonetheless; fifty-six people, none of them marchers, were arrested.

The man who had stage-managed the marches, or had made the issue as big as it had become, was a black Atlanta city councilor, Hosea Williams, called simply Hosea by everyone who spoke of him. He was sixty-one, and had been an associate of Martin Luther King's in the civil-rights movement. Hosea had since brought a lawsuit against some Klan groups for violating the civil rights of the people on the first brotherhood march; and he had also come up with the idea that some claim might be made against Forsyth County on behalf of the blacks who had lost land when they had been driven out in 1912.

Tom Teepen, of the Atlanta *Constitution,* with whom I had break-fast one day, spoke almost with affection of Hosea Williams. "A pri-mary force, a rabble-rouser in the tradition of the Paris barricades, and canny."

But I couldn't see Hosea that week.

Tom said, "He's in jail."

"Jail!"

"It's all right. He's often in jail for some thing or the other. He'll be out in a few days."

When I looked at some of Hosea Williams's own publicity material, and especially a *Who Is Hosea L. Williams?* pamphlet, I saw that his jail record mattered to him. There was a photograph of him in a cell. "Rev. Hosea holds the civil rights arrest record for jailings. . . . He has gone to jail about as many times since Dr. King's death as during his life (a total of 105 times)."

He was born in 1926. So for very many years his racial protests and battles would have been desperate affairs. But Hosea had won his war; and (though he was still a brave man: the first march at Forsyth had required courage) I felt that Hosea might now have become licensed, a star, a man on the news, someone existing in a special kind of electronic reality or unreality. And his political life required him to beat his own drum. In *The Dimensions of the Man—Dr. Hosea L. Williams—A Chronology,* with a photograph of Hosea in an academic gown, appar-ently receiving an honorary degree from another black man, there was this: "Today he's not content to watch things happen. HE MAKES THINGS HAPPEN."

THE NORTHERN suburbs of Atlanta almost touched Forsyth County. The freeways, which made Georgia look like Connecti-cut, enabled people to work in downtown Atlanta, where there were blacks in the streets, and then to drive twenty or thirty easy miles (in air-conditioned cars) to their houses in the suburbs, where there were few blacks—this part of Georgia had not been plantation country. There were branches of famous stores in the luxurious suburban shop-ping malls. The white suburbs could get by quite well without the black-run city center.

There was a news item in the paper one day that some of these suburbs didn't want to be plugged into the Atlanta city-transit system, because they didn't want to be infiltrated by blacks. No Forsyth-like shouting, no Confederate flags, no white hoods and gowns—that wasn't the way of these new suburbs. A transit official said, "It's such a subliminal issue that it's extremely difficult to deal with."

A lawyer I met said that, to understand, it was necessary to remember that 120 years or so ago there had been slavery. For poor white people race was their identity. Someone well off could walk away from that issue, could find another cause for self-esteem; but it wasn't that easy for the man with little money or education; without race he would lose his idea of who he was.

I spoke about my weekend with Howard and Hetty. Hetty had a strong idea of her racial and family identity, and yet she also had a high regard for Mr. Bowen, whom she considered a good man. Did that mean anything? The lawyer thought not. Southern white people would do anything for black families with whom they had a relationship, but that attitude stopped there; it wasn't extended to blacks in general.

We were lunching, the lawyer and I, in a big club in downtown Atlanta. The club had been started in the days when there had been a general movement out of Atlanta, and business people had felt the need for a place where they might meet in the middle of the day. It was part of the bubble in which the white professional people of Atlanta lived: the house, the air-conditioned car, the office (perhaps like an office in the Georgia Pacific building), the luncheon club.

I asked the lawyer whether he personally felt threatened. He said the feeling was with him sometimes when he was out in the streets. He meant the fear of violence. But he also meant the larger fear of a world grown unstable: the more protective the bubble in which one lives, the more uncertain one's knowledge becomes of what lies out there.

And this was why the lawyer thought it would be good if the black middle class could grow, if the blacks could become more active commercially. But—and like everyone talking about blacks now, he searched for words at once neutral and true—blacks (whatever their yearnings) didn't have the business sense, the business vocation. In a society that was economically driven, blacks didn't have the economic drive. But now there were immigrants of a new sort in the United States—Latin Americans, Asians. The lawyer thought that, when the blacks had a better understanding of what the presence of those immigrants meant to them, black racial sentiments might change.

It was there, then, as Tom Teepen had told me, at the back of everything, however unspoken: the thought of race, the little neurosis, the legacy of slavery.

The topic came up again when I went to see Anne Rivers Siddons, the novelist. She lived in North Atlanta: hilly plots, tall pines, dogwood, azaleas. The spring I had seen in Howard's home town was at its peak here, and the houses along the suburb's curving roads looked quite embowered.

Anne Siddons had just published a novel, *Homeplace,* and was doing promotional work on it, at some cost to herself: she had got started on a new book. She was a little withdrawn, living internally, holding on to her new book. She lived in such beauty now; but—as I saw when I looked at her previous book, *Fox's Earth*—her thoughts (like those of many Southern people) went back easily to a poorer time.

She said that Margaret Mead had made an important observation about the South: the relationship of the white man and the black servant woman, man and undemanding mistress, had left the white woman and the black man neutered. The black men, Anne Siddons said, were the disaffected ones.

And the newspapers—the *Constitution* and its sister paper, the *Journal* ("Covers Dixie like the Dew" was the slogan on its editorial page and its delivery vans)—were full of racial items, interwoven with the running serials: Forsyth County, and the ramifying story of the private life of a black politician accused of using cocaine.

One day there was this story. IBM sent a black executive to Columbia, South Carolina; but there was no room for the black man in the country club, no party invitations for his children. The next day there was this story: a black woman of thirty-one, a mother of two children aged five and two, took a revolver to work and shot herself in her office at Georgia Power. She felt she was being discriminated against by the company and passed over for promotion. She said in her suicide note that she wanted to give the managers and supervisors something to think about.

Desperation; but there was also the kind of playfulness that a political cause attracts when it has become safe. There was news of a black arts festival. There was news of a mighty piece of sculpture for Atlanta by a New York sculptor, *Nelson Mandela Must Be Free to Lead His People and South Africa to Peace and Prosperity*. The rock sculpture weighed seven tons and was too heavy for its first site, which could take only a hundred pounds per cubic foot. So the sculpture was going to be moved to Woodruff Park in downtown Atlanta. (Woodruff was the great man of Coca-Cola, running the company for sixty years; Coca-Cola and *Gone with the Wind* are the two fabulous success stories of post–Civil War Atlanta.) A twelve-foot iron fence, with a working gate, was to be welded into the rock. The gate was to be locked with a real key, and the key was to be given to the city of Atlanta, so that— assuming the key hadn't been mislaid—the gate could be opened when Mandela was freed.

From Tom Teepen's column in the *Constitution*: Metro Atlanta is a big city of 2.2 million; Atlanta is a medium city of 450,000; black Atlanta is a small city of 300,000. "The black leadership circle is a small town." A good journalist finds good clear ways of putting things. Tom Teepen also said this: white people in the United States don't have "leaders"; only black people have leaders. And I felt he had said that because (according to some other columnists in the paper) the current scandals about black politicians in a number of states were being used to run down black people generally.

I liked the point about leaders. I thought it could be applied to many black or backward or revolutionary countries, where the leader is everything, and where journalists and others from outside, falling un-wittingly into a version of the explorer's attitude ("Take me to your leader"), bestow on the leader alone the dignity that, in another kind of place, they would bestow more widely, on the country and the people. But then I began to wonder whether—since black politics in the United States were still racial and redemptive and simple—black people in the United States couldn't after all be said to have leaders, people they simply followed. And I wondered whether it was possible in these circumstances for black people to stand apart from their lead-ers, any more than it was possible for people of the Caribbean or Africa to stand apart from the racial or tribal chiefs whom they had created.

I HEARD more about identity.

Tom Teepen—shedding the suit and tie that he said was regula-tion office wear, and appearing instead in a many-pocketed vest or *gilet* —took me one Saturday morning to a century-old Appalachian settle-ment in East Atlanta: a big old red-brick cotton mill, white frame houses, a cemetery on rising ground beyond a busy road. Mill wages at the beginning had been very low, 5¢ an hour, it was said; but for the mountain people the regularity of the wage had been a kind of security, and the community established around the mill had survived, though many people had gone away at various times, and the mill itself was now closed.

We went to a community-and-craft center in the settlement. It was run by a woman with the beautiful name of Esther Lefever. She had come to the settlement many years before as a folksinger—a ten-year-old photograph in the Atlanta *Constitution* showed her as a pretty woman with a guitar. But then, from being moved by the response to her singing—an old woman had got up and done a special dance, and other people had cried—she had become more deeply involved with the Appalachian community, and had even become a city councilor.

She was small and slender, still attractive and clear-voiced. She was not herself from an Appalachian community, but she understood their closeness. She was a Mennonite from Pennsylvania, the eighth child of a preacher. She spoke of what it had meant to her to move from the strictness of her Mennonite background. She had felt alone, she said. What did it mean to be alone? She said she had the picture of being the last tree on the hillside: the other trees had all been cut down. It hadn't been easy for her even to give up the bonnet; all her life she had been taught to wear the bonnet out of respect for God and man. Even when she was in her twenties it made her nervous to be in the streets of Chicago. It wasn't a fear of black men so much as a dread of white men who (according to what she had been told) drank liquor and were gross.

And then she had discovered the cruelty of the world outside, the cruelty of America. How had she discovered that? She told a story. One of her Appalachian women came to her one day and said she needed a job, "maid work." Esther Lefever took the woman to see someone, a woman with a lot of blonde hair combed back, a woman (Esther Lefever said) just a step or two above the woman looking for maid work. And the blonde woman said, "Why does she want to do maid work? That's for colored people."

It was a simple incident, I thought; something that should have been passed over. The blonde woman herself (from the story) was as much a sufferer as everybody else. But the incident had many layers of meaning, and Esther Lefever had been upset and humiliated by it. She said, "They want to keep you in the slots they have fixed for you." Who were "they"? She thought, and said that they were the people who had arranged the system and wanted to keep everyone in his place.

I asked her in what way identity was important, and whether there was some practical way in which it helped. She said that, if you moved to a new neighborhood or took a new job, and people were not too friendly, then it could be a help if you knew who you were; you could last out the hostility. If you didn't know who you were—if (and this was my extension) you were dependent on other people for your idea of your own worth—then you were in trouble.

She was giving the view from below, the view of the poor people she was concerned about. And from what she said I got the impression that these people had raw sensibilities and lived on their nerves. I found that hard to imagine.

(And yet, at another level, and with another, half-buried part of myself, I understood. Perhaps in a society of many groups or races everyone, unless he is absolutely secure, lives with a special kind of stress. Growing up in multiracial Trinidad as a member of the Indian community, people brought over in the late nineteenth and early twentieth centuries to work the land, I always knew how important it was not to fall into nonentity. In 1961, when I was traveling in the Caribbean for my first travel book, I remember my shock, my feeling of taint and spiritual annihilation, when I saw some of the Indians of Martinique, and began to understand that they had been swamped by Martinique, that I had no means of sharing the world view of these people whose history at some stage had been like mine, but who now, racially and in other ways, had become something other. And eight years or so later, in Belize in Central America, a similar feeling of the void broke through my other preoccupations when I saw the small, lost, half-Indian community of that wretched British colony, coastal timberland poached from what had been the Spanish Empire, peopled with slaves and servants, and then more or less abandoned: New World debris.)

And I heard more about the ways of identity in the South from a religious scholar. Among the people he instructed were men and women studying for the ministry. I thought that people who wanted to be ministers might have been moved by some religious experience. But that attitude was a reflection of my own temperament and background, my own lack of a religious faith, and my thirty-five years and more in England, where formal religion had all but withered.

In the United States, and especially in the South, religious faith was almost universal, and a religious vocation was as likely as any other. It was something a man could turn to for a number of reasons; and what I heard from this scholar was that some of the people he was in touch with (and he meant white people) had turned to the religious life in order to be confirmed in their identity: people from poor families who felt racially threatened by the new developments in the South, people who, in the booming new South, had gone into business and had then felt themselves drifting so far from the Southern world they had known that they had given up, to return to God and the life they felt more at ease in.

I heard this talk about religion and identity far from Atlanta, at an open-air party on an estate in northwestern Georgia: hills, woods, long views, range beyond gentle range, blue upon blue.

The party was in a rough, long-grassed field between woods, and in front of a gray, patched-up wooden hut on low pillars. The hut was said to be very old. It stood almost at the foot of a slope; and when you looked through the back door and window directly to the green of the land sloping up in the shade of pines, the site did have the feel of an ancient, protective solitude, quite different from any solitude one might arrange for oneself today.

(Driving out from Atlanta, into the hills, aware of the fewness of blacks in the small towns I was passing through, I had felt I was driving into the wilderness. Some months later, when I was almost at the end of my journey, I was to approach Atlanta from the other way, from Nashville and Chattanooga, and this part of Georgia was to seem more used up and trodden over.)

The party was "Southern" in its motifs. A Confederate flag fluttered in the sunlight in the rough field between the woods. A skinned pig, fixed in the posture of a hurdler, had been roasting all day, held on poles a little to one side of slow-burning hardwood logs. (On a table were more contemporary fast foods and dips and things in waxed paper.) And a band played bluegrass music from the wooden hut. Flag, pig, music: things from the past. The musical instruments were big, the music simple and repetitive. I was told that it was the words of the songs that mattered. The accents were not easy for me to follow; but the effect, especially from a little distance, of the unamplified music and singing in that enclosed green place was pleasant.

Our hostess said, "Indians might have lived here."

With that idea of being in the American wilderness, I felt a chill, thinking of them in this green land with its protective slopes, its shade, and rivers. Later I learned the ground was full of flint arrowheads.

34

It was in this setting, with the bluegrass music coming from the wooden hut, that I heard about the religious faith and identity of the people who had come after the Indians. And I had a sense of the history here resting layer upon layer. The Indians, disappearing after centuries; the poor whites; the blacks; the war and all that had come after; and now the need everyone felt, black and white, poor and not so poor, everyone in his own way, to save his soul.

The musicians were young and friendly; there was a girl among them. When they finished they put their big instruments in their pickup truck and went away. When the sun went down there was no wind; the flag drooped. It became cold very quickly; it was still only spring.

THE Atlanta *Constitution*'s file on the affairs of Forsyth County didn't come as a set of date-stamped newspaper clippings, but as computer printouts. The story of the events of 1912, as researched by one of the newspaper's writers, was terrible in every way.

The white woman who had been dragged into woods, raped, and beaten—and died two to three days later—was the nineteen-year-old daughter of a well-known farmer. A hand mirror near the scene led police to a deformed eighteen-year-old black man. He confessed, and said that other blacks were also involved. Altogether, eleven blacks were arrested as suspects. Two days after the woman's death a crowd broke into the Forsyth County jail, shot and killed one of the suspects, beat the body with crowbars, and hung it on a telegraph pole. Three weeks later the deformed man and another black man were tried for the rape and murder and found guilty. The sister of the second man testified against him. Both men were publicly hanged a month after the trial, before a crowd of ten thousand. The few hundred blacks who lived in Forsyth were chased away.

The destroyed young woman, the deformed black, the lynching at the jail and the hanging of the mangled body, the black woman giving evidence against her brother, the public hangings (ten thousand people turning up for that, in a county that fifty years later, before the Atlanta boom, had a population of under twenty thousand)—the story is unbearable in every detail. Yet what seemed to have survived in Forsyth above everything else was the knowledge, a cause for pride to some, that no black lived there.

The man who had sought to challenge this pride was a white Californian, a karate teacher who had been living in Forsyth for five years. He called for a March of Brotherhood to mark the anniversaries of the death of Gandhi and the birth of Martin Luther King. He changed his mind after getting abusive telephone calls and threats. But the idea of the march had been taken up by another karate teacher, also white, from the next county. This was the march—about fifty people were expected to take part—that Hosea Williams had intervened in. This was the march that had been attacked by Klan groups and others, and had seeded, a week later, the big march of the twenty thousand, with the protection of three thousand National Guardsmen and state and local police officers. So that within a week what had been a brave and lonely cause had been turned by Hosea and a few others into a safe cause; and it had become safer and safer.

A radio show had been taken to Forsyth. A very famous afternoon-television talk show with a witty black hostess had gone to Forsyth, and a program had been recorded in a local restaurant. Hosea, applying equal passion to the safe cause as he had to the brave one, had picketed this show, because only Forsyth residents were allowed to have a say, and they of course were all white.

Hosea had managed to be arrested, to add to that record of his— 105 jailings at the time his *Who Is Hosea L. Williams?* pamphlet had gone to press. According to the Atlanta *Journal,* Hosea had shouted as he was being put into the police van, "This is Forsyth County! This is what you see!" And Hosea's married daughter, who was with him, had shouted, "My daddy! I want to go with him!" And she too had been put in the van.

Tom Teepen hadn't been able to arrange a meeting with Hosea when he had first told me about him, because Hosea at that time was in jail for a few days. And Tom couldn't find Hosea when he came out of jail. But then, late one morning, Tom telephoned me with the news that if I hurried to a certain building I might see Hosea. He was being arraigned on another charge at a federal court at eleven-thirty. It was almost that already, but Tom said that these affairs usually ran a little late.

I took a taxi. It was driven by an African, a man from Ghana. It was a short run for him; in almost no time he had set me down again. An open paved forecourt, the big building set back; a security doorway; an elevator to the sixteenth floor. Hardwood doors, low ceilings, a brown-carpeted corridor, neat nameplates: formal, without drama, safe, even cozy. But the hearing was over. And in a room that was like a small lecture room or classroom there was a little group in one corner, like the subdued group that sometimes stays behind after a school examination to talk over the questions.

In the little group I recognized Dick Gregory, gray-bearded and white-suited, a man grown old in the wars, and now really looking quite saintlike. And there was a squatter man with a bigger beard who could be none other than Hosea himself. Even in this moment of stillness in the courtroom his eyes suggested bustle—a man with many things to do and little time to spare. He had a toothbrush in his top pocket—a man ready to go to jail.

He also had a press officer with him, a slender brown woman. She had a handout "for immediate release." And it seemed from what she said that my chances of meeting Hosea and having a heart-to-heart talk with him were not good. Hosea and Dick Gregory were going to fly to Washington that afternoon to picket the CIA. After that they were going straight off to Europe, to London and the Vatican, to do some work about apartheid. The handout from the press officer was about drugs: Hosea was saying that certain recent incidents were being used "to defame black leaders," and that the Mafia and the CIA were the ones most involved in the drug trade, which was "destroying our children and the future of our nation." That, in fact, was why Hosea and Dick Gregory were going to picket the CIA.

And suddenly, before I could fully take in Hosea's eyes and beard and toothbrush, the little group had gone.

Four or five minutes had passed since I had arrived, no more. And to add to the randomness of the occasion in Court No. 1, there was my encounter with someone who, when the little group had gone away, had been left behind, like me. He was a reporter, quite young. He too had come too late for the arraignment. He too was new to Atlanta and didn't know a great deal about the affairs of the city. In the courtroom, in the brown-carpeted corridor, and in the elevator, we talked about his time in England. He had gone there to study the ancient Roman walls, Hadrian's Wall and the later Antonine wall. I had never seen those walls and was interested in what he had to say.

We separated downstairs. When I was going out of the front door of the building I saw a small group around a bearded man. It looked so much like what I had seen upstairs that I thought the man was Hosea, giving an informal interview. It was only when I was almost in the group that I saw that the talker wasn't Hosea, was blacker, differently dressed, without the toothbrush, and that he only had the big stiff beard.

THE CONVENTION business was important to Atlanta, and there were many big hotels in the center of the city quite close to one another. It was hard to think that these hotels could all be full at the same time. But it sometimes happened. A girl in the Ritz-Carlton dining room told me one day that an important convention was in town. What was this a convention of? Dry cleaners. And they were important because there were so many of them—as there had to be, if you considered how many dry cleaners there must have been all over the United States—that they had filled the Atlanta hotels.

No hotel gave off such a company-holiday or convention feeling as the Marriott Marquis. And none was so overpowering. To enter it was like entering a gigantic, hollow, twisted cone. It had an atrium forty-seven stories high: gallery upon curving gallery, following the twist of the cone. That twist was unexpected; the eye was always led upwards. Great red streamers, like something from a Chinese festival, hung down the middle space. And all the time, like fairground conveyances, tall glass-walled elevators, their ribs picked out in lights, slid up and down the atrium wall.

But the black man who worked for the Hilton (atrium-style there too, with the internal galleries, but not so sensational), with whom I had a talk one evening about the hotels of Atlanta, thought that I had done well by going to the Ritz. He said, "That's where the 'lite stay."

As if in confirmation of this, I heard one day (with what truth I don't know) that Gloria Vanderbilt was staying in the Ritz and had been seen in one of the elevators.

She was in Atlanta to do a promotion. Two weeks or so before, in New York, I had caught her on a talk show. She was talking about her life and about the way a woman is defined by the men whom she loves. And I assumed when I heard she was in town that she was here to promote her book. But there was much more to this promotion. "The Enchantment . . . The Heritage . . . The Prestige . . . MACY'S Proudly Introduces GLORIOUS by Gloria Vanderbilt. . . . Only a truly

great fragrance has the power to stir our emotions. Glorious by Gloria
Vanderbilt . . . Gloria Vanderbilt will autograph a complimentary
photograph and any Glorious purchase."

That was going on in Macy's, just across the road from the Ritz, on
the morning Anne Siddons came to the hotel, to talk to me about
growing up in the South. She was as intense and intelligent as I had
expected; and though she was a little withdrawn (because of the book
she was writing), and though the promotion she was doing for her
publisher (on a different scale from Gloria Vanderbilt) was a further
depletion, she spoke with a full heart, offering me a little of the experience that was her capital as a writer.

She was Southern and Georgian, and almost Atlantan. She was
born in Fairburn, twenty miles south of Atlanta. Fairburn was an
agricultural and railroad town. Her father was a lawyer; though they
were not rich, they were comfortably off. Her father was the first of his
family to go to college.

"We came down from Virginia around 1820. Our branch of the
family farmed the same piece of land for seven generations. It makes
me feel wonderfully rooted. But at the same time I feel it can be a yoke.
I feel that we Southerners can be too deeply and narrowly focused into
that land."

I told her about my trip to Howard's home town and what I had
seen there of black farming families.

She said, "It's one thing Southern whites and blacks have shared.
We have both been landowners since abolition." And she told me what
Howard and his mother had told me: that land had been given or
bequeathed to black people by the white men for whom they had
worked. Some decades ago, she said, it had come out from a study of
oral history that this giving of land had been seen by black and white
as a benign aspect of the master-slave relationship.

I asked, "In what way can the land be a yoke?"

"We don't tend to lift our sights to get a broader vision."

People settled too easily for staying on the land. They tended to say
or feel, "Our sort don't go to college. We are farmers."

Anne Siddons said: "I was a bright only child in a grammar-and-
high school dominated by children from the surrounding farms. And
everything I was naturally, I felt ashamed of. I spent twelve years
trying to hide the fact that I was a bright child. Intellect has had no

place here. The people who came to lead us obviously had intellect. But they had other things as well, to make it go down more easily. They had great charm, for instance."

When we had first met she had said, "We are a colonial people." She made the point again. Southerners, she said, were uncertain of themselves.

"I am talking about white people. At the time I was growing up, the white Southerner in the rural and small-town South felt threatened by the blacks. You don't hate what doesn't threaten you. As long as somebody was below you, you knew you had power. It was all about power, really. We were a conquered and occupied people, the only people in the United States to be like that. And this—our attitude to blacks—was the only way we could feel or exercise our power at all. We were a poor agricultural community, and we had bone-deep memories of real conquest and occupation and total humiliation.

"We were untraveled people, the bulk of us uneducated. The only way we had of coping with change was by pretending it wasn't there. When the civil-rights movement was beginning, though it was just there, in Alabama, we could pretend it wasn't there. And when change did come it was brought to us right to our door by those black hands, which we hated and feared more than anything else in the world. These feelings are here still. What thoughtful Southerner couldn't know they are still there? This would be the background of a lot of thought."

"Isn't it fatiguing for you, always to be with this idea of race?"

"A lot of us find it almost too stifling to live in." That is why, she said, many Southern intellectuals had moved out of the South.

I asked about racial protest. Hadn't it become formal, almost ritualized? There was the affair of the marches at Forsyth. It was clear, from the newspaper accounts, that only the very first protesters had risked anything. After that, the mood and tone of protest had changed. It had become the popular cause, the protected cause; some commentators had become self-righteous.

"Of course the idiocy up in Forsyth needs to be dealt with. But the response can—and did—become banal."

She had been shocked by the first news from Forsyth. But then she had had to acknowledge her own personal limitations as someone over fifty, someone who could now wake up in the mornings with the knowledge that death was going to come.

"Active revolution is romantic for the young. The problem is: how do you deal with passion in middle age, when you must hoard passion? There can be no resolution of this problem, or at any rate not a neat one. And, aside from media notice and marches, I don't know how to deal with it. The form of the protest has got to be a cliché—Lord knows, Americans will protest anything."

But race as an issue—it couldn't be avoided. "I deal with race in some form in every book I've written. It's my great war, I guess. I write to find out where I am now, what I think, to make order and simplicity in my own world. It's an impossible task. You can't simplify that. You can only clarify bits of it."

I talked of the oddity of slavery in the New World, of the two far-removed races it had brought together, African, European. Now there was a common language and even a common religion.

"I tend to think that they have enriched us more than we have enriched them. Perhaps we do on some deep level realize how very similar we are."

She said a little later: "I feel very guilty about the civil-rights movement. I didn't march, back when marching would have been passionate and real and spontaneous. I was a young woman newly come to Atlanta and still deeply caught in that web of what is seemly and what is not."

When was that real and passionate time?

"I think the great marches in Selma were about 1965. Although I got into trouble for a column I wrote for our student paper. I was at a small college. This was when Autherine Lucy entered the University of Alabama. And there were cavalcades from all over the state going over to heckle those two poor blacks, heckle and worse. Nobody went from my college. It was because they were lackadaisical, really. I wrote a column praising the noninvolvement and made a few of those simplistic and sophomoric statements about race and about whatever—"

" 'Whatever'?"

"How we must keep calm, and this had to be a good thing. And I got hauled up before the dean of students, asking that I reconsider and not submit the column for publication. Which I would not do."

I wondered how, coming from her background, she had arrived at that position.

"I recall in high school a little epiphany. We were in something to do with black and white. It was an American-history class. I can't think what it might have been. But I remember feeling very strongly: this is *wrong*. I had never had that feeling before. And I blurted out, 'That is not right.' And one of the great big gangling country guys, who must have been twenty years old at that time, got up and called me a nigger-lover. Of course I had heard it all my life, but I had never been on the other side of it. I just remember the profound, simple shock of that moment.

"My consciousness was raised a little. But not totally. I was still interested in fraternities and dances. You see, we were raised to be belles.

"We all knew—nobody ever told us, but we knew with a deeper wisdom than words—that the highest we could aspire to was capturing a husband who would then provide for us. And we believed that. At fourteen I was constantly in love. Our mothers and grandmothers believed it was the best they could give us, the protection of a man. I have a theory that Southern madhouses are full of gifted women who were stifled."

I said, "A pastoral or country society surviving in an industrial world?"

"Yes, I think so." But I had interrupted. She went on: "In high school I did everything I thought I should. I was homecoming queen."

"Homecoming queen?"

"It's at a big football game. And when the alumni all come back there is a queen in her court, and she is given roses and presented to her court at half-time. And I was a cheerleader, and all the things you were supposed to be. I was a popular girl. And that was what we all thought we had to do, to get this man and to have a good life.

"And most of us could learn to do that. But the other side of us that wanted to *learn*—we were always ashamed of it. We never prized our minds. We never prized our individuality. It was all right to make good grades. It was all part of being a good little girl. But to be a great thinker, to have a great talent and pursue it, would cut you right out of the herd. And that was the thing we were most afraid of. It could send you walking alone. I mean it almost literally in some cases.

"I knew a girl at college who was a wonderfully gifted painter—and, oh, she was good—and she spent all her working time in the art-department laboratory, painting. It was all she did. She was extremely reclusive. She was the only woman at that college allowed to have a room alone. The stigmas she bore were cruel."

I wanted to know more about being "cut out of the herd." I remembered what Esther Lefever had said about leaving her Mennonite community and feeling "alone": feeling yourself the last tree on a hill, all the others having been cut down.

Anne Siddons said, "The feeling you get is of being totally exposed, totally vulnerable to *chaos*.

"I think that goes back to safety. I think I can tell you why Southern women teach their daughters that, or that they must have a man to protect them. After the Civil War those women had lost their entire worlds. Their homes were burnt, their slaves (if they had had them) were scattered, their men might have been killed. And I think they perceived that this had happened through the sheer folly and childishness of these men of theirs. That was a *silly* war. It was quixotic, romantic in the extreme. It was foolhardy. We fought a ridiculous war that any reflection would have told us we couldn't win.

"And these women who had lost everything determined to ensure that their daughters and granddaughters would never again hand their power over to men who would toss it away so lightly. Never again would they allow their men to throw their very lives away. And they determined then to control those men by guile and charm and feminine wiles, because those were the only weapons they had.

"If we lived in the East—of the United States—we might have used our minds. In the West we might have exercised a physical initiative and bravery. But we were here, and many of us were trapped here economically. And you can't aspire to what you can't imagine. And so, to survive, we had to hook up with a man. My mother to this day would be happier if I had a teaching certificate and was married to a lawyer. 'You should get a teaching certificate. That way you'll always have something to fall back on.' "

And Anne Siddons herself still had something of her old anxiety about chaos. "What I am most afraid of is a very real vulnerability to forces I can't control. This thing about control is important to me."

She spoke again about the conventions of her adolescence. "The very things that could have enriched us and set us apart were the things that we learned, by omission, were wrong. We grew up without prizing what was real. The South is dreadfully hard on its women, and what we allow it to do to us . . . I suppose this is true of other regions as well, but I think it is more true of the South. It would be interesting to know *why* we are so suspicious of eccentricity."

"Did it affect your emotional life?"

"I've only begun to know now how much it affected my emotional life. It kept me from examining myself. It terrified me. Consequently I came to that examination twenty years later than many people do. What I resent is the power that examination might have liberated earlier. In my writing and my life.

"I am regretting the years of waste. I am trying to deal with anger against my parents for bringing me up as they did—though that anger comes out of the deep knowledge that they acted out of the highest love they had in them.

"I am glad it happened to me. I might have become one of those beautiful tragic drunk women in the South, on a country-club terrace somewhere. There are many drunk women in the South."

But there was the comfort of the land that the family had farmed for seven or eight generations, since the family had moved down from Virginia in 1820.

"I'm glad I have those ties. The feeling of floating free is frightening to me. I go back almost every weekend. I have dinner with my parents."

And now came the explanation of the "hoarding" of passion she had spoken about earlier: the need to spare feeling for private life, private ties, to divert at least some passion from public issues.

"I've talked about this with two or three women friends. And we find that we are now irrationally angry with our parents. And I think that it's because we sense that the original contract—the contract between parent and child, the contract that says, 'I will always take care of you,' and is an impossible commitment—that contract is going to be broken now, and they are going to die soon. That is what I mean by our passions having to be focused."

Still, what thought was there now, from her side, about the blacks, people equally obsessed?

"If we, Southern women, feel strictured, I wonder how the Southern black, who has had so many more overt strictures, must feel about them. Though I suspect that I may have highly romanticized whatever they may feel about them—I have a tendency to do that."

"Do you think protest is being so formalized that even black people are beginning to lose contact with what they feel, and often say what they think is expected of them?"

"I think that rote and rhetoric have replaced outrage. The first thing that happened after the very real shock about the business in Forsyth County—the shock that *it,* the Southern violence, wasn't dead

—what swung into action then was the *perfect* march. And we knew just exactly how to do it. As though some cosmic march chairman pulled all the switches—and, goodness, in a week we had the perfect march.

"We had the right component of public-safety awareness, the right component of media awareness. The right crowd makeup, a nice balance of young blacks and old battle-scarred lions; and we had the right component of white liberals. You wouldn't have found an ex-president marching in that first civil-rights march. You know, the organization! The buses appeared, just like that. That's Hosea. Boy, can he stage a civil disobedience now!"

Wasn't it good, though, that protest in the United States could be ritualized like this?

"I don't want to sound pejorative. How else would I have it? I am so thankful no lives were lost in Forsyth County, no harm was done. What I miss are the howls of pure outrage that greeted the murder of the three civil-rights workers in Mississippi. In the 1960s. But it was the spilled blood that called out the outrage. And we must not have the blood."

But there was this to the formalization of protest: there was an orthodoxy of thought about race and rights. Perhaps people would be censoring themselves sometimes, to appear to be saying the right thing.

Anne Siddons said, "I guess that happens in all revolutions. They don't end. They just pass into caricature over the years. And therefore they lose their credibility. The civil-rights movement will lose its energy and peter out into a series of sporadic brush fires, as other things come up. The civil-rights movement began to die as the peace movement and the women's movement came to life in the sixties. As I said, Americans protest anything. We are protesters. But protest made the country. It's what we know how to do."

We had talked for two hours. And across the road from the Ritz, on the ground floor at Macy's, smiling uniformed young men and women, like a kind of ceremonial designer-guard for Gloria Vanderbilt, walked lightly—lightly, like dancers—down a walkway between dark-red rope barriers, while a small band played and Gloria Vanderbilt herself—impossible to imagine that a real person possessed the name and actually was at the heart of the fame, the goods, the book, the talk show—Gloria Vanderbilt herself, dark eyes in pale, blooming skin, in the fluorescent light of the department store, the light matching the air conditioning, completing the bubble world, Gloria Vanderbilt sat and signed things for people waiting in line.

TOM TEEPEN walked me over to the gold-domed Capitol building. In the big central hall, hung with portraits of people famous in the political life of Georgia, there was a display of flags from the Civil War. Tom Teepen said, "A lot of history here."

And the lieutenant governor, Zell Miller, was in his wood-paneled office. He was from the northeast of the state, which he said was Indian territory, Cherokee territory, until the 1830s, when the Cherokees were sent to Oklahoma along the "Trail of Tears." Was that what the trail was called then? Possibly not; it was hard and painful to think about now. The settlers who took the Indian land were Scottish and Irish and some Germans, moving down from Carolina and Virginia. And the northeast of the state remained isolated—American history busy about other areas, leapfrogging or skipping over the hills of Appalachia and the communities in the "coves" and "hollows"—until the 1930s and 1940s. There were few blacks; that area was not a "racist society." But now, with the newcomers from other places, mainly from Florida, he said, there were prejudices among the local people.

That was the lieutenant governor's background. His mother came to Atlanta in 1942, when he was ten years old, and she worked for two years at the Lockheed plant. She saved up and took the children once for lunch at the Biltmore Hotel. For two years they stayed in Atlanta, and then they went back to the mountains. And now the lieutenant governor was in the wood-paneled office.

And to the paneled bar of the Ritz-Carlton later that evening came Atlanta City Council President Marvin Arrington, as concerned with his own past as the lieutenant governor was with his.

But Marvin Arrington was black. He was heavy and strong, though with noticeable bowlegs. He was forty-six, by profession a lawyer. And his talk, open and unabashed, and fresh still, though he must have spoken the lines a hundred times, was about the difference between today and yesterday, between today, when honor was his, and yesterday, when Atlanta was so segregated that the only place where black people could use the lavatories was the bus station. So that his mother, when she brought the children to town, urged them to use the lavatories there if they didn't want to walk back the miles to it.

The black bar attendants, women, were pleased to see Arrington. Smiles came to their faces, though he was not a glamorous man, and had a heavy, long face. He wore a pale-brown suit; he seemed to sit low in his chair. He told Tom Teepen he had lost twenty pounds. But his long day—he had come quite late for our meeting—had exhausted him; and though he had a cranberry juice only, he dipped his large hand into the nut bowl and drew out nuts by the handful.

We talked about the rich blacks in Atlanta—were they real? He said (as in the reprint of an Atlanta *Constitution* article I had read) that he earned a six-figure salary. But he didn't think there were all that many rich people among the blacks of Atlanta; and the figures he gave, of salaries and expenses, were really rather modest.

He said he was sorry he couldn't talk more just then, but he would like to see me; and he gave me a two-hour appointment in his law office some days ahead.

"CUT OUT of the herd." Anne Siddons had used the words to describe one of the anxieties of her Southern upbringing. And I heard almost the same words from a woman at a theology school, where I went to follow up the idea that had been given me in northwestern Georgia of religion and identity.

The woman who spoke the words—"I didn't want to be not part of the herd. That's where my identity came from"—was, like Anne Siddons, from a long-established family, not in Georgia, but in Mississippi. Mississippi, this woman said, had a history of 250 years; her family had lived in the same house for nearly two hundred years.

"The way my identity was formed was by my family and by who we were in Jackson and in Mississippi. In the Presbyterian church we had our own pew. And that was your identity. My aunt was shocked one day when she went to church and found a stranger in her pew."

Didn't the idea of piety and correctness contain the idea of service?

No, she said; that idea wasn't for her family. Other people had the idea of service; the idea was for other people. Yet she had spent much time in Atlanta serving the black community.

"There is a noblesse oblige that separated you but imposed an obligation, but with no person-to-person connection. And I think the reason I've spent so much time in the black community in Atlanta is that I was *hungry*."

"For what?"

"Hungry for . . ." She had trouble finding words. "For contact. With people who were living lives that were more real than mine was. We were real cold folks."

She meant the decorum, the rigidity, the manners of the family. When she broke away she welcomed even the idea of tears. In the idea of service now, and in the dream of becoming a minister, she had found a new idea of community.

"But remember," she said, talking of the identity that had been hers and probably still was, "this is a very specialized herd. White upper-class Mississippi people."

And while she was reaching towards a new community, the old way of things she had known was changing. The family was now scattered all over the United States; and the old family house, the "plantation," was probably "going to disintegrate." "And my mother is distraught in a way I've never known her. Because a lot of her identity is going to go. That house has been the gathering place; many people can stay there. For my mother it's a sense of place. That house, those trees, that dirt. My aunts talked about the Civil War as though it was yesterday. And the people there show off the old houses, you know. It's part of the economy of the place. They put on the old costumes and show the houses."

I said, "A kind of masque."

She said, out of the security of her new idea of community, "It's more like religion."

Identity as religion, religion as identity: it was the very theme of another theology student, a young man from a background quite different, a mountain community in northern Georgia.

He said, "When I think of growing up, the two things are very much the same thing—family and church. The church was a small church, with about forty-five members, all related. Seven or eight generations ago the first member of our family moved into that area and bought four hundred acres, and we still live on that. It isn't a plantation. There might have been slaves early on, but that disappeared pretty soon. We were a family of small farmers. My grandfather had fifteen or sixteen brothers, and their descendants all live within three miles of one another. It is very rare that anybody moves away. When you go up there you know people, and you know them as relatives.

"At the same time it is very easy for your own identity to get lost.

But I have since grown to appreciate how wonderful that is: a warm, loving, open kind of family, not just father and mother and brothers and sisters, but cousins, aunts, and uncles.

"The church is very much the same thing. Family members. The Holiness Church is a very emotional religion, and what struck me early on was how very different people were in church from what I knew of them at home. The emotion they expressed in church was different. There would be a lot of shouting. The preacher would try to work them up to the sinfulness of human nature. There would be moments during the service when people would get up and speak in tongues, and people would try to interpret what was being said. And there were times when people would get saved."

"This religion was not a reaching out to the world?"

"This religion was a calling away from the world, an excluding of the world. I still struggle to find how I relate to all that now. The first year in college I spent alone in my room. I was scared to go out. Then I became angry with some aspects of the faith that had such a rigid view of the world."

But now (like the Mississippi plantation, and for the same, economic reason) the mountain world was changing. "A lot of the people have to go away to get work." They came back, it was true; they never lost touch. But: "The twentieth century is pouring over the mountain."

Mountain family, old planter family: old ideas of community no longer served, and the descendants of those families were finding a new community in the ministry. But it hadn't been quite like this for Frank. He grew up in a blue-collar white urban neighborhood. It wasn't "ethnic," and it had no sense of community. It was Southern, but the Southern history and Southern past that were bred in the bones of the mountain boy and the plantation girl had had to be learned, studied, by the boy from the city. Because he had been born into a crowd, his early ambitions had been different.

"I wanted to be an individual, a nonconformist, a person with his own rights, opinions. But at the same time I did want an identity. And I found that in the Democratic Party. It started at high school. I got into the Democratic group and quickly became a leader of the teen Democrats. It became my religion, because I evaluated everything according to the party's success or failure. When I left school I went straight into the party organization. The party became my community. But it wasn't a real community. It didn't have the caring that a Christian community should have. In the navy I had the sense of meeting Christ in reading the Scriptures, and I was touched by that. But it was isolated until I came here, which makes real on earth this relationship with God. I have found the real community here, in theology school."

CITY POLITICS in Atlanta were mainly black politics, and Michael Lomax was one of the up-and-coming black politicians. He was only thirty-eight, but it was said that he would be running for mayor in 1989. He was not from Atlanta, but from Los Angeles, and he had style. He was tall and slender and well dressed and educated and softly spoken. He was of a pale complexion. He did not have a black man-of-the-people reputation; but service to the black cause was in his family tradition. His knowledge of black writing was considerable; his hero was the early black radical William Du Bois, the critic of Booker Washington. And he was a dedicated politician.

Everything about him was considered. He had the politician's heightened sense of the self, as I was aware when, after our talk, we walked back together for a while in the city center, and on the Macy's side of Peachtree Street. He was known; people looked at him. He made a joke about it, but this kind of public response mattered to him.

We met in the library, for which, as chairman of the Fulton County Commission, he was responsible. The people he greeted so affably in the forecourt were architects. He said grandly, but with a smile, "I like building things." And in the library council room upstairs there was tea: a silver service and white Wedgwood cups and a selection of pastries of small size, laid out for us by someone from the Commission, a white man, young, smiling, happy to serve his elegant chairman.

Blacks had to look inwards, Michael Lomax said. The need now was not for marches so much as for an internal revolution.

"The civil-rights movement distorted our conception of human relations. It made it completely adversarial. In an adversarial relationship there is a good person and a bad person, a victim and a victimizer. We were the good, we were the victim." None of the current black leaders talked of black responsibility, he said.

And yet for him, with all that he had become, and all his future, there was still the burden of being black. He spoke of the burden in this way (and he might have spoken the words often before): "There's not a day, not a moment in my life when I don't have to think about the color of my skin. And being black is not just about what I see. It's about what I feel about myself. It's as much internal as external.

"I think sometimes that an exorcism has got to happen for all of us, where you pull out all of those evil demons of race. They're still inside us, fighting with one another.

"Ten years ago I went to Brazil. And I went to a place in northern Brazil called Salvador which has a very mixed population and where having skin the color of mine was nothing unusual. And I felt a tremendous sense of liberation and freedom. But I also felt a sense of loss because people weren't dealing with me negatively because of my skin. That was the freedom, but I had so many expectations inside me as a black person that I couldn't accept the ignoring of that person—it was another kind of invisibility.

"You have to confront your own demons. For me it's confronting the fact that I am a black person and that every time a white person sees me I may be no different for him than seeing a drunk on the street. And that colors the way I think about myself. I have been angry about being black, saddened by it. And I cannot deal with the white person or the black person until I look in the mirror and accept the man I see there."

IT WAS generally agreed that the correct behavior of the sheriff of Forsyth County had done much to take the poison out of the situation at the very beginning. When I spoke to him on the telephone I found him easy and businesslike; many people had been to see him. He told me how to get to his office. It was in the Forsyth County Jail, he said. And that made me think of any number of Western films.

It was about an hour away from Atlanta. The holiday setting, of woods and well-kept roads and an enormous artificial lake created by the Army Corps of Engineers, was hard to associate with the blood tensions of 1912: the lynching of a man in the jail, the public hanging of two others, the roving crowds giving notice to the blacks. And the county town in the midst of these spring woods was very American: the fast-food places, the banks looking like churches, billboards—ordinary.

A woman stepped out of her grocery shop to direct me to the sheriff's office. Across the main town road, past the cemetery, and then on to a low brick structure. And there, in the busy little red-brick town, it was: a new building, not the one of 1912, but still as flat and basic-looking as a sheriff's office in a Western film; assertively labeled (as in a film) FORSYTH COUNTY JAIL, but with a large asphalted fore-court full of parked cars—the jail and the sheriff's office, like the fast-food places, serving a motorized community. The United States flag and the Georgia flag hung side by side from flagpoles.

Two sets of glass doors led into the reception area, where two elderly white people were sitting on low chairs. A secretary sat at a desk with papers. And at her back, on the concrete-block wall, was a seal-of-Georgia plaque: roughly rendered motifs of civility from 1776: an arch on two classical columns, a scroll hanging loose in the space between the columns, with the Georgia motto: WISDOM, JUSTICE, MODERATION.

The sheriff was in a meeting, the secretary said. A man in blue jeans came in to talk about a parking ticket or something of that nature —giving an idea of the day-to-day business of a sheriff's office. The sheriff himself came out after a while, jacketless, a paisley-patterned tie on his white shirt. He said, "Be with y'all in just a moment."

And soon I was called into his office, where, on an old-fashioned hat-rack, at the very top, was a black cowboy hat with the sheriff badge. The sheriff said he had worn the hat only once, on the day of the big Forsyth march. Also on the rack was the very clean pale-blue jacket of the sheriff.

He was in his forties. He said he had been twenty years in the county. He had "taught school" for some time; he had been sheriff for eleven years.

Years ago, he said, Forsyth County had been isolated, and the folks were very clannish. The same thing could be said of "the entire North Georgia area." "The liquor industry came along, and a few folks made moonshine here, because it was very isolated. And that was the only means of income." Later there came the Lockheed and General Motors plants; and there also came the poultry industry. "The poultry industry brought our community out of its low socioeconomic situation. You began to see better roads, a great influx." At the same time there was the Atlanta boom. "What we are attracting now is a lot of people." Land had tripled in price. In 1970 there were sixteen thousand people; in 1986 there must have been forty thousand. "We are becoming an affluent suburban county of Atlanta. So we are in a boom growth situation."

So, though "folks threw rocks" at the first brotherhood march, the cause of the rock-throwers couldn't really succeed in the new Forsyth. The second march, of the twenty thousand, wasn't a racial occasion, the sheriff said. The marchers were white as well as black, and they were making clear that they didn't want to see violence. "The American public will not tolerate violence."

About race as race, the sheriff said, there was nothing that could be done. "The real problem is social and economic. . . . There's nothing you can do, because people migrate where they feel comfortable. They migrate to their social-economic status." A black doctor who wanted to settle in Forsyth County might fit in. But it would be different for a lower-class black. People needed to feel comfortable with people. "If you have two sorry black folks and two sorry white folks they're gonna fight because they can't get along."

About the big march itself, it had always been a media event, the sheriff said. A lot of people came to that march because it was the first march in twenty years. People who had missed out on the marches of the civil-rights movement in the old days wished to take part in one now. "It gave a lot of people an opportunity to take part in something they thought was going to be historical." So there were these two "volatile" groups—the marchers, and the people who were opposed to them. What sort of people were opposed? "A lot of the people I deal with on Saturdays. Law enforcement deals with ten percent of the population ninety percent of the time." This was how the sheriff talked: he was as much sociologist (and former teacher) as law-enforcement official. He made the affairs of Forsyth County seem much more manageable.

And though he didn't say so, there came out from his talk the idea of two sets of people looking for attention. The civil-rights groups, their major battles and indeed their war won long ago, now squabbling, and looking for causes; and the white supremacists looking in almost the same way for publicity and patronage. The great Forsyth march, as the sheriff described it, was like a ritual conflict, played out before the cameras, and according to certain rules. Out of this formalizing, the issue had died. Overexposure was a very American aspect of this formalizing, I also felt. Everyone had been interviewed and interviewed; everyone, including the sheriff, had become a personality; everyone had now exhausted attention.

So, as the sheriff said: "The issue is dead."

And the sheriff made a further point. The marchers had won, but in the three months since then no black had moved into Forsyth. The county remained all white, proving the first point: that the issue now wasn't racial, but social and economic.

He was impressive, Sheriff Walraven. He was an elected official, and he saw himself representing the will of the American people—who had turned their face against violence. And though he wasn't willing to play up this side of things, he was also doing his Christian duty, Christianity being a religion that taught love and peace. (Christianity, at one time, in this setting, stood for other things; the Christianity of the Ku Klux Klan still had to be taken into account. But the sheriff saw the events of 1912 as historical, seventy-five years old. He represented the current will of the American people. There was to be no violence; it was his duty to see that there was none.)

Did he see a situation where that might change?

He thought for a while and said, "If the system falls down." But then almost immediately he added, "The system can't fall down. Individuals might fall down."

To meet this educated man with an almost philosophical idea of his duties was to see how far away from the center the Ku Klux Klan groups of Forsyth were. The point had in fact been made by the black mayor of Atlanta, Andrew Young.

"I don't view the Klan action as just racist," the *Journal* reported him as saying three days after the big march. "These are the desperate acts of people who find that history is leaving them behind. Basically what we need are some job training programs that help people get into the mainstream. What we are dealing with in Georgia now is a problem of the underclass—black and white. The black underclass gets caught up in drugs and crime. The white underclass gets caught up in drugs, crime and Klan. You can march until your feet drop, but you ain't going to change it that way."

The point wasn't taken up. It wasn't made again; it was lost in the good, safe cause.

A KIND of victory had been won. But little had changed. The message of Forsyth County was also the message of black Atlanta. It was of this special frustration that Marvin Arrington, president of the Atlanta City Council, spoke or appeared to speak.

Our meeting was not a good one. I had telephoned his law office just before going over and he had said I was to come right away. But when I got there he wasn't in. He was said by his secretary—who gave me a Coca-Cola—to have stepped out. And he didn't return for half an hour. The offices of his firm were impressive. They were in a nicely refurbished old building in downtown Atlanta; an article in the *Constitution* had said that the building had cost $1 million.

When he came back he took me into his own office. It was sunny, overlooking the street, and warmer than the inner rooms. It had many diplomas and family photographs on the wall; and African statuary, tourist curios, on the windowsills.

The failure of the occasion was partly my own fault, because when Arrington took off his jacket and urged me to begin, just like that, I could think of little to say. I had been hoping for a little chat beforehand; and hoping that during this chat I might see ideas or themes I might want to follow up. But this blunt request to get started filled my head only with what was most obvious. It didn't help that he was restless. He often got up and walked about; often spoke to his secretary through an open door; looked through papers on his desk. He said he did forty things at once.

And all that came out of this unsatisfactory meeting was what might have been gathered from the *Constitution* and *Journal* file and from his own publicity: a man of the inner city, growing up when all facilities were segregated, father a truck-driver, much of the ambition of the children being derived from their mother. "I broke out." An athletic scholarship helped him break out; he thought of all those who couldn't get such scholarships. And little had changed. Little economic power had come to black people with their political power; even the black business street, Auburn Avenue, was now neglected. Black people needed opportunity; opportunity could be provided only by the system. So that he seemed still to be laying responsibility on others. No thought here of the internal revolution Michael Lomax had spoken about. Still the rage.

When I said that there had been movement for black people, he said, "Wait for another 350 years?"

He smoked a big cigar; stubbed it out and created a cloud of aromatic smoke near where I was sitting. He apologized for that; there were, with his brusqueness, always these little moments of concern for me as a visitor. A colleague came in and was more interested in me than Arrington had been. His son came in, and Arrington momentarily softened at the sight of the big, confident boy, who told me he had been to England and had spent two and a half weeks there. After a time the boy went out. Arrington later referred to him. The world would be different for people like his son, he said. But that was the one touch of softness and optimism in his general spikiness.

A spikiness about race. About the Atlanta newspaper that had tried to destroy him, he said—and he took me to an attached room to show me the attack on him in the Atlanta *Constitution:* he had had it framed, together with a printed protest, signed by Martin Luther King's father among others, about the attitude of the press to black elected officials. And there was a spikiness, above all, about Michael Lomax, who was his opposite in so many ways: Arrington big, heavy, strong, brown-black, self-made; Lomax slender, light-complexioned, of an educated family, and conscious of his charm.

Arrington had defeated Lomax for the Atlanta City Council presidency some six years before. And it was said that if Lomax ran for mayor in 1989, Arrington intended to run against him. He wanted me to read a profile of Lomax that had been written for an Atlanta paper. He spoke to someone in his office on the telephone and asked in an executive way for a copy of "the Lomax profile." Later again he spoke on the telephone to someone in his office, to ask for a copy of his own publicity pamphlet, *The Arrington Commitment.* Eight pages, sixteen photographs; professionally produced.

He made other telephone calls. And once, while I was reading something on the wall—the past laid out in diplomas and photographs and newspaper columns—I heard him talking firmly to someone on the telephone, perhaps about the thing that had called him out of the office just after he had told me to come over. It was as though that day he had found many things to abrade him.

He spoke again about his son. That softness led him to thoughts of London, where his son had been. But: there were riots, he said. And when he was there: "I didn't feel at ease in London." He added, "I went to the Shakespearean theatre. Didn't understand it, but I went for the culture." I would have liked to know more. But this was one of the many threads that were broken by his getting up and walking, his looking for papers, his smoking, his little bursts of courtesy. This trip to England—it would have been interesting to see the country through Arrington's eyes—was something we never got back to.

I felt soon that there was nothing new for me to ask, that all the points I might raise would founder on the subject of black disadvantage.

It was something I had worried about: that these figures of Atlanta, because they had been so often interviewed, and though they might appear new to the out-of-towner, might in fact have been reduced to a certain number of postures and attitudes, might have become their interviews. Like certain writers—Borges, to give a famous example, who had given so many interviews to journalists and others who, in the manner of interviewers, had wanted absolutely the set interview, the one in the file, had wanted to leave out nothing that had occurred in every other interview, that he, Borges, had finally become nothing more than his interview, a few stories, a few opinions, a potted autobiography, a pocket personality. Which was the way, I had been told, the media created two or three slogans for a politician and reduced him to those easily spoken words. I had worried about this, about not being able to get through the publicity; and with Arrington it had come to pass. I had not been able to go beyond the file.

On the wall was a framed saying of Abraham Lincoln's: A lawyer's time and advice are part of his stock in trade.

I got up to leave. He was courteous, and as a farewell offering he gave me a little tour of his firm's offices. The people I met were friendly and attractive; there was a white office manager. The quality and mood of people in an office or in any organization tell you immediately about the employer or management. So there would have been a much better side to Arrington than the side he had shown me that afternoon.

Going down into the street, where the people were black, and Atlanta as a result appeared different from the areas I had so far seen, with a Caribbean, Latin American aspect to the crowd—and even to the city, since downtown Atlanta is not a city of solid, built-up blocks but, rather, a city of tall buildings and empty spaces, parking lots, so that it quickly acquires a semiderelict look—going down into the street, I was assailed by a very old feeling of constriction and gloom.

I was taken back to some of the feelings of my childhood in Trinidad. There, though most of my teachers were Negroes (brown rather than black), and though for such people (as well as for policemen,

Negroes again) I as a child had the utmost awe and respect, and though in my eyes people like teachers didn't really have racial attributes but were their professions alone, yet the minute I found myself in an out-of-school relationship with them I became aware—a child from an Indian family, full of rituals that couldn't be transferred outside the family house, rituals and attitudes that had day after day to be shed and reassumed, as one went to school and returned home—I became aware of the physical quality of Negroes, and of the difference and even, to me, the unreality of their domestic life.

Something like that had happened in Arrington's office. His spikiness, his stress on race and the inner city ("Inner city is my ball game") and the strength he drew from the poor among blacks, had put up that old barrier around him.

The spikiness was understandable; rage was understandable. But I also felt that rage and spikiness could make demands on other people that could never be met. He had said, "I'd like to be free. I cannot fly like the bird." Many people could say something like that; not everyone could make it a political statement. And I felt, especially in the Caribbean-seeming streets outside as I walked back to the hotel, that there were two world views here almost, two ways of seeing and feeling that could not be reconciled. And this was depressing.

I had with a part of my mind been trying to find in the black politicians of Atlanta some of the lineaments of the black politicians of the Caribbean. In Arrington, for the first time, I thought I had found someone who might have been created by Caribbean circumstances. In the Caribbean such a person, proclaiming his origins in the people (like Bradshaw of St. Kitts or Gairy of Grenada) and claiming because of his early distress to understand the distress of his people, might have gone on to complete colonial power, might have overthrown an old system and set up in its place something he had fashioned himself.

But here in Atlanta—though, as president of the City Council, Arrington had power of a sort, the power to say no—the power was circumscribed. And perhaps the very dignity that the politics of the city offered a black man made him more aware of the great encircling wealth and true power of white Atlanta. So that the politics of Atlanta might have seemed like a game, a drawing off of rage from black people. Just as civil-rights legislation gave rights without money or acceptance, so perhaps city politics gave position without strength, and stimulated another, unassuageable kind of rage.

Hosea Williams, after picketing the CIA in Washington about drugs, was to have gone to Europe to do some work about apartheid. Either he didn't go; or the trip was very short. Because a few days later Tom Teepen arranged a meeting for me with Hosea in Atlanta. The meeting was to be in East Atlanta, in one of the "neighborhoods," Tom said; and he drove me there to introduce me.

The building we stopped at looked like a small factory or warehouse, and it stood next to a broken, three-walled shed. There was a central corridor, with people sitting at a desk. Stickers printed HOSEA were on walls and doors, and gave the place the feel of an election campaign headquarters. We were shown into an inner office, past a room with a secretary at a full desk.

The walls of the inner office were hung with many big black-and-white photographs of the civil-rights marches: Hosea, much younger, in some of the photographs, with his amazingly young leader, Martin Luther King. There were photographs of arrests by police. But the most moving photographs were those that stressed simpler things: the overalls of the marchers, and the mule carts—the twin symbols of the movement, affecting, and inevitable, and right, like the Gandhi cap and homespun of India. Tom Teepen, looking at the photographs with me, said that when Martin Luther King was killed it was decided to carry his coffin on a mule cart; but the only one that could be found— and was commandeered—was in a museum or a fairground.

Also on the wall were many shields and plaques given to Hosea for various things. And there was a poster with a Black Power twist on the Aunt Jemima theme. The big black woman didn't smile; she offered a big black fist; and the words were "No More" and "Net Weight 1000 lbs."

Hosea (he had been busy somewhere in the building) finally came in, a man in his own place now, deferred to by the people there, and stiller than when I had seen him, in the federal courtroom.

Tom Teepen introduced me; told him of my interest in Forsyth County. I saw in his eyes an immediate acceptance. And right away, even before Tom left us to go back to his paper, Hosea began to talk, began unaffectedly to act out the story, giving off energy, walking about, coming right up to me sometimes, while I sat at the long board table that was there in the big office in addition to the office desk.

He took the story of Forsyth back to the beginning of the year, when the karate instructor from California had decided to have a Walk for Brotherhood to mark Martin Luther King Day in Forsyth. Hosea heard about that on television, and became interested.

"He didn't know that violent and rabid racism existed up there. They came after him so vicious he began to realize, 'I mightn't get out of this town alive.' In places like that the major weapon is fire. Burn them out, burn down their houses. A martial-arts student from the next county came forward to help this fellow. The martial-arts fellow has the reputation of being a tough guy. He said to the Californian, 'We are white males. They can't do this to us.' He's a tough guy. But they not going to go after *him*. What they'll do is go after his family. So he began to reach out for black help. He became more shaky.

"When I heard of this the first thing that hit me was this: 'Every movement we have ever been in, some whites came to our defense. Here are these white boys in trouble. If Dr. King was here, what position would he take?' I said, 'Hosea, pack your bag. We've got to go to Forsyth.'

"I finally got the name of the martial-arts guy through a newspaper. I called the guy. 'My name is Hosea Williams. I offer you my help.' He was overwhelmed. He said, 'I know of you. Before I accept your help I want to talk face to face with you.' But I wouldn't drive to Forsyth that night. He said, 'I'll drive down to Atlanta.' I was afraid of him. I didn't know who he was. He might have been from the Klan. I staged a meeting in the lobby of a big hotel. He drove down that same night, he and his father-in-law. He said, 'I know you. I know your reputation. I know you're a tough man. But I tell you one thing. If you come to Forsyth and march with me you ain't gonna leave that place alive.'

"I know how tough Forsyth is. But I thought he was being too pessimistic. I called a press conference. I announced that we are leaving from Dr. King's grave at nine o'clock and we are going to Forsyth. I didn't think nobody was going with me. Black people are afraid of Forsyth. They know the reputation. Black people don't even like stopping for gas at Forsyth.

"Dean Carter, the martial-arts man, said: 'These people are ignorant. They are told to keep niggers out, don't care what it takes. They are taught from the cradle to the grave to keep those niggers out. You do whatever you have to do—you beat them, you kill them—to keep niggers out of the county. It's like their culture.' That's what Dean Carter said. 'It's like their *culture*.'

"I thought I knew how bad the place was. I didn't know how bad it really was.

"The next morning there was about thirty-five to forty people.

"I sensed, going up, that these people had a deep frustration. I got up and taught and talked and taught and talked and preached all the way up there. When we got there, there was about thirty or twenty people waiting to join us. One or two was the Ku Klux Klan waiting to infiltrate. But at the same time there were about fifteen hundred people all around—the papers say two hundred, but I say fifteen hundred—and they were having a Ku Klux Klan rally and they were shouting, 'Kill the niggers! Kill the niggers! Run the niggers back to the Atlanta watermelon field.' Fifteen hundred. All around.

"The sheriff tried to discourage us getting off the bus. I said: 'We are Americans. Marching is a matter of free speech.' I wasn't going to let anybody stop us marching.

"Those people all around were so souped up they were diving and running over four-foot fences like Olympic hurdlers, shouting, 'Kill the niggers! Kill the niggers!' "

When I had seen him in the courtroom—doing nothing, saying little—he had seemed harassed, agitated. Yet now, though he was walking around my chair and acting out his story, stamping his feet, jabbing his fist down, he seemed lucid. His talk didn't seem exaggerated or quirky. And what increasingly came out was how practical he had been. Like the Indian mahatma, he knew how to organize things, how to use the institutions of the society: the law, the press.

The opponents of the march had also organized. According to Hosea, they had laid by stores of missiles.

Hosea said, "The press kept coming up to me"—odd, this description of a dangerous march, with the press on hand: how had he got them there?—"The press kept coming up to me and saying, 'Is this bad? Is this bad, Hosea?' And I said, acting, 'No, it ain't so bad.' And one of my own staff members came and said to me, 'Reverend, it's *bad*.' And he was right. It was bad.

"One man, one of the Forsyth crowd, was running up to the front of our bus and then to the rear of the bus—the bus that had brought us to Forsyth, the bus I had rented—running back and forth trying to get to me. I realized what he was doing. He seemed to be a leader, and I thought I would try to communicate with him through the eyes." (I remembered what Howard had told me: in moments of street danger avoid eye contact. It was Howard's rule for avoiding trouble generally; and I saw it practiced all the time by black waiters in Atlanta.) "And when he came back up to the front of the bus, I smiled at him. He went berserk. He started screaming: 'The nigger smiled at me! You gotta kill these niggers! I don't want these niggers march. But the nigger *smiled* at me!' "

The sheriff then asked Hosea to get his people back on the bus.

"I got the people on the bus and take them down a lil ways, to give him a chance to contain the Ku Klux Klan."

Hosea drew up the bottom of one trouser leg and showed the dark-red bruises on his pale-brown shin and calf. He said the bruises had been caused by a brick thrown during the march.

That was the end of the march. On the bus going back to Atlanta a thought came to him, and he began to smile. His son asked why he was smiling, and Hosea said to him, "I feel like I've really celebrated Dr. King's birthday."

It was his storyteller's way of rounding off the story, which had begun with his strictures on the false ways people, and black people among them, had begun to celebrate the birthday of "Dr. King"— which was the way Hosea invariably referred to Martin Luther King.

Hosea said, "On the bus coming home I told my son, 'Them's some of the baddest white folks I've ever seen.' "

"I've faced mobs before. But they usually were older white males. If there was any women they was only one or two and they was quiet. But at Forsyth, oh God, they had a large number of women, many holding little babies in their arms, and screaming all kinds of vulgarity, especially hatred. 'Kill the niggers! The niggers get AIDS!' The number of young people, the teenagers! I thought: 'Oh my God, we got sixty more years of that kid standing over there.' "

After that first march, Hosea said, some newspapers had reported that he had been run out of Forsyth County. That had encouraged him to organize the second march. Forty thousand people had marched then. The newspapers said twenty thousand, but he thought forty thousand.

"Racism is coming back, man. Just like it did after the Civil War.

They described that then as the ending of the Reconstruction. Well, we're now at the ending of the second Reconstruction."

But the Forsyth issue was dead now, as the sheriff had said. Had anything been served?

Hosea thought that, though no black had moved to Forsyth, a lot of good had come out of the affair. He offered a list of the good things. One: the good white people up in Forsyth had been able to stand up to the Klan. Two: the fragmented civil-rights groups had come together, in a way they hadn't been together since the death of Dr. King.

"Three: Forsyth kind of forces so-called leaders to stop jiving and *lead*, not to wait for things to happen naturally. Forces leaders to go out and initiate and provoke confrontation. Four: the greatest thing. It proved that Dr. King's strategies didn't become obsolete with his death, as other people say. They say to me, 'Hosea, you're just a battle-fatigued old general. It's time to stop demonstratin' and start negotiatin'.' They've taken the movement out of the street and into the suite. Out of the street and into the suite. That's what they spin around doing. But they have to come back to my position and admit that the street is where it's happening."

"A primary force": that was how Tom Teepen had described Hosea. But I hadn't seen it like that. I had seen him more as a performer, acting up to the public character he had created for himself. I didn't think so now. The City Council politics he was engaged in required him to be a showman; but through his showmanship—now, in the privacy of his office—I was aware of his lucidity and goodness; and I felt that the mahatma himself—with all his own awkwardness— might have radiated something of that quality.

As it happened, among the books on a bookshelf against the wall there was one with *Gandhi* on the spine. And when Hosea had to go out of the office to talk to someone who had arrived, I went and looked at it. It was a paperback. It wasn't the mahatma's autobiography, as I had thought; it was the screenplay of the film *Gandhi*, and on the fly leaf there was a dedication to Hosea from the writer, Jack Briley: a dedication that said it was (if I remember rightly) from a man who wrote words to a man who took the blows. The dedication, it seemed to me, did honor to both men, and hinted at one explanation (out of many) of the extraordinary power of that film. And the story Hosea had told (and I was an audience of only one), the energy he had given off, added a new meaning to the big photographs on the walls: the mule carts and overalls, and the young Martin Luther King, whom Hosea honored and adored.

When he came back to the office a little of the energy that had come to him during his telling of the Forsyth story had gone away. In its place there was authority; he was now in my eyes absolutely lucid.

I asked him about his recent campaign about drugs, and his picketing of the CIA.

He said, "The drug thing, it's bad. Drugs are destroying our people more than anything—segregation, racism—since slavery. The fear of the drug-traffickers, the fear that results from the drug-trafficking, is worse than the drug. Nothing have they feared like those drug people. I was born in the streets; I was raised in the streets; I still live in the streets. And even I have just discovered how bad the drug business is."

So there was logic in his behavior, as there had been in the mahatma's, the switching of reforming attention from public issues to private, from the external foe to the internal. And the impression he gave of being a very practical man was added to when I asked him about the building where we were. Was it his political headquarters in a "neighborhood," or what? He said it was his business place. He made chemicals. This was unexpected. I must have read about it somewhere, almost certainly; but it hadn't registered.

He said, with as much gentleness as pride, "Come, I'll show you."

We went out into the corridor and went past the desk where, ever since I had come, there had been two young people, a young woman and a young man, as still as students, serving some purpose in Hosea's affairs. At the end of the corridor Hosea pushed a door open, and there, attached to his office building, was a warehouse with barrels and on one side stacks of cardboard that would fold into cartons.

"I make janitorial chemicals," Hosea said. "Floor-cleaners, window-cleaning fluid. Everything to do with janitorial cleaning. I had to make myself independent of those people downtown."

He employed twenty people. The business was bigger than I thought; and in this business side of the man there was again, and more than ever, something of the Indian mahatma, who had started his professional life as a lawyer, was scrupulous about accounts, was careful about things like newspaper presses, and in South Africa in the 1900s, for this very purpose of independence and Ruskinian virtue, had started a farm. Strange fulfillment sixty years later of the mahatma's creed, and perhaps the achievement here had been bigger than the mahatma's in India: the winning of legal rights, against a background of slavery and violence, for a people long humiliated and disenfranchised.

He took me outside, to wait for a taxi. There appeared to be none. He said, "I will stop someone I know and make him take you back." But no one he knew came along. In the end he asked two of his people, waiting in a shabby van, to drive me back. "Give them something for the gas," he said. And, driving back along Highway 20 to Atlanta, in the company of these followers of Hosea's, poor people, in their littered van (the radio turned on), I felt myself in another atmosphere, and felt the distance between the people Hosea led or spoke for and the setting, the towers of central Atlanta appearing in the distance above the freeways.

F ROM SCATTERED impressions (and really more from stories of Shango and Shouters in Trinidad and memories there of black street-corner preachers and beach baptisms) I had thought of black-American religion as the religion of ecstasy and trance. I was not prepared for its formality or its communal-social side, as in Howard's home town. I was not prepared for its purity, as in Hosea. Or, later, in Robert Waymer.

He was a handsome man of forty-nine; formal clothes became him. He was on the Atlanta School Board. He came from a black South Carolina family. There was a family farm of fifty acres—not big, but it had maintained many of the family. And the family had been well known in South Carolina, in Orangeburg, for three generations. "Maybe four."

I told him that family continuity like this had formed no part of my idea of black life in the American South.

He said, "It was a secret."

"Secret?"

"You don't tell white people everything." And this was so strange from him, in the paneled lobby of the Ritz-Carlton, where he sat confidently, fitting the setting.

He said: "They were hostile. People who understood their circumstances and took pride in doing something for themselves knew that if you were black you were living in a hostile environment."

He told me about his extended family. "There was quite a resonance in the extended family. And from that resonance and cooperation my father's two eldest sisters married brothers who were tobacco farmers, cattle farmers, general truck farmers. It was from that beginning of farming we came. And we were quite ingenious people, I think. There were sixteen of us. My mother was the oldest daughter of an A.M.E. minister."

He told me about the initials. African Methodist Episcopalian. The church had had its two hundredth anniversary that year, he said. African? Did it have something to do with Africa? No. It had been established by an ex-slave, Richard Allen, when he found that he was shut out of the white churches. And that was Bob Waymer's theme: the solidarity that had come to black people from being shut out, the necessity that had driven them to found their own institutions—and the breakdown that had occurred with the ending of segregation.

His father was the eldest son of a farmer. So there was a tradition in his family. And yet there was a certain modesty.

"We're really not leaders. Really not. You and other people haven't had an opportunity to learn about blacks the way they really are. My family doesn't consider themselves outstanding. We are good committed people, committed to helping each other. A kind of dedication that started with my grandfather and continued with my mother.

"You got to know that you don't know anything about blacks.

"The civil-rights movement was great for everybody. But it freed up whites more than it did blacks. We were a closed, segregated, persecuted group in America, and we knew that. Everything that we learned, my age group, we knew that we had to be good at what we did. We had to be curious. Patriotic. Better than the other guy. Educated. And religious. And *cautious* too. We had to be cautious because we had to negotiate the hostile system in order to earn a living, to survive and exist with a feeling of well-being. We did well, as a general group of people. We established our institutions, educated our own. Public education is a relatively new concept. The first high school in Atlanta, the Booker T. Washington, was built in the 1940s."

"Do you talk much about this now?"

"No. Not much. There is nothing to say. If you said anything you were bragging about how well you were able to survive. Which is nothing. Or you would be boasting. Which among my family and other families like mine is tantamount to sin—it's vanity."

I asked him about the place of the church.

"The church is basic. And I'm not specially religious. The church is where I learned how to have respect for myself and others. And that's basic. And the Ten Commandments—that's the law. That's it. I used to think when I was a child they were my mother's laws, and I wondered how the other children had got to hear of the same things."

He was calm. Yet there were others—I mentioned Marvin Arrington—who were not calm.

He said that people like Arrington were "actors." He stressed the word, and then he explained it.

Arrington was a lawyer. "There is a difference in the attitudes of black Americans who were educated solely in black institutions, and those who went to higher education in white institutions.

"Everybody wants to be successful in what they do. Learning is a very painful changing of you and your mental attitudes. If you are going to be a success as a lawyer in America you are going to be successful only if you emulate or become a white lawyer. The profession—and this is not only for the legal profession—orients you in that direction. And you become an instrument of your own demise."

Demise—death. That was a strong word. But he meant the death of the soul; and, as he saw it, it was the kind of death that had come to black people in some ways with desegregation and the consequent loss of community. This was the very subject that Howard—and it seemed now so long ago—had touched upon, as we were walking back from church to his mother's house.

Bob Waymer said, "I mean demise. Let me tell you why. In the teaching profession and the legal profession and any other profession you learn certain things from white institutions about blacks. And they are ninety percent derogatory. Frederick Douglass—he is one of my heroes—and other people have said it—says that there is no planting without the tilling of the soil. For a while, because of the love and compassion which Dr. King was able to communicate to the rest of the world, there were many people all over the world who felt that something was askew, wrong, about the race question and the treatment of blacks. But these good people always knew that. They knew that already. What Dr. King did was to act as a catharsis for white people. He was a great mental-health cure for white Americans. What he did for blacks was to make their rights legal and to inspire tremendous numbers of blacks to take action for their people and themselves.

"But once blacks got into white institutions they found that being in their own institutions was a lot better, and that being a white American wasn't all that great. We thought that once we had the same rights all our problems were over. What happened was that we retained eighty percent of the historical problem that we had, and that now we also had to deal with all of those things associated with being white.

"Let me give you a comical example. If you were a domestic and you cooked dinner for a white family, you knew how much they would eat and you knew that if you cooked a little more you could always take that home with you. You always did that. It was part of the built-in economy, the hidden economy."

And there were other examples, which were not so comical; were in fact humiliating to think about. In the days of segregation blacks could not stay in hotels or motels or be served in restaurants. Some places served blacks at the back window; and it often happened that when the cook knew his order was a back-window order he put on, if he were serving a hamburger, an extra piece of meat. This was the origin of the cheeseburger. And since there were no hotels for blacks there grew up, in certain black families or houses, the "tourist home," where blacks might stay. Local black people usually knew where these places were, and could direct the traveler. The "tourist home" was usually a room in someone's house; it provided a livelihood for some people.

"The civil-rights movement made us equal. We didn't have to be resourceful any more. All we needed was a credit card and a good job. So, what's lost? Mrs. Smith, who operated her tourist home, can no longer earn a living. We went from four dollars a night for a family—which included breakfast and a sandwich to take with you, and communication—to fourteen dollars a night in a Holiday Inn room."

Communication through the tourist homes: it was one of the unexpected fruits of segregation, and it was something Bob Waymer stressed. New dances, he said, traveled very fast between blacks because of this communication. In those days without television it was like magic: blacks from different parts of the country could always dance the same new dances when they met. With desegregation this was lost.

"There was a tremendous boost for hotels like the Holiday Inn all across the United States. I remember people who weren't traveling anywhere who would go downtown and check into the Holiday Inn just because they had the right."

R ELIGION WAS like something in the air, a store of emotion on which people could draw according to their need. The religious vocation could come to many. For some the vocation contained the ideas of service and community. For others, with a stronger sense of self, who had gone out into the world with a will to win but had then withdrawn for various reasons, the vocation came as a wish to expound the word, to preach, to make an offering to God and men of the life that had been lived.

The white former businessman I met, in a group of mature students in a religious school, had felt "humbled by God." It was only after he had made his religious decision that an offer had been made of the capital he had been looking for to keep his business going. That offer of capital had been a temptation; but he hadn't fallen. He was a handsome man, with arresting blue eyes; he couldn't have been unaware of his looks; he might have expected an easier passage through the world. The same could probably be said of the striking black woman from Alabama. She spoke of her beauty as of something to be taken for granted; and something still an asset. But her life after she had left the South had been one of poverty and disorder. And there was Danny, a musician. He too, like the former businessman, had felt humbled by God—he used the same words.

Danny said, "I pictured my life as a shattered mirror—a piece here, a piece there."

I was so taken by that—the kind of chaos Anne Siddons had talked about—and so interested by what he had to say about the development of his religious life, that I wanted to talk to him again. We fixed a time. He didn't come. I telephoned. He was eating; I could tell by the noises; he said he had had a lot more to do than he had thought. We fixed another time. And he came.

He was black and stocky; in his short-sleeved open yellow shirt he looked very casual in the lounge of the Ritz, where that morning they were making a video about the hotel, with a male model, and they were shifting very bright lights about. This was the background to our talk of religion and the vanity of the world.

I asked him about the feeling he had had of being humbled by God. And that was where his story began.

"All my life I was such a winner, always seeking fame, even in high school. Everything I did I was number one. In music I have to be the leader. I was captain of the football team, the basketball team. I was the valedictorian of my class—I had got the highest grades of any graduating senior in my class. Even doing domestic work around the home, I would give it my very best because I knew my parents would praise me. I just loved people to brag on me. I thought I was something special in the world—I think it had a lot to do with grace and gifts that were naturally given, God-given, to me.

"And also my parents were professional. My father was a minister and also a teacher, and my mother also. And, the small community we lived in, by both of them being professional was kind of unique. It made me proud, even as a small child. We lived in a little place in Texas.

"I could even think we had indoor restrooms when most people in the community didn't. And though I would never brag about anything like that, it always had an effect on me. We were the first or second to get a TV set. My father was actually like the leader in the community. The first black to be on the school board after integration.

"I was aware of the fact that being boastful and wearing pride—letting it show on the outside—would cause people to not like you or resent you. So throughout my life I always knew how to be modest. But the purpose was for praise.

"I had a music scholarship, a football and a basketball scholarship. And I really didn't accept any of them because I didn't know what I wanted to do. I figured out eventually that music would be my best route. My mother taught me in the first and second grade, and my sister and I were always on program—always acting or singing solos—in the church. So music was always a way where people focused on me. It wasn't something I was thinking. It was something I just knew—that when you sang everyone sat down and listened to you, focused on you. I even used to go down to the grocery store and sing solos for the man, to get some candy.

"When I went off to college I went and looked at the football players —and my decision was made about music. The guys on the football field were so large and brutal. It would have been a hard way to go.

"There was a talent show at the college. I was walking through the dormitory and I heard someone playing a guitar downstairs, and so I went down to see what was going on. I went back to my room and got my clarinet and went down and started playing with this guy—songs. It drew crowds. People started coming down to listen. After that more musicians came. And we decided from that moment to perfect a couple of numbers for the talent show. We were successful that night. A nightclub owner was in the auditorium, and he asked us to come play in his club that night. We didn't play for money. We played for doughnuts. We loved it so much we didn't know but those two numbers. And that was when it started. And the group became the most popular group in the city. We got a manager. We toured the country. We made a reputation for ourselves.

"I was making so much money and was so popular, and I was only nineteen, just a senior in college, and living in a fabulous apartment, I thought I was God's gift to women. Until all of a sudden school became unattractive. It actually seemed irrelevant, because I was already on my way to fame and fortune—and I put *fame* before fortune.

"So I left school, to concentrate on being a star. And after seventeen years of being with several recording companies touring the United States and Canada, Africa—my life became shattered."

This was sudden, in the telling. But Danny's hidden point was that he had misread the music world, had misread his position in it. His position had always been subsidiary, supporting. He had been too quick to see himself as a star, had allowed himself to be deluded.

"I began to sense that I wasn't in control of my life. Even that God was being unfair to me. Because I knew I had as much or more talent than anyone in the business. But I would always get exploited. They would take ideas from my songs and never release my material nationwide."

"You mean you had no manager? In all those years?"

And it turned out that the first manager he had had, while he had been in college, hadn't lasted. "One thing was that all my life everything had always been *me*. So I was everything. I figured I could be my own manager, everything. I wasn't submissive. My pride blinded me from the wisdom of what my very first manager said to me—he was offering to support me financially if I stayed with his group. But I wanted my own name up front. And so throughout the years we floated around. The record companies and promoters know that entertainers are addicted to one thing—entertaining. So they exploited us, and we allowed ourselves to be exploited.

"I lost my group. That was the very point when the crisis came. I was in a club and I remember thinking, 'The time that I was most successful was the time when I was an apprentice.' That word came to me: *apprentice*. 'An *apprentice* to someone that had connections and money.'

"Reflecting back, I realize that the Lord was dealing with me then. I was being in a way humbled then—to even recognize that I need to be following someone, rather than being in direct control. But I was thinking strictly musically—maybe I need to join a group that's doing something, going somewhere, and be a follower rather than a leader.

"Then a big opportunity came up. I remember I was in a recording studio, getting ready to do a song on an album for the company who had made the offer to me—it was like an auditioning. And I was *horrible*. I broke down in the recording studio and cried like a baby.

"And I remember praying in the studio. I said, 'Lord, why are you letting this happen to me? How can I go to my family and tell them I have failed on my big break?' I had phoned people all over the United States and told people to look out for me, because this was it—I was going to be a big star at last. And even though my parents never agreed with what I was doing, I could even sense that they were hoping I would make it, my dreams would come true. The main thing I dreamed of was surprising my mother with a Rolls-Royce and a million-dollar home."

"Why do you think you failed so badly in the studio?"

"I just didn't seem to have it. I was embarrassed. I was depressed. Felt like my life was over. I felt like that was the last shot for me. It just shattered everything. To have your pride fed all your life and then to be denounced was like calling me counterfeit. Maybe I never was what I thought I was.

"So it was during that time that I began to think of another way. And that was that all my life at the back of my mind I had always like heard a voice saying, 'If you would be a songwriter, first. Let other people record *your* songs—that would be the best route for you.' I just sensed that. But I had too much pride. I didn't want to make it as a songwriter. I wanted to sing my own songs. But now I had reached the point where that was a last alternative. Because, even though I was at rock bottom, I never totally gave up. So this was a point of humility for me—that maybe I should try being a songwriter. So I gave one of my songs to a local musician, a tremendous vocalist, and I became his producer and manager. And we, on a local level, were successful.

"It was at that time I met a man that told me about Christ. He was a minister. He was a black minister. In his early sixties. He was also a musician. I went to the office to meet my wife, and I met this man. And when I met him his countenance was like there were *lights* coming from his eyes—just glowing. The smile just cut right through me. He looked at me with so much *love*. And at the same time I felt his countenance was drawing me to him. But inside I felt dirty and unclean and ashamed. And I wanted to go in another direction. All this was in the office of the insurance firm where he worked and my wife worked.

"All he said was, 'I've been looking forward to meeting you. I've heard so much about you.' He was a saxophonist, but he told me he only played *hymns*, and he asked if we could get together and play some hymns on the saxophone. Inside I had no desire, no intentions of doing that. But I told him yes.

"Before he came, about a week later, he sent me a Bible. It was a Living Bible. Up front it had selected scriptures that addressed specific issues. And one was: What does the Bible say about success? It gave all the scriptures relating to success and what to do when you are distressed and frustrated. All those scriptures related to trust in the Lord. Trust, and He would do. The emphasis is on *He*. All my life the emphasis was on *I*. *I* would do, or *I* can do. Or *I* have done."

And at the thought of that *I* having done, Danny laughed, as though he had made a joke.

"When I got together with the old musician, I accepted Christ. He shared Christ with me. He opened the Scriptures up to me.

"He came to my house a week after he had sent the Bible. My wife wasn't there at that particular time. He came with his saxophone. We played a little. And he really became interested in my singing. And he shared Christ with me. We had prayers. And I knew—but it was primarily reading the Bible for myself and seeing that where I had been carrying the burden of living, being successful, being happy, carrying that burden on my own shoulders—I knew, I saw through the Scriptures, that God, through Christ, offered everything I had been in pursuit of.

"So I prayed and invited Christ to come into my life. I believe that

God became human to take on our sins so that we could live in the righteousness of God. There was a scripture pertaining to that that really grabbed me. It was Galatians 5:22. The Living Bible put it this way: The Holy Spirit wants to produce fruit in you. 'Fruit.' Singular, but plural. Fruit, which are: love, joy, peace, patience, goodness, meekness, and self-control. That really grabbed me. To be successful is to have all of that living within me, because it wouldn't be my circumstances that would determine my happiness, but my relationship with God. So to be successful no longer depended upon personal achievements, but just simply having the peace and joy of knowing that God loves you. So much so that he would forgive me for all the things I have done.

"That very night, after the prayers with the old musician in my house, I went to a jail with him and participated in a worship service. And this became a nightly thing—visiting the jails. He would preach and I would sing."

"What did you think about the people in jail, the prisoners? How did they look upon you?"

"I *loved* them. I began to *see* people. All my life all I had ever seen was myself. My love was a self-directed love. I began to see that people had a lot more to offer me than I had to offer them. In other words, I began to see people in the way that I saw God.

"At this particular time I was still playing with a band at the weekend. But my songs changed. I started turning the secular words to songs about Jesus. I started preaching onstage."

"How did people take that?"

"As a joke."

"Black audience or white audience?"

"Mixed. I started having Bible studies on the way to the gig, as we called it. With the musicians. Bible studies during the breaks. And the group was becoming more popular than ever before. At the same time the gentleman who had led me to Christ was patiently—and lovingly —telling me that there would come a time when I would have to make a decision—to absolutely surrender to Christ.

"And that's when I wrassled—I struggled. Because I told the Lord day after day, night after night, that I could be a witness in a nightclub, because people there don't go to church and don't want to go to church. But I kept reading scriptures, and hearing in my mind, 'Be you separate. Come ye from among them. What fellowship has light with darkness, or righteousness with unrighteousness?'

"That's when, one night, my wife and I were at home. And I had a vision. I was in my home town in Texas. About two hundred yards from our house there is a pond. It is my favorite place, even now. Where I go to fish, to shoot my rifle, to swim. And I saw myself walking through the field going to the pond. When I heard a voice calling me Moses. And I looked up, upwards. And I recognized the voice. I knew that it was the voice of God, saying: 'You've gone as far as you can go.' Immediately I closed my eyes and lay down in the field. And suddenly another image that was transparent at first grew out of the image laying in the field. This image was muscular. I could see the intensity of the veins in my arms and muscles as it popped the shirt open. And on my face was self-determination, ambition, very powerfully prideful. And I continued walking towards the pond, each step growing more intense, ambitious, and confident. When suddenly again I heard a voice saying, 'Moses, this is as far as you can go.' This time I looked up with resentment. In my mind I was saying, 'No, you can't stop me now. I'm almost there. I can make it.'

"The power that came from above suppressed me into the field, the power which all the time I was fighting. As I was on my knees, still fighting, my skin began to melt and my bones began to melt also, till finally I was a horrible-looking creature, like something in a scary movie. But I continued to resist until there was nothing but liquid—I was a liquid mess. And then another image, transparent at first, grew out of that image on the ground. This time I was peaceful—this image had peace on its face, my face, and there was love and joy in my heart. Submissive, willing to be obedient and to trust in the voice that was directing my path.

"When I woke up I was—in the vision—touching my feet in the water. And my wife woke up as I was sitting in the bed with tears running down my face like water, chill bumps racing all up and down my body. And the power that was present woke my wife up as I was sitting up in the bed. My wife woke up in fear, and she was crying. 'Honey, what's wrong? Honey, what's wrong?' And I began to sing: 'Nothing is wrong. God is calling me.' And she immediately lay down and went back to sleep.

"Shortly after that I surrendered totally and entered the ministry.

Walked away from what was potentially a hit record. Knowing that the love of God and being submissive to God's will is success.

"It was some time later, on my thirty-fourth birthday, that I promised the Lord that I would go where he sent me and do what he wanted me to do. And he led me to the Methodist church, where I became a candidate for ministry. Now, this church insists that one has to go to seminaries. The college I chose, in my home town, is very, very expensive. And I didn't have a dime. I went there. I was rejected. I was told I had to have money to come to that college. The person who rejected me was a minister on the council. He said, 'Sir, you have some nerve coming here. And you don't have a dime.' I said, 'The Lord sent me.' "

Danny, telling this story of his rejection, laughed.

I asked, "What did he actually say?"

"He said something to this effect: 'Let the Lord give you some money, then come back.' " And Danny laughed again, as though he understood how tempting it had been, to someone in the minister's position, to reply like that.

Danny said, "He was rough. That was on Friday. That Sunday I directed the choir and played a saxophone song in our church. The district superintendent came by that Sunday. He was impressed after hearing that I was a candidate for ministry. On Monday morning I received a call from the gentleman who had sent me away. He said, 'God must have sent you. We are going to get you in school.' And all my schooling was paid. Over twenty thousand dollars so far. That was three years ago."

I asked about the old musician.

"He is still my closest friend. I *love* him. I call him my father, my brother, my friend. I tell this story, and would like it known, so that some people might be touched by Jesus."

2

◩◩◩

The Religion of
the Past

THE INTERSTATE highway goes right into the Charleston peninsula. So you arrive quite easily in the historical area. And after
Atlanta it was like arriving in Toytown. The people in the hotel lobby
were in tourist clothes; their footsteps and voices ricocheted off the
walls and the marble floor and hung in a roar above the extravagant
chandelier, at which from time to time a new arrival aimed a camera,
as though this too was part of tourist Charleston, together with the
many shops of the hotel lobby; and the Slave Mart and the Confederate
Museum in the eighteenth- and nineteenth-century streets outside; and
the renovated old market with its many stalls and boutiques, and with
grave black ladies sitting out on the pavement and weaving baskets.
The tourist Charleston not only being the eighteenth-century town,
and slavery and the Civil War, but also having something of the tourist
Caribbean of today.

In the historical area the horse-drawn tourist carriages moved up
and down all the time, and the horses had "diapers," to catch the
droppings. Other visitors walked about and looked. And others again
—in curiously ritualistic postures, appearing to lean slightly backwards
—pedaled themselves about, two at a time, in their pedal carriages, a
new tourist style.

The historical area is small. It doesn't seem possible that anything
real can survive. But Charleston does have its pretty eighteenth-cen-

tury streets and churches and graveyards; and in the historical area there are still people who carry the names commemorated in the names of the streets. ("What are they doing now?" a tourist asked his horse-carriage driver late one morning. He was asking—in his innocence still believing in the completeness of the world to which he had bought a tourist ticket—about the old families in the old houses they were passing. And the driver, living up to his role as a retailer of wonders, said, "Why, they haven't got up yet." The exchange, as it happened, was picked up in one of the houses. That was where I heard it—as an illustration of the little distance that can exist in downtown Charleston between the tourist and the thing toured.)

It is in fact the tourist trade that keeps historical Charleston in working order, keeps the old families where they are; though it is possible in a foreseeable future that the tourist trade, by pushing up property values, might drive some away. The story in Charleston is that money has begun to come back to some of the old families; and money, it is said, has become a motive where once people were content with the antiquity of a name. Names—they are really what is celebrated in the plaques on some of the buildings. The events themselves are small, colonial, not memorable to a visitor.

In this tourist Charleston the visitor soon stifles. But there is a larger town. There are the rich suburbs outside the peninsula. There is the Charleston of the naval station. And there are the various black areas. There is a large and pretty middle-class area, acquired and consolidated during a time of white panic. In the center, on what must have been the site of old houses, there are black housing projects, bald brick buildings going baldly down to scuffed earth, buildings that drive people out of doors and expose them and their children and their washing lines, so that the impression of slum, of many people living publicly in a small space, is as unavoidable as the impression of black faces. The east side of Charleston is also black. The houses there—some looked after, many not—are old, in the old Charleston style; but there are no tourists. So, after the Toytown aspect of the rest of old Charleston, the blacks seem like squatters, intruders at the Charleston ball. Yet they are as old as the old families.

It is only when you cross over from peninsular Charleston to what were once the slave plantations, the town's vast hinterland, that the slave past becomes vivid—though there is now just forest for the most part.

The land is flat and marshy, and it goes on for miles. The forest—oak, gum, maple, pine, sycamore, magnolia: tall forest—speaks of the fertility of the soil. The flatness and easiness and the extensiveness of the land make clear the need in the old days for abundant slave labor; and they also make painful the thought of that labor.

Now all is peace. From time to time there is a gateway in the forest, indicating land acquired by a big company; there is an old church; and there are black settlements. These settlements have a history. Most of them are on the site of old plantations that were taken by the federal government after the Civil War and broken up into sixty-acre plots for former slaves. Old property now, historical, some of the houses good, some poor; but after 120 years of land being passed on without wills or deeds, most of the titles are impossible.

I saw this coastal South Carolina forest on a Sunday morning. My guide was Jack Leland. He was a retired Charleston newspaperman, and he was of an old family. All this land and forest—so much the same to the visitor—was known to him in detail. This vegetation was the vegetation he had known as a child; it was still magical to him. Very few of the plantations now grew anything. Cattle were raised on some. Wealthy Yankees had bought others and turned them into hunting preserves.

"This second Yankee invasion, as my father called it, began in the 1880s, and continued to the 1930s. And it was a good thing, because it preserved the old buildings and gave jobs to the local Negroes and added a lot to the economy."

The land and the black people who worked on it, the memorializing of the past—these were still among Jack Leland's concerns, though his own family plantation had been alienated more than fifty years before. And our Sunday-morning excursion had a memorializing purpose.

We were going to Middleburg Plantation. A chapel of ease there that was more than two hundred years old, and was in danger of being washed away, had had its foundations consolidated with the help of a federal grant. There was to be a service in the chapel that morning—a special spring service, but also one of thanksgiving. Middleburg Plantation had been in the possession of the Gibbs family until six years before; and old Mr. Gibbs, Jack Leland's father-in-law, had sent out invitations for the service to people who he thought would want to attend. Afterwards there was to be a picnic in the grounds of the plantation house. That house had been restored by the estate agent who had bought the property.

The chapel of ease was at the end of a long lane in the forest. The lane was unpaved, soft; there were very bright spots of sunlight on the ground. It was cool in the forest shade; in the open sunlight the heat was immediate. The chapel was called Pompion Hill Chapel; in the flat coastal land of South Carolina a hill was anything a few feet high. The chapel stood beside a marsh where rice had once been cultivated. The surface of the water was in patches bright green. The original rice fields of this part of South Carolina had been created by Dutchmen who had learned about rice and dykes in the East Indies. Now the water level in the marsh had risen, because of some dam or hydraulic works some distance away; and it was this rise in the level of the water that had threatened the 1763 chapel of ease. With the grant from the federal government a rock revetment had been constructed around the "hill" at the water's edge.

The cars bumped down the soft lane to the chapel. Old Mr. Gibbs, in a jacket with a big check pattern, welcomed each, and directed each to its parking place.

The chapel was a single-chambered red-brick building, entered by the two side doors; whitewashed inside, undecorated; and, except for the baroque dome and pilasters at one end, without architectural flourish. The floor was tiled; paving tiles, Jack Leland said, were especially hard for colonials to make. The only notable furnishing was the pulpit, of local cedar, which was contemporary with the chapel and was the work of a Charleston cabinetmaker whose name was still known. IHS, the piety of the planter and slave-owner; now the sign of another kind of piety. And, indeed, after old Mr. Gibbs had been recognized and had shuffled up along the paving tiles and had spoken his thanks to everyone who had helped with the preservation, the theme of the sermon—a noisy motorboat racing about on the marsh from time to time, but its waves were now striking harmlessly against the gray rock revetment—the theme of the sermon was religion as a binding together of people. Community now with a special meaning, at once diminished and grander.

Then we went on to the plantation house. Brick pillars, green gates, a gateway without a wall, led from the road to a very wide avenue of oaks. The oaks were 150 years old; and these oak trees of South Carolina had the shape and spread of the saman trees of Central America, which had been introduced in the Caribbean islands as a shade tree for certain crops—cacao and coffee—and had been taken on from there to places as far away as Malaysia; so that tropical plantations and colonies of the imperial time acquired a similar look, with the vegetation that had been brought together from different parts of the world. Here, in South Carolina, was something like the saman trees of Trinidad.

And again the bright sunlight, coming through the foliage, fell in dazzling spots on the shaded ground. But then, after this long wide avenue, the restored plantation house was quite modest, a white-painted wooden building with three rooms upstairs and three rooms downstairs. This was upsetting to one's ideas about the grandeur of plantation life. Jack Leland said the house was small because the builder had been a Huguenot. English planters, when they did well, could become flamboyant; the Huguenots remained economical and austere, investing and reinvesting in land and slaves. (And the very first plantation house, according to the booklet about the restoration, had been even more modest, with a sitting room and a dining room alone on the ground floor, without a veranda or a back porch.)

Separate from the main house was a "dependency," as an ancillary building was called; and this dependency, more or less in order, was a cookhouse with a brick chimney. Another dependency had burned down, and nothing remained now but its brick chimney. Black servants were careless, Jack Leland said. It was because of this carelessness that in Charleston there had been regulations forbidding the building of wooden dependencies. The main house could be of wood; the dependencies had to be of brick.

There were other dependencies in the grounds of the Middleburg plantation house: stables at the end of an open field, and a commissary. Jack Leland thought I should go and have a look at the commissary. It was a two-floored building, wooden shingles on the upper floor, brick on the lower. Rice would have been stored on the upper floor. On the lower floor there were two cells with bars on the windows. These had been for slaves; not punishment cells, but "holding" cells, where difficult new slaves would have been broken in or reconciled, one at a time, to plantation life.

The difficult slave would have been held in one cell. In the other there would have been an old slave, someone used to the ways of the plantation. The old slave—not locked in his cell, but free to come and go—would have talked to the new man and tried to calm him down;

would have eaten food, shown how good it was, would have offered food; and the new slave's fears and resentments would have been soothed away.

I walked across the bright field to the commissary. It was hot, stinging; not truly a spring field. On one side of the field were greenish ponds—like marshland breaking through the ground—and they were full of white water lilies. Lotuses, Jack Leland had said. But they were not the delicate red lotuses of India. These white lilies, which had naturalized so easily in South Carolina, had become like things of the marsh, growing thickly together, choking themselves out of the water. And, on the far side of the commissary building, were the two slave cells, separated by no more than a lattice partition, with the earth for floor, and with the small barred windows high up, too high to reach.

They were really small spaces, tall boxes. It was easy to enter into the terror of the new man from Africa, the "new Negro," as he was called in the West Indies, who might have been snatched weeks or months before in the interior of Africa, marched or taken to the coast, held there in a dealer's stockade or compound in a place like Gorée Island off Dakar, and finally transferred to a ship for the passage across the Atlantic. Easy to enter into his terror, the terror of the man taken away stage by stage from what had been reality. Easy too to enter into the heart of the other man, the trusty slave on the other side of the partition, who sat with him and talked to him and tried to present the new life to him as one of ease and plenty, the only real life.

Old Mrs. Gibbs wanted to know, at lunch, if I had seen the cells where the new slaves had been "acclimated." (I hadn't heard the word before; later I was to understand that the word was in general use in the South.) It was something that should be seen, she said; it showed the trouble planters went to, to make things easier for their slaves; that was a side of plantation life that wasn't generally known.

The picnic was laid out on folding tables in the shade of trees. And all around, below the great oaks of the plantation avenue, there were picnic parties—the communion of the church service extending to this big picnic lunch, in the grounds of the restored plantation house.

In the dining room of the house itself there was a spread for visitors on one table. On another table were photographs of the restoration work; photographs, too, of old black people who had worked in the house. There were no black people at the picnic; but these servants were remembered. And Mr. Hill—of the family who had bought the plantation from the Gibbses and had gone to so much trouble to restore it, as a gesture to the community and history and the land—Mr. Hill told me that among the house papers were documents that enabled you to trace the ancestors of many black people. He was in a blue-striped seersucker suit, a big, plumpish, friendly man, offering a formal welcome to the house.

Many firms and many individuals had made gifts towards the restoration. The rooms themselves had been done up by different interior-decorating firms. This explained the puzzling description of the house in the advertisements I had seen: "Middleburg Plantation Designer House 1987." The nineteenth-century "State Room," for instance, had been done up by Lowcountry Decorators and Lowcountry Antiques. They had gone in for "dramatic upbeat fabrics on traditional upholstered pieces." As accessories they had chosen, among other things, "a beautiful oil painting of a black servant girl circa 1894," and "new silk trees and plants, the modern homemaker's answer to her 'too little time' problem."

The rooms were, in effect, exhibition rooms aiming at a period feel; the restored house was for show. And for the visitors who were expected there had been incorporated, at one end of the back porch, a gift shop, and at the other end a kitchen.

The restoration had been carefully done. No attempt had been made to make the house appear grander than it had been; and it was thought that what had been done would enable the house to live for a while. The magnificent grounds remained. Jack Leland's old father-in-law, who had lived in the house for some time, was greatly moved that the house would survive. And so was his daughter Anne, Jack Leland's wife. She had come to the house as a child to spend time "in the country." There was no electricity in those days, and she had had to go up to bed with an oil lamp.

The land and the past were being honored, the plantation and the river at its back which had made for the rice paddies, as in the East Indies. But what was missing were the slave cabins. The plantation house, even with its surviving dependencies, was without what would have been its most important—and most notable—feature. Jack Leland told me that the slave cabins would have been set beside the oak avenue. The cabins were known as "the quarters" or "the village."

They would never have been out of sight of the plantation house. And, considering the sanitation of those days, there would almost certainly have been a physically squalid side to the slave plantation.

But now the plantation was cleansed of its cabins. There remained the wonderful oak avenue, ever growing. Hard, mentally, to set the cabins in that grandeur that spoke more of old European country houses. Only the heat of the marsh, and the light, assailing one whenever one moved out of the forest shade, brought to mind the idea of tropical crops growing fast: labor, sweat, people, squalor.

The empty Sunday-afternoon road led through forest again, seen now with a slightly different eye; and led through the scattered black communities descended from the slaves who had, fleetingly, triumphed over their masters a full 120 years ago.

Indigo, rice, cotton—all the big slave crops had collapsed here, just as, in the Caribbean, coconut had suffered from a kind of "rust," and cacao, which had once in some islands been "king," in planter language, had been all but wiped out by the blight known as witch broom. So that it appeared that certain crops, when planted beyond a certain human scale, became afflicted in some way, economically, or by some disease that redressed the balance; as plagues reduced human populations, and myxomatosis kept rabbits down when because of their numbers they ceased to be charming.

Not far from where the country road met the highway, a black crowd was coming out of a big church. Suits; dresses; hats; cars. After the Middleburg picnic, an answering idea of community: the vanished slave cabins transformed into something quite different now, not only the old country communities in the forest, but also black settlements in Charleston itself, some middle-class, many more in projects, or in old houses on the east side, avoided by the holiday tourists in the horse carriages and pedal carriages.

AN ELDERLY lady living in one of the houses of the historical town, when she heard that I had been born in Trinidad, said, "There is a story in my family that our Burke ancestors from Philadelphia had been left the island of Trinidad."

We were sitting out in the small garden, drinking lemonade. The house next door, though of brick, looked extravagantly antique, small and crooked and quaint.

I said, "The whole island?"

"The whole island. That is the story. Southern people like to feel that, once upon a time at least, they were rich. But they died, the Burkes, in the Windward passage, when they were going to claim the land."

I asked for a date.

The lady went inside and then came out with a family tree, sketched out literally like a tree. Her mother had spent some time on that. And there on a lower left-hand branch was the inscription about the Burkes: "Died May 1795 when going out to claim land in Trinadad." *Trinadad* —that was the inaccurate spelling in the family tree, indicating the romantic distance at which, in the family stories, Trinidad lay from Charleston and from Philadelphia.

The story was interesting to me. Trinidad, for nearly three centuries after its discovery, had been an all but forgotten part of the Spanish Empire. Late in the eighteenth century, out of a wish to protect their South American possessions, the Spaniards had decided to open up the island to immigration, and to convert an island of bush into a slave sugar colony, on the pattern of Santo Domingo and Jamaica and Barbados. But the Spaniards couldn't provide the immigrants themselves. They didn't have the people; their empire was too big. To protect themselves as best they could, the Spanish authorities required immigrants to Trinidad to be Roman Catholic; in return they promised free land in proportion to the number of slaves a settler brought in. The people they had in mind, and the people who mainly went, were French, from the French West Indian islands, in turmoil after the French Revolution, and then the black revolution of Toussaint L'Ouverture in Santo Domingo, and all the upheavals and changes of flag that occurred in the Caribbean during the conquests and reconquests of the Napoleonic Wars.

The story of people going out to Trinidad to "claim land" in 1795 was therefore not fanciful. It even in a way made sense to say that the whole island was to be claimed. What was news to me was that Irish people in Philadelphia—who couldn't have had many slaves and wouldn't have qualified for the free land—had thought of going.

But the Burkes of this story didn't make it. They were drowned, and Trinidad became a myth of their great fortune. And, in the family chronicle, there was a sequel. The Burke family lawyer, the Charleston lady said, married the family nurse. Between them they did the Burke orphans out of their patrimony. Generations later the wickedness came to light. It happened one day that one of the lawyer's descendants was entertaining a descendant of one of the orphans. The lawyer's descendant showed some ancestral china plates. There were only eleven. The descendant of the orphan said, "I have the twelfth. It is one of my greatest treasures. The tradition in my family is that the other eleven were stolen."

A Southern story: a story of old family, a dream of wealth in the past. But it interested me for another reason. One of the very first books written about the affairs of Trinidad was by a pamphleteer from Philadelphia. His name was Pierre Franc MacCallum. He was a man of radical, even revolutionary views; a hater of authority, in his own narrative. He went out to Trinidad in 1803, six years after the British conquest. He was hostile to the British governor, and hostile to British authority generally; so hostile, in fact, that he was eventually deported —taken from the very rough jail in Port of Spain to the harbor, and put on a ship for New York.

MacCallum's French forenames suggest that he was partly of French origin. This may explain some of his radical or anti-British feeling. But what also comes out in his book is that, in his campaign against the British governor and British authority in Trinidad, he was driven more by rage about the way poor Scottish and Irish people had been dumped in the Carolinas. He had always been a mystery to me, this pamphleteer with the half-French name from Philadelphia. He was less so now. In this Charleston story of a family fortune lost two hundred years ago in Trinidad I thought I could see a story of remigration and fortune sought: some sort of movement of impoverished people from barren Philadelphia to just-opened-up Trinidad.

There must always be certain things that drop out of history. Only the broadest movements and themes can be recorded. All the multifarious choppings and changings, all the individual hazards and venturesomeness, and failures, cannot be recorded. History is full of mysteries, even as family histories are full of gaps and embellishments. Certain things are lost, the way for me, the grandson of immigrants from India to Trinidad, ancestors as close as grandparents are mysterious, and some unknown, making it impossible to give a good answer, after just a hundred years, to a question like: "Where did your people come from?"

What is not easily called to mind now is how close, in the slave days, the slave territories of the Caribbean and the South were. When the French planters of the West Indies were negotiating terms with the Spanish authorities for settling in Trinidad, one of the pressures they applied was a threat to take their slaves to the American South. That would be better for them as planters, they said, especially since after the war—the War of Independence—the United States seemed likely to be of some importance in the hemisphere (and therefore better able to protect people). And how rich and tempting the flat, well-watered lowlands of the Carolina coast must have appeared to people who knew only the islands!

And how strange to reflect that the black people of Trinidad I grew up among might, with another twist, have been born in the Carolinas and might have had an entirely different history. The chief difference lies in the distance of the two societies from slavery. Slavery was abolished in the British colonies in 1834; and the Caribbean colonies were thereafter neglected. So 150 years separate the black people of the British Caribbean from slavery. American slavery ended with the Civil War. But it might be said that freedom came to the black man only in 1954; so American blacks have reached where they have reached in just thirty years. In those thirty years American blacks have grown to see opportunity; while the larger independent territories of the British Caribbean—Trinidad, Jamaica, Guyana—have in their various ways been plundered and undone.

I T MIGHT have been that I was getting used to the Southern accent. But I felt from time to time that I was picking up something of the distinctive Barbadian enunciation—known to me from my childhood —in the speech of black people in Charleston. Strange—tiny Barbados finding an echo in grand South Carolina! But in the eighteenth century Barbados, sugar-rich and slave-rich, was the colonial land of opportunity. In Benjamin Franklin's *Autobiography* it is the place to which people ran away to try their fortune as clerks or lawyers, Philadelphia itself being so poor that sometimes there wasn't even coin. And Barbados was the model for the South Carolina plantation colony. And Barbados was an element in the aristocracy of Jack Leland as an old Charlestonian.

Two of his most valued possessions came from Barbados. They were sea chests, and they had been brought by an ancestor from Barbados in 1685, fifteen years after the founding of the South Carolina colony. The chests had been in Jack Leland's possession for forty years; they had been passed on to him by an aunt. He had talked to a historian about the chests, and he had been told that chests like those would have been made to measure for a voyage, to fit between the beams of a ship. They were carpenter's work or joiner's, not cabinetmaker's. They were high and undecorated, mortised at the corners, without extrusions, altogether plain; and they were prominent in his dining room.

He lived in an old, very narrow "single house" in the center of old Charleston. The house was about fifteen feet wide; the plot was small; it was a house one would have passed by. To that extent, then, living in a very simple house in a narrow street, he was representative, almost emblematic, of the old Charlestonians, proud of family rather than money, proud of the land and his old connection with it.

He carried its history with him. And one of the first things he did when I went to call on him after the Sunday at Middleburg was to show me a map of the district, made some years ago, with all the old plantations. There were many. The road along which we had traveled, though very much longer and straighter than any in Barbados, had shown only a fraction of what had existed. Each plantation had been an entity, each a little kingdom ruled by the planter; each had had a house, and quarters; and in each, according to Jack Leland, the quarters had been in the middle, to prevent communication between the slaves on different plantations.

The map was on the landing of the staircase of his house. The staircase was in the center of the narrow house, separating the front room from the back room. The entrance to the house was on the side. That central side entrance and staircase was fundamental to the idea of a "single" Charleston house, a single house here not being, as I had thought, a small detached wooden house; but a house in which, for the sake of privacy, the entrance was not at the front but at the side, and in which there was a single room on either side of the entrance and staircase. A double house had two rooms on either side of the staircase.

It was said that the idea of the single house had been imported, with the idea of the plantation slave colony, from Barbados and the West Indies generally. I hadn't seen anything like the Charleston houses in Trinidad. But Trinidad was a late West Indian foundation;

and its origins were Spanish and French. The West Indian colonies to which Charleston looked were the older, British ones.

It was always strange to me in Charleston, this harking back to the colonial British West Indies as to a mark of blood and ancestry. That idea, of a colonial aristocracy going back to the foundations, never really existed in Trinidad in my time; and doesn't exist in the former British West Indies now. The reason is simple: the British West Indian colonies more or less closed down in the 1830s, with the abolition of slavery, and became stagnant. The British Empire moved east; then moved into Africa. And there is no point in the former British West Indies now in claiming to have been among the first there. Perhaps there cannot truly be said to be an aristocracy in a place that came to nothing—they are just people (like Robinson Crusoe) who went to the wrong place. Whereas Charleston was claimed by the large events of a continental history, and its small-time beginnings are now indescribably romantic, when it was on a par with slave colonies like Antigua or Barbados or Jamaica, and looked to them for trade and support.

The importance of a colony depends principally on its economic possibilities. The French exchanged Canada (or their idea of Canada) for the very small West Indian sugar island of Guadeloupe. The Dutch gave New York to the British in exchange for the South American coastal colony of Surinam in 1667. (When I was in Surinam in 1961 I was told by a Dutch woman teacher that in Dutch schools it was said that the Dutch had got the better bargain, because the British had lost New York, while the Dutch—in 1961—still had Surinam.) And without the United States at its back, post-plantation Charleston might have been like Surinam or Guyana in South America, or Belize in Central America, former continental slave colonies from which, after the money went, the slave-owners or their successors had finally to go, leaving the place to the slaves and the people who replaced the slaves. Whereas the Charleston that survives, the Charleston of the old families, the romance the tourist travels to, is a white town, where the black people (though they outnumber the white) appear as intruders.

So, just a five-hour drive east and south from Atlanta (founded as a railway terminus in 1837), was a history quite different from Atlanta's. Though, as in Atlanta and northern Georgia, that history could be seen layer by layer: the tourist town, segregation, the Civil War, the plantations, the large slave population, the wealth, the eighteenth-century colony.

IT WAS in indigo that early fortunes were made, Jack Leland said.

"When the revolution started, Great Britain was paying a bounty on indigo. Indigo was a good dyestuff. India was not yet in the picture. The bulk of British indigo came from here. After the revolution there was no British market, and indigo faded out. No indigo was planted after 1800. The planters concentrated on rice and cotton. These were crops they already had, together with the indigo.

"The rice-planters were at the top. The cotton-planters were just under them. The run-of-the-mill farmers were down at the bottom with the shopkeepers. It was like a caste system. You still hear people saying of somebody, but not so much nowadays, 'He's in trade.' And that means he's a little bit outside the pale. It's changing rapidly now. Money has become a big factor. Before, family was always more important than money."

The social prejudices of England, reinforced by colonial wealth—it seemed from this account that (even apart from the fact of slavery) success, when it came to the Charleston plantations, began almost at once to undo itself. But the land was blessed: it was so fertile and well watered, so flat and easy.

"After the loss of indigo this area became very prosperous. This strip of land which runs from North Carolina to Florida became probably the wealthiest agricultural area in the world. And these planters were the people who started Newport, Rhode Island. They built their summer residences there.

"The Civil War was the first big blow. The war freed the slaves, and the planters had to pay them to work. And after the war the plantations fell apart, literally."

That was easy now for me to imagine. I had only to think of the oak avenue at Middleburg, set slave cabins below the oaks, imagine a slave population on holiday or disaffected; imagine the rice growing in its water-logged fields, growing fast; think of the great distances, and the heat; the numbers of the blacks and the fewness of the whites. And it was easy to see how the little kingdoms that had created wealth for a few generations, had built houses in Charleston and summer houses in Rhode Island, could just collapse.

"The final blows were the big hurricanes. There were three of them —1885, 1893, 1912. They broke the dykes, and there was no means of repairing them. At the same time rice began to be produced in Mississippi and Louisiana and Arkansas and East Texas. It was grown on high land, and it simply knocked these planters out of business. So by 1920 no more rice was being grown commercially here. We grew a little, but it was just for our own needs.

"The boll weevil came in about 1915, and within three years it had killed the Sea Island cotton crop. Then the farmers went into truck-farming. That is, growing vegetables—potatoes, beans, tomatoes, squash—for New York and Eastern markets. That lasted until California came into the picture, after the irrigation of the desert. The desert soil is very rich, and all it needed was water."

"So, after a certain stage, the plantation story is a story of bad luck and decline?"

"It makes me very sad. My family owned slaves. I think they were very kind masters. Some years ago I interviewed some of the former slaves—they are all dead now—who had lived on my family's places. And they were very complimentary on the way they were treated. Slavery was wrong. I can't make any brief for that. But it existed. It was used to build the agrarian economy we had, and it was a fairly good, workable institution."

"Was there a particular moment when you became aware of the plantation past?"

"I grew up on a plantation where there were still twenty former slave cabins, and they were all occupied by Negroes. And right from the start I realized that these people had at one time actually belonged to my family. And we were friendly."

"At this time the family fortune was already on the wane?"

"Rice went, then cotton, then truck-farming. Then the Great Depression came. And my father had to sell it. And that was the end of that."

This was also the time, as I heard later, when much of the furniture of old Charleston houses passed into the hands of dealers. Charleston furniture is now scattered over the United States and is very valuable, especially those pieces made by Charleston cabinetmakers (like the man who had made the pulpit for Pompion Hill). This story of loss reminded me of what Parkman had seen on the Oregon trail in the 1840s, when emigrants to the West, worn out by the dangers of the trail and the harshness of their travel, abandoned the precious pieces of furniture they had hoped to take to their new homes.

Though this land had gone, Jack Leland was still romantic about it.

"The land is not mine. But I feel it is my heritage." And this word, "heritage," I was to hear more than once from him, as though it was the word that explained much of his attitude to Charleston, his family and ancestors. "That particular plantation, the one on which I was born, was bought by my family in 1832. And my father lost it in 1935. So it was in my family for one hundred and three years. But there were other properties that had been in the family longer than that.

"One of the unusual things about my family was that my Leland ancestors were really New Englanders. The first Leland in South Carolina was Aaron Whitney Leland"—he was particular about all three names, repeating them slowly so that I could write them down—"and he was from Massachusetts. And he'd just graduated from Williams College in Massachusetts, and he'd come down here as a tutor in the Hibben family"—important again, the name of that family—"which at that time owned what is now Mount Pleasant, the eastern shore of the harbor. And I think that, being a sharp Yankee trader, he changed his religion and married one of the daughters. And that began the Leland family here. He changed his religion to Presbyterian from Unitarian, and he even became a Presbyterian minister.

"But my mother and my father were members of families that had come in here at the beginning of the colony, in 1670." And it was from one of those early families that he had inherited the sea chests that were in the sitting room, on the other side of the central staircase.

How had he become aware of the poverty of his family?

"We had a very good life. There was plenty of food. And actually I didn't realize that we were poor. Of course, we were better off than the Negroes and what we call the backwoods whites. And I didn't realize that we were economically poor, that very little was coming in.

"I had one year here at the College of Charleston. It was a private school then; my grandmother paid for it. Then she died. I was looking for a summer job, and I found this job on a Norwegian freighter which was hauling bananas from Cuba up to Charleston and Jacksonville, Florida. Then the captain, who owned two-thirds of the ship, got a cargo of coal to take to Argentina. And while we were in Argentina he got an offer to go to Australia. So I wound up in Australia, on a triangular run from Sydney to Singapore to Manila and back to Australia. In August 1939 we came back to this country and picked up a load of bananas in Honduras and came up to Mobile, Alabama. The day we came into port, Hitler invaded Norway. Which made the ship a belligerent-nation ship. The U.S. Border Patrol advised me to get off. I came home and went back to the College of Charleston. And of course the next year was the draft for World War II, and I was one of the first men to be drafted from Charleston."

So he had missed some formal education. The years he might have spent at university had been spent as a seaman. Did he feel he had missed the company of his peers?

"A lot of people on the ship spoke English English. British English. It was a tremendous education. The war was another educational experience. England, North Africa, Sicily, Italy. And having the background I had—my father and mother were great readers, and they had instilled in me the ability and desire to read and learn things.

"I came back in 1945, and went back to college again. And I got a job with the local newspapers and stayed with the newspapers from then on."

"You've seen Charleston rise again?"

"I've seen it change too. When I was a boy there was no black district in Charleston, and no white district either. White people and black people lived side by side. The change began during the Depression, when a tremendous number of farms and plantations went out of business, and the Negroes who had worked on those places began moving into Charleston and also going north. And then World War II came along, and there was a tremendous economic thrust, because this was a major naval station, and they developed an airfield, and that drew a lot more of the Negroes from the rural areas into the city.

"After the war the young men began coming back. The areas where most of the nineteenth-century immigrants had lived—Germans, Irish, and Italians and Greeks—these families were still living in what is now the black district. A middle- to low-income area. But the young men coming after the war couldn't get loans from the banks to buy old houses in the city. They had to build new houses in the subdivisions. And as they did that their parents' houses became vacant, and the blacks moved in. And today we have a tremendous black section. And the old Charleston, peninsular Charleston, is sixty percent black and forty percent white. The public schools are ninety-five percent black."

"What a fate for a city that lived off the plantations!"

"It really has been a tremendous upheaval. Consider this. This house, the house where I now live, was restored about seven years ago. The house was built in the 1840s by an Irish carpenter who had come over perhaps to escape the potato famine. The rooms are terribly small. The architect who opened it up was a good architect, and he utilized every bit of space. And right now we are the only white family on the block. I should say, on the street. The street is only two blocks long. All the rest are Negroes.

"The house next door, now. You may or may not be interested in this. Some years ago my mother-in-law, Mrs. John E. Gibbs, discovered that some old Gibbs retainers—as she called them—were being taken advantage of. And she bought that house and restored it, made it into two apartments, with a little dependency in the back yard. And the old Gibbs servants now live there, and she only gets enough money out of them to pay the taxes and insurance. They are wonderful people to have. They look out for us.

"We have, right down the street here, one of those low-cost housing projects. And those people are terrible. They're all black in that one. That project is a crime-producer. There is always something bad happening there or being done by people who live there."

"Is it hard for you to live with Negroes without having authority over them?"

"I've always lived with Negroes. Always done it. And they've helped me. We're good friends. But socially we are separate. There is no way to get around it. But last year, when my stepdaughter got married in Saint Philip's Episcopal Church, which is the mother church of the Anglican communion in the Southeastern United States —a big formal wedding, with a reception in the South Carolina Hall afterwards—the servants came to the wedding, and they were like part of the family. No getting around it. There's one old man who's the same age as my father-in-law—he's eighty-two. He grew up in a dependency of the Gibbs house on Logan Street. And he, the old servant, cannot read or write. He's legally blind. And my mother-in-law gets his food stamps and cashes his welfare checks. And he really thinks he's a Gibbs, one of the family. I feel very fortunate to have them." The old family servants, living in the restored house next door. "They look out for us."

"When you think of the way the race issue has developed, do you feel sometimes that slavery was a calamity for the South?"

"Slavery *was* a calamity. The outcome was always inevitable. But you've got to remember that the people in New England also had slaves. They didn't have so many; they had small farms. The Southern economy depended on Negro slaves. The beginning of the end occurred shortly after 1800, when Great Britain outlawed the slave trade. And, then again, the United States passed a law against the importation of slaves."

"So the end was visible even when the plantations were at the height of their prosperity?"

"The great wealth was just building up."

"Considering the effects now, do you see it as a weakening of the country?"

"It is. The younger Negroes, the Negroes under sixty, have never been able to really associate with the way the white man lives." He meant that blacks of that age group lived in their own community, didn't serve in the houses of white people, as their parents and grandparents had done. "They stand on the outside and look in. And they don't adopt the white man's standards.

"Now—just a matter of childbirth. As you probably know, the Negro woman keeps the family together. And they have a tremendous number of children. In South Carolina, at least, the number of illegitimate children born every year is predominantly black. And there's no stigma—of course, that's changing today in the white families as well. And these people are willing to live on welfare—or they *do* live on welfare, I don't know how willingly. The Negro churches, which at one time were the center of the Negro communities, have never put any stigma on illegitimacy. They accept it. It's really a tragic situation, these young black girls having children when they are thirteen or fourteen years old, and no husband to provide money."

I asked him about civil rights and postwar politics.

"In 1947 a federal judge, Julius Waties Waring"—he stressed the three names, and he spelt the tricky middle one for me, and it was only later that I got to know how notorious this particular name was in Charleston—"Julius Waties Waring. And he was from a very old Charleston family. And he handed down a ruling that Negroes could no longer be excluded from the Democratic Party primaries. And his ruling was correct. Negroes shouldn't have been excluded. At that time, the Democratic Party primary was the real election in the state, because there wasn't any opposition. And by 1952 the Negroes were beginning to vote in large numbers. They are now a potent force in the election system. They've come a long way. Unfortunately, their leadership is sadly lacking. Their leaders tend to be negative, politicians with a lot of rhetoric but very little understanding of the true working of government."

That was the point he stressed: the true working of government. Charleston had a "rabble-rouser," but among the black officials there were some good people. And, having lived through so much change, he was now philosophical. "I think we are coming along wonderfully."

I wanted to know about the evolution of his thought on racial matters.

"I grew up in a family where we were told we could be friends with Negroes, and had to respect them, and couldn't take advantage of them. But you couldn't elevate them to being social equals. I grew up believing strongly in that."

Another day, when I was reflecting on what he had told me and I went back to this point, he said, "The Negroes had their own caste system. In Charleston there used to be a brick-mason contractor called Pinckney. He was a mulatto. He did a lot of the brickwork on the old houses in Charleston when they were being restored. But he knew that on his father's side he had come from a top-ranking family in South Carolina. And he would refer to his workers as 'my niggers.' This shocked me, because my father had told us never to use the word.

"The Negro house servants looked down on the field hands. They referred to them in a derogatory way. 'A cornfield nigger.' The house servants started that word. The house people associated with themselves.

"I was only seventeen when I went to work on that ship. At that age you don't have big ideas about anything. But, going into ports in the Caribbean and South America and Manila and Singapore, I began to change my mind a little about people of other races. Back here the Chinese were called Chinks. Over there in Singapore they ran the show. They were top of the heap.

"Let me tell you this story. When I was in the Army Air Corps I went to Chanute Field, Illinois, to study meteorology. In my class there were four Negroes who had studied at Tuskegee, and they had a tremendous problem with mathematics. In the study of meteorology you study all sorts of things—the various forces of nature—and a lot of mathematics with it. And these young Negroes—it was incomprehensible to them. Most of the people in that school were Yankees. I was one of the few Southerners, and I realized the problem these Negroes had. I offered to help and I did help, and these Negroes were able to graduate. And I will never forget: I was getting ready to go to Florida, where I had been posted, and I had to catch the bus right there at Chanute Field, and these four Negroes showed up and brought me a bottle of whiskey as a farewell gift. The Yankees at that school would pal around with the Negroes, but they didn't see that the Negroes needed help and they didn't do anything to help them. But I had been brought up that you had to *help* the Negroes. This was part of your duty, your heritage.

"I guess it's just a part of your life. For instance, today, if I'm walking down the street and if some white man tries to panhandle, I ignore him. But if it's a black, I stop and talk with him, to see if he really needs help or if he's trying to get a drink. I think a lot of the blacks—the ones I know intimately—understand this about me. But to the other blacks I'm just a honkie, the enemy, the archdemon personified. And I'm perfectly willing to admit they have some reason for not liking whites.

"It is really difficult to get a black person to sit down here." He gestured towards his settee, placed against the wall of his single house, next to the door, with, on the other side of the door, the two sea chests from Barbados, which had come into his family in 1685 and were the mark of his Charleston aristocracy, the mark of the colonial ancestor from Barbados. "Difficult to get a black person to sit down and talk to me. They don't say what they feel. They don't trust the white people. The Uncle Toms—there's no truth in them. In 1952 I was assigned to cover all the counties in the lower part of the state and find out how the Negroes were going to vote. The 1952 election was the first one in which Negroes were going to vote in some number. In Beaufort County, down the coast, I was amazed myself. The Republican Party was the party of Lincoln. But I found, after talking to about a hundred blacks, that they were all going to vote Democratic. I turned in a story to that effect, and my editor, who had a lot of Uncle Tom friends, refused to believe it."

I asked Jack Leland whether he took an interest in the affairs of the Caribbean islands, and whether this to some extent affected his view of American blacks.

He said, "Well, look what happened in Santo Domingo. That island was divided into two parts, Haiti on one side and the Dominican Republic on the other. In Haiti they killed all the white people. And when you go to Santo Domingo there is the difference between night and day. The Dominican Republic has a stable economy. The Haitians are starving. I had it tremendously impressed on me when I was on that ship—and we went to the Dominican Republic and we were loading bananas. I met some English people, and they took me over to Haiti. It was like the difference between night and day. I hate to think it's because there's no white connection in Haiti and there is in the Dominican Republic. But somewhere along the line something went wrong. And when I look at what's happening in Africa today—I don't think my point of view gets any hearing. The American people have closed their minds to thoughts like that. They think globally. They've turned their thoughts to one world, one people. It's unpractical, unfeasible. I don't think the way a native of Nigeria thinks, and he doesn't think the way I think. We are different people."

I was aware the first day we had met that Jack Leland had a bad leg. The third or fourth time we met he seemed to be in especial discomfort, and I asked him about his leg. He said he had damaged both legs in North Africa, in February 1943. He had gone on a bombing run over Sicily, and the last bomb had stuck in the rack. Orders had been given to the returning crew to jump, and he had jumped; it was the first time he had ever used a parachute. He had landed on a rock and had torn the ligaments of both ankles; it had taken him two and a half months to recover. An irony was that the pilot who had given the orders to jump had managed to land the plane without accident.

That was how the war had gone for him. Yet he had spoken of the war as a time of learning and adventure; he had never referred to this lasting damage until I had asked. It was like an aspect of his training, his fine manners, his "Sir?" when he hadn't quite caught what I had said: the manners that were part of the South's idea of itself.

"IT'S MORE like religion," the upper-class woman from Mississippi had said, speaking of a certain attitude in her family (and other Mississippi families like hers) to the Civil War and the past; and the old family houses; and the dressing up in period costume on some days, when the houses were shown. Not a masque, not vanity: more like religion. And in Charleston too there came to one that idea of the past as religion.

It wasn't only the old houses and the old families, the old names, the antiquarian side of provincial or state history. It was also the past as a wound: the past of which the dead or alienated plantations spoke, many of them still with physical mementoes of the old days, the houses, the dependencies, the oak avenues. The past of which the more-black-than-white city now spoke, the past of slavery and the Civil War.

Not a day had passed since I had come to the South without my reading in the newspapers about General Sherman, or hearing about him on television. And—in that newspaper or television way, when a well-known name is to be stressed, ironically or otherwise—he was often given his full name, with the strange American Indian middle one: William Tecumseh Sherman.

Charleston had survived the war. Columbia, the state capital, hadn't. It had been burned by Sherman in 1865. It was of that burning that the elderly lady, a guide to the cathedral near the State House in Columbia, spoke to me; and she spoke as though it had happened quite recently. And perhaps Hannibal had been remembered in Italy and Rome in a similar way a hundred years after he had passed. The cathedral was one of the few things in Columbia that hadn't been burned by Sherman, the lady said. And this might have been because he thought it was Roman Catholic; Sherman's wife was Catholic. And towards the end of the tour, when we were talking of the stained glass (so fragile in a city about to be razed), she broke off and said, as though offering thanks again, "It's a miracle the cathedral wasn't burned."

I had read about the burning of Columbia. But the fact wasn't at the front of my mind that afternoon. And this talk of burning—from an elderly lady, in the cathedral—made a fearful impression. I hadn't been looking for the cathedral. I had gone in after noticing the graveyard. I was on my way to the State House grounds to look at the Confederate Memorial. I had been directed to that by a judge I had come to see. He had said that the inscription of the memorial was something that should be studied. It was poetic and contained much of the South's idea of itself.

On one side of the monument was engraved: *To South Carolina's dead of the Confederate Army 1861–1865.* On another side it said: *Erected by the Women of South Carolina. Unveiled May 13, 1879.* There was rhetoric in that reference to women; monuments of grief and revenge, or grief and piety, are most unsettling when they depict women bowed in grief.

On the other side facing the busy road the monument read: *This monument perpetuates the memory of those who, true to the instincts of their birth, faithful to the teachings of their fathers, constant in their love for the state, died in the performance of their duty: who have glorified a fallen cause by the simple manhood of their lives, the patient endurance of suffering, and the heroism of death, and who, in the dark hours of imprisonment, in the hopelessness of the hospital, in the short, sharp agony of the field, found support and consolation in the belief that at home they would not be forgotten.*

On the other side, facing the State House, and read with difficulty from an oblique angle if one didn't want to walk on the grass at the monument's back, there was this: *Let the stranger who may in future times read this inscription recognize that these were men whom power could not corrupt, whom death could not terrify, whom defeat could not dishonor, and let their virtues plead for just judgment of the cause in which they perished. Let the South Carolinians of another generation remember that the state taught them how to live and how to die. And that from her broken fortunes she preserved for her children the priceless treasure of their memories, teaching all who may claim the same birthright that truth, courage and patriotism endure forever.*

On one side: birth, faith, duty, suffering, and death. On the other side: the nameless, undefined cause, ennobled by these virtues. The words are grand, nevertheless. The pain of defeat is something that can be shared by everyone, since everyone at some stage in his life knows defeat of some sort and hopes in his heart to undo it, or at least to have his cause correctly seen. But the pain of the Confederate Memorial is very great; the defeat it speaks of is complete. Defeat like this leads to religion. It can be religion: the crucifixion, as eternal a grief for Christians as, for the Shias of Islam, the death of Ali and his sons. Grief and the conviction of a just cause; defeat going against every idea of morality, every idea of the good story, the right story, the way it should have been: the tears of the Confederate Memorial are close to religion, the helpless grief and rage (such as the Shias know) about an injustice that cannot be rehearsed too often.

And there was more of that in this central square of South Carolina, the state that had started the war: more pain, more humiliation, more exposing of a wrong that was one day to be undone. On the lower granite steps there was a life-size bronze statue of George Washington. This plaque had been affixed: *During the occupation of Columbia by*

Sherman's army February 17–19, 1865, soldiers brickbatted this statue and broke off the lower part of the walking cane. The cane had been left hanging in the air. On the pillar at the foot of the steps was another plaque: *Construction of this State House was begun in 1855 and continued uninterruptedly to February 17, 1865, when Sherman burned Columbia. Work was resumed in 1867 and carried on irregularly to 1900.*

The Confederate Memorial, the one erected by the women of South Carolina, had been put up in 1879; when the Northern occupation army had been removed and the state had been redeemed from Reconstruction. The State House plaque, with all its grief about Sherman and the burning, had been put up more than twenty years later, when the world had changed even more. There was evidence of this change right there: the other memorial in the paved forecourt of the State House was a jaunty one, a celebration of the Spanish-American War of 1898, with a Kiplingesque inscription.

It was as though the grief of the Confederate Memorial had found its expiation in the jauntiness of the other memorial; as though the unmentioned Southern cause had lived on and found justification in the later imperialist war; as though the unmentioned racial anguish of the period after the Civil War, the later hardness towards blacks, had become incorporated into something a good deal less squalid than the slave cabins with the very black and ragged slaves of South Carolina, had become incorporated, as some Southerners had said, into the wider cause of white civilization, spreading to Africa, Australia, and the East Indies.

But the true past of the South was the thing that had been lost: the world before the war, and then the war itself. That grief was special and was like religion; it would last beyond the decline of the nineteenth-century empires, beyond the idea of empire itself. And, now that the memorial about the Spanish-American War was embarrassing, the episode itself hardly remembered, what remained moving in the State House grounds, what could still be felt to come from the heart, were the words of the Confederate Memorial. And there was still that difficulty about the cause.

How could such a cause be defended?

In the library of my Oxford college, one day in 1952, I came across a small book, privately printed, a gift to the college from the author, possibly an old American member of the college. The book, which had been printed in the 1920s, was about slavery. The author wished to clear up the misunderstandings the rest of the world had about American slavery. That was what the author said. But the little memoir he had settled down to write in his old age was about his childhood and the pleasures of his childhood. Slavery had been part of his childhood; his childhood could not be imagined separate from the background of slavery, and its special rituals. White children, the writer said, were often given slave children of their own age to play with and knock about. The writer said that he too had had his "own negro boy." The fact that this had been so, that the writer had had his own slave boy, was offered as sufficient explanation of the practice.

And something as simple and heartfelt as that was at the back of a beautiful, celebratory book, *A Carolina Rice Plantation of the Fifties*, published in New York in 1936 by William Morrow.

The fifties of the title were the 1850s, before the Civil War, when the slave-worked plantations were still going concerns. The historical core of the book was a short memoir of that time by D. E. Huger Smith (Huger one of the old Charleston names with a special Charleston pronunciation: "ewe-gee," just like the two letters "U" and "G"). To this had been added thirty water-color paintings—done seventy or eighty years later—by Alice R. Huger Smith; and a "Narrative"—really a historical essay—by Herbert Ravenel Sass (another old name, Sass a name of German origin, Ravenel pronounced in the French way and in Charleston in 1987 still a name seen on signboards).

The water colors, of plantation scenes, were romantic: sometimes dealing with plantation work, black men in a work gang mending a broken embankment, women loading rice onto a flat plantation barge; sometimes atmospheric studies of water and forest; sometimes pure calendar (or "Soviet") art, the planter and his wife (like father and mother in an illustration in a children's book) moving white and gracious among the smiling blacks, with—in another picture—a little blonde girl receiving a bouquet from a black child.

A big reproduction of the embankment-mending scene I was to see later in a Charleston restaurant, as something from the old days—and romantic, suitable for the tourist town. And the romance of the paintings was genuine. They hadn't come from the 1850s, the slave time. If they had they might have been different—more topographical and descriptive, and for that reason upsetting. The paintings had been done by someone who (as she said in the foreword) wished to record a world that was vanishing; and they had been done by someone who had been born towards the end of the Reconstruction period—in the 1870s—when the vast plantation world, the ordering of so many millions of acres, had been turned upside down. Shame and anger at the Reconstruction, grief for the defeat, nostalgia for the world as it had been, or an idea of the past: all of that mingled—in these water colors—with the delight in brush and color and paper, delight in the natural world, the painter's sense of her own delicacy.

And there was something of that mood in Herbert Ravenel Sass's essay. He too dealt in romance: the oak avenues, the beauty of the river onto which the plantation houses fronted; the organization of the great plantations; the technical skills connected with the flooding and draining of a tidal plantation; the self-containedness of each plantation, each almost a little state with its own lord, who had certain legal punishing rights over his subjects.

It was that idea of the plantation state that no doubt made the writer see the Rice Coast as "in essence an attempt to recreate in America the classic Greek ideal of democracy." And in a curiously written paragraph that makes no reference to Africans or slaves or black people, plantation slavery is incorporated into this Greek ideal as "the most complete 'economic security' " ever offered certain people in America. "For this security, covering the whole period of their lives from babyhood to old age, a price was paid." "A price"—that is the silent way in which, to preserve the idea of the classical world, slavery is referred to. And this "price," the writer adds, was "perhaps not wholly excessive," considering the people—again never mentioned—to whom this security was offered.

But—when this Greek aspect was set aside—there was another way of talking about slavery. "For the South the slavery problem became the negro problem, and what in reality the Carolinian state strove against from 1831 to 1865 was a threatened 'solution' of the negro problem which would destroy them." The state required slaves; without slaves it couldn't get by; but the slaves threatened the state with extinction always. So the planter's special way of life in the ricelands of Carolina became "white civilization"; that was the thing that had to be preserved.

There was a torment in this way of reasoning, this unwillingness of educated men and religious men—and sensitive men—ever to say that what they were defending was simply the world they had known. And there is always the silence—the lack of reference to Negroes, the slave cabins below the oaks—when the plantation world becomes something nobler than itself, becomes something like the Greek city-state. That had been the silence as well, fifty-seven years before, of the Confederate Memorial in Columbia; the virtues of the dead men ennobling the cause, the cause itself never defined. But how else, in 1879 or 1936, even at that time of high imperialism, could educated men defend slavery?

I had come across the rice-plantation book in the collection of a lady with a famous name. She lived with unusual simplicity in an old house in Charleston, with a piazza (Charleston for "porch" or "veranda") looking out onto a green yard shaded by an old oak, a yard neither ordered nor overgrown. At the boundary of the plot (or beyond the fence) there was the windowless back of the neighboring house. This was the Charleston style, the piazza at the side, for privacy. But the house next door rocked with a radio; no protection against that.

And it was there, on that piazza, where the furniture was simple, weather-hardened, with ingrained dust (the breeze in Charleston, Jack Leland told me, was from the south or the west, and that was where people placed their piazzas, to catch the breeze), it was there that, through the courtesy of the lady, I met the son of the man who had written the "Narrative" for the plantation book of fifty years before.

Marion Sass was in his fifties, tall, thin, stooped, excessively wrapped up for this hot Charleston afternoon: a brown tweed jacket worn without stylishness over a pullover. He had small, sad blue eyes in a thin, gentle face. He didn't want to sit with his back to the breeze; he sat with his back to the wall of the house. The air was full of pollen. My own eyes were heavy; I felt a cough building up; and, like Marion Sass, I was wearing a jacket. And on the sagging floor of the piazza, facing the unkempt garden or yard, almost as on a stage set of a play about the South, and in the sound of the next-door radio, we talked.

He was shy; he spoke softly; he looked down and away. As a Charlestonian he went right back, to Henry Woodward, who had explored and prospected the land for the foundation of 1670. I asked whether such an ancestry in Charleston wasn't a burden, whether it didn't constrict a man. He said it was a burden. His ancestry was one of the things that kept him in Charleston. There was a large part of him (in spite of his German surname) that would have liked to live in England; his late wife had been English. It was of England, and its curious effect on people—so many people, he said, seeing England for the first time, felt it to be their home—that he talked for some time; and it was of England, I felt, he would have preferred talking, if such a thing, so simple and free of complication, had been open to him. But there was the burden of the ancestry; and there was his Southernness. And it was to that, without my prompting just then, that he turned the talk.

His father, Herbert Ravenel Sass, had been born in 1884 and had died in 1958. So his father was fifty-two when the rice-plantation book was published in 1936. Eighteen years later, when his father was seventy, the main civil-rights cause had been conceded. Marion Sass himself had been born in 1930. He would have shared some political defeats with his father; but the Southern cause, as he saw it, lived on in him.

He told me that at the time the schools had been integrated his father had broken through the "paper curtain" the North had imposed on Southern views, and had published an article in the *Atlantic* magazine suggesting that mixed schools would lead to a mixed race. That had been proved wrong, Marion Sass said; with integration the races had in fact kept more to themselves socially. But that didn't lessen the need for his political work, to which he now gave more time than to his law practice.

This talk of political work, he said, might sound as though he were engaged in getting people elected to office. He had done that as well. But he was now more concerned with "resistance." Resistance to the conquest by the North and resistance to Americanization, which was really Northernization. Though it was ironical, he observed, that some of the most important "American" things—Coca-Cola, and country music, and even the idea of supermarkets—were Southern. (Just as there are Swedes who can recite the five—or six, or seven—industrial inventions that made Sweden rich, so Marion Sass appeared to have at his fingertips the Southern contributions to the idea of America.)

There was no need to define Southern values. "Southern culture is not simply a matter of the agrarian culture versus the industrial, or the ideals of honor against the crass values of commerce. Southern identity is important because it is Southern. We are Southern. That's enough. It's like the Irish. But they—the Irish—don't have this terrible burden of an alien population in their midst."

There, again, a full fifty years after his father's essay in the rice-plantation book, was the vagueness connected with "the problem." How did he deal with that—the question of race—as a thinker?

He said, "Our way of dealing with that? I try to have as little as possible to do with the race problem. A lot of the white-supremacist cause is in the North and has nothing to do with the South. The Southern cause and the Southern problem are really different things. The North uses the blacks all the time against the South. They did it in 1860, and they've done it in this century."

The North was now very concerned with all its minorities. It might have been thought that they would have considered the South a minority area. But they didn't. The official Northern view could be put like this: "The white Southerner is not a minority. He is a backward fellow American who oppresses a minority, the Negro."

Had he looked at his father's book about the plantations recently?

No, not recently. But he knew the book well, and he had some of the feeling for the old plantation life.

I said, "But you can't feel nostalgia for what you don't know?"

"Although I didn't grow up with any knowledge of the working life of the plantation, still, life on the plantations—when we went to visit them when I was a child—it was more like the old Southern country-side, even though we didn't have slavery. It was the old easygoing rural life, and relations between the races were much more what they had been. So I can feel nostalgia for a past."

He was as concerned, even obsessed, as his father had been by the superficial destruction of the South—the highways, the fast-food chains—and pained by the alienation of some of the plantations to people and firms from outside.

The past as a dream of purity, the past as cause for grief, the past as religion: it is the very prompting of the Shias of Islam to nobility and sacrifice, the dream of the good time of the Prophet and the first four caliphs, before greed and ambition destroyed the newly saved world. It was the very prompting of the Confederate Memorial in Columbia. And that very special Southern past, and cause, could be made pure only if it was removed from the squalor of the race issue.

When—again as in a stage set—we got up from our chairs and went inside, for a salad provided by our hostess, I said I felt he was dealing in emotion without a program. He agreed; but then he said the program was being created.

The talk became general. We looked at some of our hostess's old books about South Carolina. We looked at copies of her family letters —many of them plantation letters—that were almost two hundred years old: the letters had been typed out and bound in heavy folio volumes. When they—Marion Sass and our hostess—spoke the names of plantations, Fairfield, Oakland, Middleburg, Middleton, Hampton House, it was as though they were talking of country houses. But then I understood that they were also talking in an allusive way of the very many families to whom they were related.

He drove me back to the hotel in his untidy old car. He was nagged by what I had said about emotion without a program; and the next morning he sent me a copy of a letter he had written to the local paper in 1983 and a copy of an advertisement announcing a Southern publishing program. These copies were left at the hotel in a very large, used envelope, with my name and his name in very small letters; the envelope carried the printed name of a health organization.

And then he telephoned; and as he spoke I could visualize his thin, sensitive face. He hadn't done the publishing the advertisement had promised, he said; but the advertisement had drawn a response; he felt he had touched a chord. He told me that because of the developments of the 1950s his father had ended as a Southern separatist; and that was where he himself was now. The defeat of the South, the surrender of Lee, was for him an unappeasable sorrow, I felt.

I asked him whether he knew the Confederate Memorial in Columbia. He said he had studied law in Columbia, and he liked the town, which some people didn't like. He knew the words of the Confederate Memorial very well; he spoke some of them on the telephone. He thought the words might have been written by W. J. Grayson, who in the 1850s had written an epic poem called *The Hireling and the Slave,* a poem in rhyming couplets in the style of Pope. The theme of the poem was the superior condition of the slave in the South to the industrial worker in Massachusetts. He hadn't read the poem right through.

His cause had come out of an unappeasable sorrow. And I felt it could lead only to further sorrow: he himself knew that there was now another, and perhaps more predominant, side to Southern thinking. I thought of what Anne Siddons had spoken in Atlanta: the need at a certain age to hoard emotion, to spare passion from public causes for one's own spiritual concerns, to make one's peace with age and the frailties of one's own human state. I spoke of that as best I could on the telephone. He said he understood; but still it worried him that at times he could so sink into himself that he could forget his cause.

Then, courtesy returning, he said he would like to read some of the things I had written. But there was trouble with his eyes—those eyes whose sensitive rims and whose smallness had made an impression on me. He needed to have a cataract operation on both eyes. That was said to be a simple operation these days, but in the leaflet he had been sent (perhaps in that overlarge envelope in which he had sent me copies of his letter to the newspaper and his publishing advertisement) he had read of possible complications. And he wished to trust to his own lenses for as long as possible.

ONE HOT morning—hot for May, everyone said, and without the rain that the gardens needed, the rain that could sometimes fall every afternoon—on such a morning Jack Leland took me through what he called his "territory."

First we went to Mount Pleasant, on the east side of Charleston harbor. It had been the "summering place" of planters, and was now a rich-looking suburb with old trees, very shady. Not far below was the sea. We saw a trawler putting out. The Portuguese were the first to use those trawlers in Charleston, in the 1920s, Jack Leland said; he logged everything connected with his town. We had come to Mount Pleasant to see the Hibben house, the house of the family where Jack Leland's New England ancestor had come as a tutor and stayed to wed. It was at the end of a cul-de-sac, a two-hundred-year-old house with columns, the house of the people who had once owned all the land of this suburb —a story of ancestors given unexpected reality.

On the road again, he pointed out where black communities had grown up on plots of ground that had been given them after the war, the Civil War. "They're not doing well. These Negroes up to World War II had land and they all had gardens. They raised a lot of their own food. Now you very rarely see a Negro family in the country that has a vegetable garden."

We drove through one black village, and Jack Leland showed the houses of two of his black "friends." These friends were people he bought things from: his definition of black friends was South Carolinian. Some of the houses suggested that the owners were well off. I asked whether they were small businessmen. He said no; the blacks in those houses probably worked in the naval yard or had other federal jobs. The local black population had lost its most ambitious section with the migration to the cities in the North; almost every Negro of ambition had gone.

"Does the name Stepin Fetchit mean anything to you?"

It certainly did. Stepin Fetchit was adored in my childhood by the blacks of Trinidad. He was adored not only because he was funny and did wonderful things with his seemingly disjointed body and had a wonderful walk and a wonderful voice, and was given extravagant words to speak; he was adored by Trinidad black people because he appeared in films, at a time when Hollywood stood for an almost impossible glamour; and he was also adored—most importantly—because, at a time when the various races of Trinidad were socially separate and the world seemed fixed forever that way, with segregation to the north in the United States, with Africa ruled by Europe, with South Africa the way it was (and not at all a subject of local black concern), and Australia and New Zealand the way they were—at that time in Trinidad, Stepin Fetchit was seen on the screen in the company of white people. And to Trinidad blacks—who looked down at that time on Africans, and laughed and shouted and hooted in the cinema whenever Africans were shown dancing or with spears—the sight of Stepin Fetchit with white people was like a dream of a happier world.

It wasn't of this adored figure that Jack Leland was speaking, though. He had another, matter-of-fact, local attitude. He said, "The ambitious people went north, and we were left with the Stepin Fetchits." Now there was a movement back; not big, but noticeable.

I said, a little later, that it was my impression that the blacks of South Carolina were very black people, not as mixed as black people in the Caribbean islands. He said there had been little mixing of the races. The planters thought it demeaning to have relations with a slave woman. There was a story that after the war the Union soldiers didn't have those scruples. But there were not many mixed people.

Did that make for more difficult relations between the races?

No; it made for easier relations. "Mulattoes and quadroons and those are the angry people."

Later, some way up the highway, we turned off to have a look at a spectacular old oak avenue, partly in ruin: the kind of avenue with which Marion Sass's father had begun his nostalgic recall of plantation days. And when we drove on, the sea was on our right, hidden by forest; and the river was on our left. Salt and fresh: where the land was salt, cotton had grown in the old days; where the water was fresh, there had been rice. Now, along one stretch of road, there was a large kiwifruit plantation.

We turned into a side road then, and suddenly, in overgrown ground, attached to a Presbyterian church of 1696, there was a little cemetery, where, Jack Leland said, some of the first settlers were buried.

We were entering sacred territory.

Beyond a certain creek the old plantation of Walnut Grove began. It was the ancestral property, acquired in 1832 and sold during the Depression, in 1935. Still with us, the roadside woodland. And, now, the black village where after the Civil War blacks had been given plots of plantation ground.

"When the children were small," Jack Leland said, "and we crossed the creek, I stopped the car and made them get out and bow three times to the east. Sacred territory."

"What did the children think of that?"

He laughed. "They got a great charge out of it. They still do it when they come here. And I do it with them. People see us bowing. They probably think we're crazy. We probably are. But it's a nice craziness."

And now, driving through his territory, memory overcoming him at certain spots, he filled out some of the things he had told me earlier. They had been poor, with little money coming in. But they had never been short of food. "Shrimps, crab, oysters. Clams. Fish. Venison. Wild turkey. Ducks, roes, partridges. There was just a wealth of wild food to be had. And, of course, my father had the farm where he grew the food." And when on a morning he, Jack Leland, went out with the shotgun, the birds he shot were for the table. The hunting life—it was important here (to blacks as well); and when you saw the land you understood. And the land concealed something else. There was a creek at some distance with very pure water. The creek was called "the branch"; visitors would be offered bourbon and branch.

We turned off into a narrower road. We passed a house in a wooded garden.

"That's a cracker house. Backwoods whites, poor white trash, as they say. And that's another cracker house, I would say. About seventy years old, perhaps. They're part of the picture. You can't leave them out."

He had the local eye—just as in Malaysia the local people can distinguish a Chinese house from a Malay one, purely by the way the surrounding ground is used. The houses he had described as cracker houses had seemed to me attractive, with trees and shade and shrubs.

He said, "They have a certain charm. But a lot of junk around. You can tell a cracker house by the trash, and the generally unkempt look of the place. Half a dozen defunct automobiles, say. That was very typical at one time."

The crackers, like the blacks, had their own place in the local caste system.

"When I was growing up we went to high school and grammar school with them. But we did not socialize. Our social lives were entirely different. Most of the crackers were Baptists, Methodists, or Pentecostal Holiness—that's the shouting religion. Whereas my family and the other families up here were Episcopalian mainly, and Presbyterian, and they were top of the heap.

"I will tell you. At Walnut Grove we had a summer cottage, where my father's younger brothers and their friends stayed during the summer. A four-roomed house on the river. This was shortly after 1902— my father had just married and brought his bride back. He was the eldest of eleven children.

"One day my father got up early in the morning, at six, for his usual cup of coffee. And he saw some of his horses standing by the gate, saddled but with their reins cut. After a while the younger brothers and their friends showed up, walking. They had been to a square dance out in the swamps, where the crackers lived. They hadn't found their horses afterwards, and they had had to walk back. And my father warned them not to go back. Because, he said, this—the cutting of the horses' reins—is the crackers' way of warning you not to meddle with their women. 'The next time they will take more drastic action.'

"But they didn't listen. They went again. They were riding back through a trail in the swamps when the crackers dropped out of the tree limbs above them with knives. Like the Indians. One of the men with my uncle was killed. It was in the night. Nothing could be proved against anybody. Nobody was brought to justice. It was the law of the swamps. You just did not socialize with those people. My father always said he preferred having the Negroes living on his property, rather than those crackers."

The blacks looked down on the crackers, and the crackers hated the blacks, because the blacks were in direct competition with them. But the crackers were as exploited as the blacks, Jack Leland said; and were probably treated worse by white employers because there was less feeling of responsibility towards them.

"The crackers began to increase in number after the Civil War. Before the Civil War in this plantation area there were only planters and Negroes, and nobody in between except perhaps the overseers."

There was a church that Jack Leland wanted to show me, the family church, the one connected with Walnut Grove—St. James, in Santee parish, Santee the name of the river. It lay along the King's Highway —the name coming down from colonial days, indicating a road made at the king's orders, at a time when most people traveled by water. The road was unpaved. If there had been the usual amount of May rain, it would have been difficult; but it was easy. And soon we were there: an old red-brick church with a portico. There was another portico at the back. The church was meant to serve French and English, but the portico for the French, at the back, was now blocked up. The red brick had the appearance of something neglected in a damp tropical climate.

"Come," he said suddenly, moving briskly in spite of his bad ankles, leading me in through the fence. "Come, let me show you where I'm going to be buried."

It was hot, no wind, and there was a hum of mosquitoes. All around, in the pines, were the cries of birds of various sorts. In the small churchyard, dry, full of brown leaves and fallen pine needles, were tombstones.

"All these people are relatives." *Jonah Collins Born 1723 Died 1786*. "He's the son of the man who brought the sea chests from Barbados." *William Toomer 1866–1955*. "My mother's uncle. A lawyer and a judge." His sprightliness at being near the site of his burial place took me aback, then imposed reverence on me.

"There."

An ordinary, bare spot of earth, a little vacant space between the headstones. That was where he was going to be buried.

"I want to be buried with a flat-topped marble tomb, right here by Jonah Collins. It will have my name, the date of my birth, the date of my death. And at the bottom there will be a line: *Have one on Jack*. And I'm leaving two thousand dollars to the church, so that every year at the spring service they can have wine, whiskey, or whatever. I think people will remember me because of that."

The mosquitoes and other insects were a nuisance. He had expected them; he had come with a can of insect repellent. Without a breeze the heat was oppressive, scorching the head. But there was often a wind, he said.

"There's no sound like the sound of the wind soughing through the pine trees. And that's where I want to be buried, so that I can listen to it forever."

Inside, the church was very plain, with the mustiness and shut-up smell of a building not often used by people, without that warmth. The church had been built in 1763. (So the Pompion Hill chapel had been built in the same year.) It had a rough, tiled floor, and the building materials were brick and stucco and timber. There was no stone in these parts; and the windows had timber surrounds, dressed like stone: local work, local trees, slave work, perhaps. The pews were enclosed; a family in its pew would have been hidden, as if in a high-walled box, open at the top. Perhaps, Jack Leland said, the pews had been built like that to keep the children in, or perhaps in cold weather they were easier to heat, with the warm bricks that were used for that purpose.

How had he got the idea of death and celebration?

"There was a Professor Ogg of Oxford University in England. He came over twenty-five years ago. He told me a story I'd never heard of. There was a rice-planter's son, a Mr. Trapier, who was visiting Oxford in the 1830s. The son of a rice-planter from Georgetown, South Carolina—making the grand tour in the 1830s. He was being entertained by the dons"—Jack Leland spoke the word precisely—"of New College. I believe it was New College. And he asked for a mint julep. They'd never heard of a mint julep. So when he came back he had a sterling pitcher made and sent back to the college as a gift, with money for mint juleps."

We went on to McClellanville, on the sea, the summer resort of the family. And it was still, literally, a family resort. There were cousins or relations in almost every house in the white part of the village. Most of the blacks lived outside the village proper. Jack Leland knew the history of every house. That magnolia tree had been planted by his father in 1892, in what had then been Jack Leland's grandmother's yard. His father had brought the seedling over from Walnut Grove in his saddle bag. And Jack Leland himself had planted a line of oaks on the street in front. He had done that in 1934, the year before his father had had to sell Walnut Grove. They were now very big trees. But that planting had been part of a federal program—and they contained a reminder of the poverty of those days. A woman ran the federal tree-planting program. She employed about fifteen high-school boys, and they were paid a dollar a day.

We had lunch at a restaurant on the highway, not far from Mc-Clellanville. The very young waitress turned out to have the name of Leland; she was a cousin.

I read him the words from the Confederate Memorial in Columbia. He was affected by them.

He said, "I think it's great."

Did he still have feelings about the Civil War?

He did. "When I was a boy there was a story in my family about the burning of one of the family plantations after the war was over. The place belonged to one of the drafters of the ordinance of secession. That was in 1860. And that, of course, brought on the war. After the Civil War this whole area was under martial law, and the colonel in charge of the area of Christchurch parish was a Colonel Beecher, a brother of Harriet Beecher Stowe. They were great abolitionists from New England, and I think I can say that that book, *Uncle Tom's Cabin,* did more than any other single thing to provoke the war. It irritated the South, where only thirteen percent of the people owned slaves, and it worked powerfully on people in the North.

"The story is that the wife of Colonel Beecher went around in Christchurch parish burning plantation houses. I grew up thinking it was perhaps a folk story. But in recent years a diary has come to light of a Dr. Marcy, who was a Union Army surgeon. He was one of the people authorized to take books, art treasures, and what not out of the houses down here and ship them north. And my daughter—she is doing research out of Middleton Place: she is part Middleton—got a copy of this diary. In it she read of the burning of Laurel Hill. That's the house owned by the drafter of the ordinance of secession. There was proof there, in that diary. She burned perhaps twenty houses, Mrs. Beecher. Torching people's houses. The Beechers were Puritans. These people have a mentality that is very hard to understand. When they sent missionaries to Africa the first thing they did was to make the Africans wear clothes, cover up."

Early afternoon. On the road again, we passed black church congregations dispersing, driving away in cars. I asked about blacks and cars, remembering that in Trinidad ownership of cars among blacks became widespread only after the second war. He said that for some years blacks weren't allowed to drive cars; they were thought to be reckless drivers. "And they were." And in the old days, he said, black churches had their Sunday services in the afternoon, because many of the black women would have been at work in the morning in white houses, cooking lunch.

The green highway signs measured off our progress back to Charleston. There came a moment when Jack Leland stopped leaning forward, his hand on the back of my seat.

He leaned back and said, "We are now out of my territory."

I⊤ was Alex Sanders, chief judge of the South Carolina Court of Appeals, who had directed me to the Confederate Memorial. I had had an introduction to him; and when we first met in Columbia he had given me lunch at the Faculty Club in the university. Our conversation had been general. I felt he had been puzzled by our inconclusive meeting. But it wasn't possible for me to tell him exactly what I wanted from him; for the simple reason that on this kind of journey one doesn't know what one wants from a man until one has spoken to him.

He was a big man with a strong accent that could divert one from the precision and economy with which, as a lawyer, he could speak. He had sent me to the memorial, he said later, to enable me to understand something about the South. He himself, though he found the words moving, wasn't certain about the cause.

"Lost causes are espoused or romanticized by the second generation." The memorial had been put up in 1879, 14 years after the end of the war. It was astonishing to him that people in 1879 had found the money to make the memorial, at a time when there wasn't enough to eat. He remembered talking to one or two veterans on the Confederate side. One of them said, "I gotten my arse shot off for other folks' niggers."

"He didn't have any, you see. And the vast majority who fought in that war didn't have any. They were fodder for the aristocracy. Identity is more than just remembering the past. We have to be like museum curators. In the dynasty of Ming there was obviously a lot that was beautiful. But I am sure there was a lot that was junk. The job of the curator is to pick and choose."

But didn't he, when he was growing up, have an attitude to the South?

He didn't, any more than a fish has an attitude to the ocean in which he swims. "It was only after I'd grown up and left that I developed an attitude. And at first my attitude was that I was ashamed of it. But the older I get the more I realize that the transgressions of the South were the transgressions of mankind, and that there were certain things that were superior. There is a cultural attitude in the South that embraces respect for family and God and in some ways for country. Although patriotism is not among the highest virtues on my list, still, the patriot believes in something larger than himself, and it is therefore a virtue. There is an attitude in the South that there is more to life than the moment."

"Honor? It's such a theme. So many people talk about it."

"I was trained that way. To believe that truth is an ultimate virtue. The watchword for life was unselfishness." He stopped. "But I don't know that any of this is peculiar to the South. I am inclined to think, however, that the closer you get to the equator, life tends to be exaggerated."

"Did you try to distance yourself from the South, after you'd become ashamed of it?"

"Particularly when I was with people from the North. And even when I was in the South I spoke out against things I didn't like. That meant the racism."

"It must create disturbance, turning against what you had grown up with."

He said: "It produces a certain schizophrenia. But as I get older I get more tolerant. I become more tolerant of intolerance. If you find a Klansman to talk to you, and you ask him what the Ku Klux Klan stands for, he would say it stands for law and order, and love and friendship, and brotherhood. If you would ask him how he would set about achieving those things, he would say, 'Whatever it takes. Whether we have to blow up that building or attack that man.' He doesn't see how those two ideas are not in harmony with one another. You can't deal with that kind of schizophrenia."

At our lunch he had spoken of the South's acceptance of civil rights as a kind of recognition by the South of the immorality of its earlier position. I wanted to know whether he could chart particular stages of that recognition.

"I have a hard time explaining that to myself. It is a wondrous thing. If you had told me in the late fifties and early sixties that in the very near future we were going to have an integrated society, I wouldn't have believed you. I thought then that it might have been a hundred years in coming. It may even be divine, the change that has come about —I don't know. It's hard to understand. But people all of a sudden saw that it was wrong. And that is miraculous, for people to say that their own behavior had been morally defective. Nobody ever confesses on that scale. And here we have not only a somebody, an individual, saying that, but a whole society."

And commercial pressures were now bringing about social change. There had been the recent uproar about a black IBM executive being denied membership of a club in Columbia. IBM as a result had dropped an idea about putting up a local plant. Neither IBM nor the executive had wished to talk about the matter or make race the issue; and it wasn't, therefore, easy for people to deal with. The consequence was that there had been no bluster on the part of the club; they had simply changed their policy and invited some blacks to join.

Judge Sanders spoke as a lawyer. Through the law he had arrived at a larger identity.

He said, "The common law is a majestic thing. It has a remarkable capacity to resolve disputes in a way which not only preserves civilization but enhances it. It is not unusual for me to find myself guided in a decision by a decision which a judge made a thousand years ago. I am aware I'm serving a larger civilization. And I know I'm *serving* it."

"So you don't have a problem of identity, no trouble between background and profession."

"Not any more. I am more at peace with myself. Of course, that may be a matter of getting old and less judgmental and more understanding."

His family had been in South Carolina "forever." An early ancestor on his mother's side had come out as a missionary to the Indians, and had then become a missionary to slaves.

3

■■■

TALLAHASSEE

The Truce with
Irrationality—I

PEOPLE IN Charleston had been complaining about the lack of their afternoon rain. As if to make up for this, on the day I left, and almost as soon as I had cleared the town and was going west, there was a fierce cloudburst. The tall trees tossed, the leaves showing their undersides, every big bough in separate convulsion. The rain slapped the windshield; nervous cars parked off the traffic lanes with their lights on. Not many miles away it became clearer, midafternoon again; though still from time to time approaching cars—when they had their headlights on—alerted one to the storms ahead.

Tropical weather, of continental violence, matching the landscape: the swamp of South Carolina running into the marsh of northern Florida, reeds green and brown, patches of water silver or black, a landscape impressive by its great size. And soon enough, from this tropical swamp, Charleston—which one had begun to take for granted: so perfect a creation—began to seem far away. It was hard to think of that town being set down here—as it was hard to associate all this coastal land with African slavery, land so much of the New World, so unlike any other, land one wanted to contemplate, to enter a little into its wonder.

The slavery of the British Caribbean islands began to seem small-scale, even domestic. Slavery in the British Caribbean was really an eighteenth-century institution; when slavery was abolished in the British Empire in 1834, England had become a manufacturing and trading country and could afford to write off both the plantations and the islands. Slavery in the Southern United States was most important in the first half of the nineteenth century—most important, that is, when slavery was on the point of becoming anachronistic, an absurdity in an industrializing country. But business people are concerned with the here and now (it is fearful to read of the slave-owners' wish to extend plantation slavery to the Western territories); and it took a war to do away with slavery in the South. The freed slaves remained, in inescapable numbers, no longer mere units of labor and wealth, a kind of currency; and it was they—for whose sake, one way or the other, the war had been fought—who bore the brunt of the South's anguish.

A slave is a slave; a master need not think of humiliating or tormenting him. In the hundred years after the end of slavery the black man was tormented in the South in ways that I never knew about until I began to travel in the region. Jack Leland had told me that in the early days of the motorcar in South Carolina blacks hadn't been allowed to drive. In Tallahassee I heard that blacks were not allowed to try on clothes in stores; they had to buy anything they tried on. In Mississippi blacks could not be educated beyond a certain point; in South Carolina there was a time when attempts were made to deny blacks education altogether.

And there was in the South something we never knew in the Caribbean of colonial days: violence, and the absence of law. How did a black family react to news of lynchings? What happened to the bodies? How were they buried? A man I met told me that when he was a child he was not allowed by his father to be a delivery boy. The father feared that a white woman might accuse the boy of being a Peeping Tom or of attempting rape.

In the Caribbean the black man, after a hundred years of colonial neglect, a hundred years of separation from slavery, found himself in a majority on his own island, with the power of electing his own leaders and his own government. The black American, at about the same time, found himself just liberated but in a minority in the world's most advanced country, and among the most denuded in that country. His possibilities, as an American, were far greater than those of a West Indian. But there could be no easy movement forward for the mass; they had lived through too much; the irrationality of slavery and the years after slavery had made many irrational and self-destructive.

It was in the news every day: drugs, crime, street life, "negative peer pressure" at school (blacks beating up those blacks who did well at school). In Atlanta, Anne Siddons had spoken of her need after a certain age to hoard emotion, to save parts of herself for herself. It seemed that blacks of all ages—living out their cause in their lives—felt a similar need. But in their more desperate condition this looking inward could separate them from their cause and often work against it.

"Finally, I suppose, the most difficult (and most rewarding) thing in my life has been the fact that I was born a Negro and was forced, therefore, to effect some kind of truce with this reality." The words by James Baldwin (among the most elegant handlers of the language) had stayed with me since I had read them, nearly thirty years before. "Reality"—it was what I remembered and what I accepted; but now, in the South, in the middle of my own journey, I began to wonder whether the truce that every black man looked for hadn't in fact been with the irrationality of the world around him. And the achievement of certain people began to appear grander.

THE REVEREND Bernyce Clausell lived in Tallahassee on Joe Louis Street. "Not in the project," she said on the telephone. "Tell the driver not in the project." And the white driver not only went straight to the house, but spotted the lady in her collar in the street, talking to a member of her congregation.

Reverend Clausell was a Baptist pastor, and she had some reputation both as the only Baptist woman pastor in this part of Florida and as someone who did social work. She had been in the news for having sent a relief mission to Mississippi, to the town of Tunica, in a poor region with the name of Sugar Ditch. She had sent a truckload of supplies. Down the side of the truck there had been a professionally lettered banner: TALLAHASSEE TO TUNICA. There had been a copywriter's feeling there for effect, I thought. But the lady I saw in the street when the taxi-driver pointed had nothing forbidding or assertive about her.

She was small and slender and mild-featured, academic-looking in her collar, someone suited to the quiet residential street, with its little houses and neat yards; definitely not a street in the "project."

She said goodbye to the woman she was with, and greeted me. She said that the woman, who was of her congregation, had stopped her just as she was on her way to the church to turn the lights off. She asked me to go with her. It was a few house plots away, on the other side of the road: Calvary Baptist Church, a white building, with a board that gave the name of her late husband, the Reverend James Aaron Clausell. He had founded the church.

The grass around the small church was as clipped and neat as the grass in the house yards. The light bulbs in the porch were burning wastefully away.

Clausell—what sort of name was that? She said it was French. It came from Louisiana; it was the name of one of the important early settlers there. Her husband had been a light-skinned man, like many of his family.

And there was a story about the founding of the church in that street. The Clausells had been holding prayer meetings in their house, and people were being saved and baptized. One day Reverend Clausell asked her, "What are we going to do with these people?" She said, "Let's start a church." He said, "I don't need a church. I pastor too many churches already." She said, "Well, honey, I wasn't thinking of what you needed. I was thinking of what the people needed." That was how the church had started. And when Reverend Clausell died, Bernyce, his wife, had become pastor, in response to the wishes of the congregation.

The church, so white and plain outside, was full of things inside. It was clearly much used, and looked like a living room or a meeting place for the congregation. The main hall was about fifty feet long by thirty feet wide. It was full of flowers, and it had a piano and an organ. The carpet was green-blue; the pews were upholstered in a green fabric. At the end of the hall was a very big picture of Jesus and Mary Magdalen. It was at least fifteen feet wide and five feet high. The picture had been bought twenty-three years before from a printing house near Boston. The Christ was noticeably white, blond, long-haired, a little bit—as I had noticed in other places—like some paintings of General Custer.

I asked Bernyce Clausell about the representation.

She said, "It doesn't worry the congregation. I teach them that color is not important. A white Christ is better than no Christ at all. After all, Christ is colorless."

But she also had a black Christ to show, a black Christ with black disciples. This picture was small, something she held in her hand.

About the carpet and the pew upholstery she said, "Everything was given. We take what is given. That's why they don't match exactly."

On the windows were stained-glass patterns on paper, strips of paper stuck on. The strips had been printed with a floral design. They had been ordered from Spencer Gifts, a mail-order business; and they had been chosen from a catalogue.

The church door opened, and a woman's voice greeted the pastor. Reverend Bernyce knew the visitor. She excused herself and went to the woman. I didn't turn to look; I looked at the Boston mural. The woman who had turned up spoke in a low voice, and Reverend Bernyce's voice matched hers. Their words were not distinct. Only one sentence, of Reverend Bernyce's, came to me out of the burr-and-bumble. "You don't have to fall on the floor and jump to the ceiling." The consultation went on for a while: the second person that morning to have sought out the pastor with a spiritual problem.

And when, after many goodbyes and thanks, the visitor left, Reverend Bernyce explained.

"Her daughter came last week and accepted Christ. She's going to be baptized. The daughter is fourteen years old. But then somebody told the daughter that she wasn't ready—and they are really trying to keep her out of the church. Some denominations wouldn't let you join until you make some kind of emotional, physical reaction. That's why I told the mother that nowadays you don't have to jump to the ceiling."

I asked her to explain a little more.

She said, "You're born a Hindu. We are not born Christian. We are born black."

That last thing seemed strange for the pastor to say. But perhaps she meant no more than that people had to choose Christ.

"To become a Christian does not require lots of emotion. In our worship services we are emotional only if we are so moved."

She led me to the room at the back of the main hall. It was an annex to the main building, and it was called the Clausell Fellowship Hall, in honor of her late husband. It was domestic-looking. There was a stove for cooking, and all about were clothes that had been collected for the church's charities, especially for Mission Outreach. The mild lady pastor spoke the slogan of the program with perfect seriousness: "It's our caring-sharing project." It was part of the "Tallahassee to Tunica" mission. There were clothes (covered with green cloths) on racks, in boxes, in sacks, and on tables. She said that her appeal for the poor of Tunica in Mississippi, some six hundred miles away, had touched a nerve in her congregation.

All around in this annex, on walls and boards, were photographs of black Americans. "We keep black-American history in front of people, so they will know some of their heritage." There were portraits of Martin Luther King, Richard Allen (founder of the African Methodist Episcopal Church in Pennsylvania), Booker T. Washington, Harriet Tubman, Frederick Douglass, and black-American service heroes; and there was a photograph of the black-owned Atlanta Life Insurance Company.

We left the annex and went back through the main church hall. On the wall next to the front door there were many color snapshots of Reverend Bernyce's European tour in 1972. This—and everything else —gave to the hall the feel of a devout person's scrapbook. But there was something more. This elderly black lady had been experiencing the larger world, the famous world, as a black person, and giving a little of the glamour of the experience back to her black congregation. Just as the honors that had been given to her were to be regarded as honors given to a black person, and honors therefore to all black people.

In the church porch there were cutouts from magazines of black and white family groups. This was Reverend Bernyce's way of reminding her congregation of Mother's Day; and she had been careful to show both black and white family groups. She said, "We're a biracial country." The word was new to me; but then she qualified and extended it. "We are black, but the country isn't all black. We are many races. So in picturing families we have families of different colors."

The air felt heavy with pollen. On the other side of the road, where her house was, the ground sloped away, so that the house was in a little dip; and the air was heavier. There was a car in a carport. And in her little sitting room, much smaller than one might have thought from the outside, there were many more photographs and mementoes and things. One wall was covered with framed diplomas and plaques. It was warm in the sitting room, even with the door open.

She had been born in Georgia, and when she was nine months old had been taken away by her parents to Columbus, Ohio. "I don't know what my dad did. My dad was a laborer. He was a little feller. He couldn't do too much." And it was probably from her father that she had inherited her own smallness. "We stayed in Columbus a little while. Then my mother died and our auntie took us to New York. I loved my aunt. I was too young to know my mother. In New York we had everything all around us—reefers, murder, dope—but it didn't influence us, because of our church life."

She broke off to talk about the accommodation black country people had to make when they went to the big city. "You lose all the ties to your family, your community, your church. But then there is the chance for you to gain new ties, even in a great metropolis like New York. You can get into a smaller group and be a viable person in that smaller group. Like, for instance, a church, a social club, a political group, or just a street group. Some young people, when they migrate from the South to the North, they still want a group to cling to. So unfortunately they become affiliated to a street group."

How did she explain the strong religious instinct black people had?

"I think it comes from slavery. And even from before slavery. From Africa. They just had a strong religious heritage. In slavery God was their deliverer. And they felt that some day God would work it out."

Was it sometimes a form of escapism?

"With some people it might be a form of escapism. I wouldn't deny it. But primarily Christianity is a way of life. I should say that the white churches that I know are similar to ours. They are doing great mission work. And more than we are, because they have the finances. Religion has had a great part in helping to break down segregation.

"I have to speak personally. I did not experience any racial hostility until I left New York and went to live in Washington, D.C. This was in 1941, when I was twenty-five. I went to work for the government. And there was this experience that tore me up—the first day. The cafeteria in the War Department building was not open yet. So about four of our black girls went to a small sandwich shop to eat our lunch, and we bought sodas, and were about to sit down to eat, and the lady there said very harshly, 'Can't you people, can't you people find some place else to eat?' Of course we didn't have much appetite after that."

"Did this shake your faith or your way of thinking?"

"What it did, it made me wonder about my nation. Before that, I was a hundred percent patriotic. I loved America. But it began to shatter a little my patriotic fervor. It didn't shake my religion. In fact, because of my religious training I didn't hold any ill-feeling against the woman in the sandwich shop. Washington, D.C., was not integrated. And *that* was mind-boggling to me, that the nation's capital wasn't integrated.

"When we went to the large cafeteria in the War Department building, where we worked, whites would not want to sit at the same table with us. If we sat down with them they would move. We just began to know that this exists. It made me a fighter, all right. We joined a group there that was spearheaded by the Quakers, and our aim was to integrate some of the lunch counters in the city. We would meet—all the Quakers were white—and have prayers and decide where we were going. And we were being told not to show any reaction to any violence that would be shown to us. We had to be trained. You can't imagine the things that were said to us. People would spit in our faces. If we drank out of a glass they would take it up and throw it away. Christ said turn the other cheek. And finally Washington was integrated, a little later."

The atmosphere was heavy, with the pollen and humidity of northern Florida. My eyes had begun to smart; and now, thinking of those prayer meetings, I began to cry.

She said, "People have changed. And now some of those people wouldn't believe that they were that cruel back there."

It was such a good way of putting it. She didn't offer a personal forgiveness. She spoke of a larger change of heart. It was immensely moving.

She said, "These experiences helped to build me and give me more character and strength."

But what of others?

"Some people couldn't take it. They just gave up. They accepted. For those people it may have been the best thing to do. It's not for everyone to fight. The Bible says, Let the strong bear the infirmities of the weak."

She, so frail and spare on her settee in her little sitting room, considered herself one of the strong.

"It's still an issue. Not segregation, but racism. It's more subtle."

I wanted to know her attitude to the past. But the past for her, as for nearly all black people I spoke to, stopped at a certain point.

"I've never dug into my roots. I can go back as far as my grandfather and grandmother. Around 1900. And that's all."

Now there were other problems beside those of racism. There were the problems of teenage pregnancies, drugs, dropouts, and the behavior of black students at schools who were reported to beat up those blacks who did well at their studies.

"We didn't have that problem when the schools were all black. Now —I hate to say it—integration has damaged some of the black children. Because in the black schools we had to visit the parents' homes periodically. If we had problems we would go to the home, and the parents were very cooperative. We had religious activities at the schools. We had fifteen-minute morning devotions. In the integrated schools what happened was that some of the black children began to role-model some of the nonproductive white children. And parents didn't have that close tie with the schools. Those of us who are in this work have to work harder. You can't do too much in the schools now."

She regarded herself as one of the strong. Her religion gave her some of her strength. Had there been any experiences that had confirmed her in her faith?

She said, "Many. All the time. God speaks to people, just like he did in olden days. I knew when I was sixteen that I was going to preach. I told my church in New York. I don't know how it came. I just knew it. And I know that in 1971, when I became a minister, God had talked to me. They are words in your heart, when God speaks. But there have been occasions when God talked to me in words, when he called my name, and I looked around to see who was there who had called me, and there was nobody there. The first experience of God speaking audibly was when I was a child. He said, 'Get up and go join the church.' I didn't do it then.

"But since I've been in the ministry God talks to me all the time. In words. He'll tell me to do something. And I'll reply to him out loud. Some of my congregation know about those experiences. One Sunday God spoke to me about a child in the congregation. I had just turned to go back to the pulpit, and God said, 'Pray for that child!' I turned around and saw this child sitting in somebody's lap. The command was urgent. And I said, 'Whose child is that? Bring that child here.' I prayed. People cried. A week later the child became ill, but the child did not die. Thank God!"

She normally didn't speak of these experiences. The one time she did was when she appeared before the Ordaining Council, a group of black Baptists in New York City. "I had to justify my calling. I told how God spoke to me. When I told the Ordaining Council, they understood quite well."

Her religion had helped her through the hard times in Washington in 1941 and later.

"You see, it's the holy spirit that guides and protects us in these instances."

"Did you ever feel abandoned?"

"I never felt abandoned by God."

"Did he tell you to be a fighter?"

"I don't know. It was in me. And I felt I had done what I could do."

She revered the memory of Martin Luther King. But the resistance she and the Quakers had undertaken in Washington was long before the civil-rights movement of the 1950s and 1960s. She was braver than she claimed. But she referred everything to her faith. "So many religious experiences, so many experiences of God." And she was pleased that both her daughters were religiously inclined, and one "totally dedicated to the church." To that extent she was passing on the torch as a woman pastor.

"When I was a child in New York we had women preachers in our congregation, so to me it was nothing rare or different. When I married a minister I lost all thoughts of being a minister myself. My husband did not believe in women as ministers. But he knew I wanted to be a minister. He was a perceptive man. He was much older than I. He knew I wanted to be a minister because sometimes in church I would get up and talk. When the spirit moves, you move. He understood I was sincere. When God spoke to me in 1971, I couldn't help what my husband thought. I had to respond to the call this time. I had to hear God's voice and not my husband's voice."

It was time for me to leave. She gave me a stapled photocopied booklet about herself, a souvenir of a celebration held in her honor six months before at the Florida Agricultural and Mechanical University. This booklet had copies of articles about her from the Tallahassee *Democrat*; it listed her many awards and honors. The frontispiece was a full-page photograph of herself; and on the cover she was described as a "servant of Christ."

She also gave me her card. On this card the Calvary Baptist Church was described—and again I thought of advertising copy—as "the friendly little church on the corner of Joe Louis and Arizona." At one time that would have seemed to me very "American." Now I understood a little more, and knew that churches like Reverend Bernyce's were more than places of worship, were community centers, social centers, and depended on the personality of the pastor.

Maurice Crockett, a big, upright, handsome brown man of fifty-six, was the Florida Parole Board commissioner. He had been represented to me as a local black success story. That made me want to see him. He had agreed to see me, but he hadn't understood what I was after. And when I was taken to his office early one afternoon —his desk was cleared, and he was resting his head on his crossed arms, but he was far from asleep—he was not immediately welcoming.

He said, and it was like a prepared statement, "Most people from outside see us as ethnically deprived, semiliterate." There wouldn't have been much in the meeting if we had gone on like that; but when he understood that I had come to listen, his manner softened. Soon his natural graces took over; he talked easily, anxious to efface the first, unwelcoming impression.

He said, "When I became a department head, over both blacks and whites, the whites were not happy, and I had to live with police protection for a couple of years."

It seemed so unlikely now, in the general civility of his office.

"It might have been an overreaction, but you never know. There were any number of threatening phone calls and innuendos. And a lot of the whites quit."

The fight wasn't pleasant, but it was necessary.

"Some people try to give the impression that when we were segregated the whites were happy and the blacks were happy. But it isn't true. I don't think any thinking person could be happy under those circumstances. I could never have *afforded* to be happy. My choices were so limited. My son today has unlimited choices of career. I did not. When, in 1964, I thought I was due for a promotion, they came and drove me around in the car and explained that I was qualified but they weren't ready for a colored person to do that kind of job yet. I went home and, I'll tell you, I cried. And it still hurts.

"My son, because of my job, has never experienced that kind of rejection. In my work here I've been surrounded mainly by whites, and that's the environment my son grew up in."

His son went to white public schools, until his father put him in a black school affiliated with the local black university.

"He couldn't take it. He had never been in an all-black situation. The music was different, the manners were different. Michael had been listening to white kids' music. In his scout troop he was the only black kid."

Maurice Crockett had lived through a hard time, and had more than survived. But had some people broken under the strain?

"Some people back away. And the way you do that is you involve yourself in your church, in things around the home. So to all practical purposes you isolate yourself from reality. The church is all black, and when you go there everybody is friendly, and you aren't threatened, and it's like being in the womb again."

But he had had a special source of strength.

"Most black kids have mainly a matriarchal system. But I grew up with a man. He was my stepfather. He was a role model and a guide for me. Mothers tend to be not as strict with boys. Boys need the kind of structure that a male provides. I think a lot of the black kids today would go to school if the basic family structure with the male was in place. But black males have a hard time establishing themselves, because of the lack of job opportunities."

I asked him about his son, who had been taken out of white schools to be sent to black schools.

Maurice Crockett said, "He's begun to be aware that he's black, and that everybody doesn't love him. He's starting his third year at Tuskegee. But Michael still has his basic cadre of white friends."

Out of success now, out of his new security, Maurice Crockett was rediscovering, reasserting, his blackness. He needed religion, but he needed a black religion.

"I'm not a shouter. But I like to be in a church where that kind of thing goes on. A lot of us want to emulate other standards, and we have to do that. But I still think that, like most ethnic groups, you shouldn't divorce yourself from your basic culture. Especially when I go to church. The church is my salvation. The church keeps me sane."

Salvation, sanity—I hadn't heard the two run together. But in the job of Parole Board commissioner there were special needs.

"Some days in this job the stress of trying to keep up sends you home with pain. One of the most stressful things we have to do is that we hold the final face-to-face interview with the prisoners on Death Row. We actually go to the prison and sit down with the inmate and his attorney. Our meeting is transcribed by a court reporter. And when the world gets too much for me, I go to church. The saving grace for us black Southerners is the church."

"Do you feel successful now? Content?"

"I'm not content. I'll go to my grave being not content. I'll constantly try to improve. People want to say we want to land from the trees and eat watermelon for the rest of our days. I want them to know that that kind of stereotyping is misplaced. I receive visitors a lot in my job. Most people from outside see us as ethnically deprived, nonverbal. I guess they see us as semiliterate people."

That was where our conversation had begun. Now he had brought it back to that point, with an explanation.

"But this is false. If you come to me like that, I will let you know that I am not the kind of person you can handle in that way."

His own truce with irrationality—how had he managed it? What was it about the past that now, from this distance, most surprised him?

"What I find hard to understand now is how I contained the anger. I suppose you have to learn that the anger doesn't solve your problems. You sometimes have to sit down and wrestle with yourself."

He still occasionally wrestled. He lived in a white neighborhood. He took his dog for a walk. At whatever time of morning or afternoon he took the dog, there was always, in a house at one end of the street, an old white man who sat out on the porch and watched him. It would appear that the old man was waiting for Mr. Crockett to go past his house.

"But what's the point?"

I didn't understand the explanation Mr. Crockett gave. "He wants me to know that he is there. He wants me to know that I'm being watched." And Mr. Crockett made a gesture with his finger, drawing a horizontal line.

"Does he say anything? Do you talk?"

"We do. And I always have to think of something to say back. The last thing he said was, 'I don't know who's slower, you or the dog.' And I have to think of something to say, something foolish like, 'You're slower than both of us.' That kind of nonsense."

But the neighbor would have been a religious man, perhaps a Baptist, a fundamentalist. Didn't that make for a certain kind of communication?

Mr. Crockett rejected that. "White fundamentalism"—putting it in quite a different category from the black fundamentalism he liked in black churches and saw as part of his black culture—"it is their attempt to go back to the good old days. The white church now has a school attached to it. They call it a 'Christian school'; the main purpose is to keep it segregated. The white-fundamentalist church has consumed these people and consumed the issues. It's a half-baked attempt to establish a structure that has long since gone by the board."

I T WAS the advice of a West Coast writer, someone originally from Tallahassee, that had sent me to Tallahassee. Northern Florida, I had been told, was quite different from southern Florida. Northern Florida, the panhandle part of the state, was part of the Deep South. But it had taken me a long time to find my way; it sometimes happens on this kind of journey.

Tallahassee, the state capital, was an artificial administrative center midway between the extremities of the panhandle, midway between the towns of Pensacola and Jacksonville. And all that I had got to know of the countryside was the few miles between Tallahassee and the beach houses on the black creeks and white sandspits of the Gulf of Mexico: a holiday landscape of food shops, restaurants, mobile homes, gas stations, places offering live bait, and churches—disposable buildings in "redneck" country, where (I was told) in the old days blacks would have been burned out if they had tried to settle, and where there were still almost no blacks.

But then, almost at the end of my time in Tallahassee, I saw something other than that holiday landscape. About an hour's drive away, and just behind the highway—American highways make one state look like another, and one part like another—I saw old dirt roads, forest where there had once been fields, houses that had been abandoned whole, barns and garages in overgrown yards. It was a little like being in an abandoned European town in Africa, in Zaire or Rwanda.

There had been an old community here. Now it hardly existed. Farming could no longer support it; farming no longer paid. And here and there among the ruined houses—trees and shrubs and bush seeming to reach out towards them, darkening the open space of yards—were places in which people still lived, black and white, people not ready to go, holding on, people who it might be said were working out the quirks of their own character. The fat young man rocking on the low porch, for instance, was the son of a black farmer. That was the way he had chosen to spend his days; he had made that choice of solitude. I thought of the drinking man in Howard's village, framed in his window on a Sunday, looking out, but far from the life of his community. Here there was no longer a community; the fat young man rocked in the middle of bush.

My guide was Granger. He was white, in his forties, and he worked in a hotel in a nearby town. He did that for the ready cash, to keep his own farm going. It was a small farm, 120 acres. But it was ancestral land. It had been homesteaded—Indian land, staked out and claimed from the federal government—in the decade before the Civil War. The local Baptist church had been established in 1856; Granger was a Baptist. The land had never been worked by slaves. "We feel like we were the first Americans," a relation of Granger's told me. And various ancestors had migrated to this part of Florida from South Carolina, Virginia, and Georgia.

There were stories in some branches of the family of old wealth. There was a story that one ancestor had owned a third of a county in England. There was a later story, from a time after the calamities of the Civil War, of another ancestor who had made good in the China trade and had brought home a chest of gold coins, which, when emptied out onto the farmhouse floor, had sent up a cloud of pure gold dust.

Now Granger worked in a hotel, two days on, two days off, and looked after what was left of the ancestral farm, doing so not for money but for the piety, the debt owed his ancestors, and doing so as well because farming was for him part of the beauty of the days. Farming meant being in these fields, these woods.

We drove in his fields in his old, un-air-conditioned pickup truck. One of his cows had just calved. We stopped in the truck among the pine trees, in the thin, broken shade, among the cowpats and the pine litter, the cones, the needles, the brittle dead branches. He got out and, keeping his distance, spoke both to the mother and the birth-smeared calf struggling to its feet. He had been waiting for this event for some days. This was the kind of farming he did and liked. It had given him his gentleness.

But development was coming. People with jobs in the towns were building houses in the villages. The old farms were under threat. A cycle that had begun when the Indian land was homesteaded was coming to an end. (The tomb of Osceola, the Seminole chief who had died at the age of thirty-eight in federal-government captivity, was not far from Charleston, and within sight of Fort Sumter.)

Fifty miles or so away, still in the panhandle, building development and agricultural failure were putting an end to another kind of community, a community of black sharecroppers. Black people had lived on this land since the end of slavery. Once everyone was related; these fields bounded everyone's horizon. Now the roads had got there; the community, exposed, was breaking up; there were pine plantations in the old fields—young pines growing out of a lot of bush. But not everyone was ready to move to a town.

The life on the land here was different from the life that Granger found on his 120 acres. There was a different idea here of ancestors, history, piety. For Barrett, the black man in his thirties who was showing me around, the agricultural life of this inbred black community was stultifying and shameful.

Barrett was middle-class, with parents who were modest professional people. He came from a biggish town where there were few black people. Until he had come to Tallahassee he had thought that black people in the South were like his family; he was still unsettled and enraged by those aspects of black life in Tallahassee that didn't fit in with his old ideas. The idea of being in a minority was so much part of his upbringing, and so important to him, that he had had trouble, he told me, getting used to the sight of all-black streets. I liked him for saying that; not many people would have confessed to something so simple and undermining. And when his work had taken him to that old black agricultural community, he said, he had suffered from "culture shock."

I didn't think that what he was showing me was all that bad. But, then, I didn't have his expectations. And, with anger building up in him again, and out of this anger wishing to see the worst again, and to show it to me, he drove me to a side road and said, "Look at that one. A house without windows."

It was extraordinary, a much-patched-up and wretched old wooden house, standing by itself in a bare yard, with no trees around, and with bush in the field at the back.

I thought I understood now what Maurice Crockett wished to save his son from: growing up "white" and then having, like Barrett, to make adjustments.

Barrett didn't think as Maurice Crockett did about black religion. Barrett didn't think that the shouting religions were part of his own black culture. After he had got married, he said, he and his wife had talked about what church they should go to. They had talked very seriously, and they had decided to go to the Presbyterian church.

He was twenty years younger than Maurice Crockett. He didn't have the older man's needs.

At the start of our drive I had noticed his racial passion. He wished to blame someone first of all; but then his own words had led him away from that, to a more general irritation. I had asked him about his racial passion; it seemed to be so much his main subject. He had acknowledged my question, but not replied to it. Now, when we were almost back at the hotel, he returned to the question.

He said, "You asked me about that. I've been thinking about it. I suppose I am angry because I am black. I don't know whether that's a good enough reason, but that's how it is."

It was a good reply. It was part of his honesty.

In the driveway of the hotel there was a black figure I had grown to recognize. He wore a black turban and a cream-colored Indian-style long shirt. He was reading aloud, chanting, from an Arabic book, perhaps a Koran. He paid no attention to the coming and going around him. He read aloud like a student; he held the fat book close to his face; he sat on a low wall; he could not be ignored.

REVEREND Bernyce Clausell, Mr. Crockett, Barrett—they were all aspects of a developing black movement forward. And Jesse Jackson came to Tallahassee one day, looking for support for his presidential candidacy. Even if the man himself was not seen by many, his presence was felt. His entourage nearly filled the Golden Pheasant restaurant. Later that evening a limousine with its hood up waited outside a club where the candidate was meeting local people. Such style, such expense; and this was just one day, and not a very important one, in the calendar of a presidential candidate.

It would have been historically satisfying, and simpler to manage intellectually, if this movement forward was, broadly, all; if black people, their legal rights won, were now becoming masters of their own destinies. But at the other end of this movement, and close enough to threaten this movement (in spite of the mighty presence in the Golden Pheasant restaurant of the men and women of the Jackson party), there was irrationality and self-destructiveness, and despair of a sort perhaps not known before.

It is like the final cruelty of slavery: that now, at what should have been a time of possibility, a significant portion of black people should find themselves without the supports of faith and community evolved during the last hundred years or so. In the Caribbean islands, in the most settled days of slavery, the slaves played at night at having kingdoms of their own: a transference to the plantations of West African beliefs—still current in the Ivory Coast—that the real world begins when the sun goes down, and that at night men change or reverse their daytime roles. No fantasy even like this, no African millenarian dream, supports the new denuded black element. It is hard to enter into their vacancy.

"I'm nothing. I'm just existing," a young black in a detention center said. "Your hands soft," another said, using words that seemed to me to come from a long time ago. "Your hands soft like cotton." His own hand was gentle. He had the intelligence and dangerous attractiveness of a kind of delinquent. But he was horribly lost; he couldn't be reached. Another man said, "It is very hard for a black man to make a very small step."

They were all going to be released in a few months. But there was nothing for them in the world outside; they insisted on that. And they all spoke as though their lives had been predetermined, and were already over.

"Nearly sixteen millions of hands will aid you in pulling the load upward, or they will pull against you the load downward. We shall constitute one-third and more of the ignorance and crime of the South, or one-third of its intelligence and progress; we shall contribute one-third to the business and industrial prosperity of the South, or we shall prove a veritable body of death, stagnating, depressing . . . the body politic."

The words read like special pleading. And they were. They come from the speech Booker T. Washington made in Atlanta in 1895, when he was only thirty-nine: a famous speech that established him in his reputation, and in which he did two apparently irreconcilable things—calm Southern white people down, and offer hope to black people at a time of near hopelessness. Special pleading, overstated; but those words of the 1895 Atlanta speech now read like prophecy.

4

∎∎∎

The Truce with
Irrationality—II

I HAD got to know *Up from Slavery* when I was a child. My father had read me a story from the book, and I believe I then read more of the book on my own. My father, born poor, and in spite of his ambition always poor, liked stories of self-help and of men rising from poverty. He suffered in Trinidad, and I would have known that *Up from Slavery* had racial implications and could be related to the way things were on our own island. But I was too young to do anything with that kind of information. I received the Booker T. Washington story my father read me almost as a fairy story, and in the part of my consciousness where it lodged it was stripped both of race and historical time.

Within the larger story of a man rising and making good, the story in question was the story of a test. The young boy, alone in the world, and just starting out in the world, had been asked to make up a bed (this was the way the story lived in my consciousness). And what was at stake, what depended on the correct making up of the bed, was the young boy's entire future.

It was hard to forget that story (and every time I made up a bed it hovered in my consciousness): the fairy-tale test, the doing of a seemingly trivial or irrelevant thing supremely well. Like the story of a temptation to an honor-bound knight or a saint who had made a vow; like magical tests in other fairy stories: picking up the grains of rice, guessing the name of the dwarf, spinning straw into gold.

But the story I carried in my consciousness was wrong in one detail. The ragged boy, born a slave, who had walked many days and nights to a particular school in order to be educated there, had been asked first of all not to make up a bed, but to sweep a room. The boy had swept the room four times. The woman who had set the test hadn't then simply said, "All right. You pass." She had run her fingers over the walls and floor, to check. The boy had judged rightly, after all. He had done the deceptively simple task very well; and in this way he had won over yet another potential tormentor, and turned her into an ally on his magical journey.

There was a reason why, in my memory, the story had changed from sweeping a room to making up a bed. Beds were important to the slave boy. In the one-room slave cabin, also the farm cookhouse, where he had lived with his mother, the boy had slept in rags on the earth floor; and when, in his rise, he was first presented with a made-up bed, he didn't know how to use it. He didn't know whether he had to sleep on both sheets or between them or below both of them. (I would have been sympathetic to that predicament, having at the age of eighteen moved to temperate England from tropical Trinidad, where we made beds in our own way: one sheet spread on the bed, another sheet or blanket folded, to be used as a loose cover during the night if it was needed. I might even have transferred an early personal embarrassment to my memory of the book.) And in the school he had later established at Tuskegee in Alabama for people who, like him, were not far out of slavery, Booker T. Washington was concerned to teach his students how to use beds, and concerned in a more general way to teach good domestic manners as he had grown to understand them.

A moving story, and a fabulous one: the boy who had slept on the floor of a slave cabin had become one of the most famous Americans of his day, had dined with the president, and had never ceased to serve the cause of his people. It is easy to see how *Up from Slavery* could have worked on a self-made man like Andrew Carnegie and drawn great sums of money from him for the school at Tuskegee.

At the same time the very fabulousness of the Booker T. Washington story had made it seem separate from the grimmer aspects of the Southern or American racial issue people wrote about in books and newspapers. What had the great fame of the man served? What had happened to the great achievement? And so the book had receded, leaving only a memory of the bed-making test (which in my mind ran together with the story of the middle-aged Tolstoy, in a peasant phase, wishing to make up his own bed). And then its very title had been undermined by the William Buckley parody title, *Up from Liberalism.*

It was only when I began to plan this journey, and had been given the idea of Tuskegee, that the book became real again for me. It became especially real when I went to see Al Murray in his apartment in Harlem.

Al Murray was the first person educated at Tuskegee whom I had met and spoken to about it. He it was who began to give me some idea of the grandeur and complexity (and anguishes) of Booker T. Washington; gave racial attributes to the neutral fairy-tale figure—the slave boy's father might have been a white man; and fitted him into historical time. When the school had begun in 1881, as a simple trades school, black men had the vote, and the school had been given some small subsidy by the state of Alabama. Twenty years later, when *Up from Slavery* was published, black men had been virtually disenfranchised in the South. It was against this background, of increasing legal disabilities, that Booker T. Washington had built up his school. What would have been hard enough in a time of stability had been made much harder, with the walls of prejudice, segregation, and humiliation constantly shifting, closing in. Booker T. Washington did what he did, Al said, because he understood the way capitalist America worked; he knew how to present himself to that side of America. What was important to remember was that Booker T. Washington was a nineteenth-century American, the counterpart of the Carnegies and others whose wealth he tapped.

Al Murray's admiration for his university and its founder made the old black-and-white photographs that he showed me, in the two volumes of Louis R. Harlan's biography, especially moving: the stately photographs of Booker T. Washington; the formally dressed young blacks, men and women, doing domestic work and agricultural work which, just a few years before, would have been slaves' work, but which was now (like their teacher's own room-sweeping test) a step to better things.

It was to a special kind of romance, then, that I was traveling when I left Tallahassee and its drugged, asthma-inducing pollens, and made for Alabama and Tuskegee—going up through the plains of Georgia and then through the extensive flat neon confusion of the camp-following town of Columbus, Georgia: sex shows and pawnshops and fast-food restaurants; crossing from that into quiet, rural, seemingly left-behind Alabama.

Tuskegee became a name on the highway boards; became the name of a forest—speaking then of a pre-1830, preplantation, Indian past, giving another association to the unusual name; and then at last became the name of a town.

I was expecting a town like some of those on the way. This was smaller, shabbier: small eating places, few of the great fast-food names (I missed the tall, bright, competitive signs, roadside commerce's equivalent of the joust and the pennants of chivalry), grimy garages, small grocery shops—a place still poor, hardly the setting for the great man's success story. But then came the campus, and it was grander than anything I, and I am sure my father, had imagined. My father, reading self-help books in Trinidad, no doubt compared himself to poor boys who had become engineers and bridge-builders in industrial England; and though my father might have found aspects of his own story in the beginnings of Booker T. Washington, a man's possibilities depend on the possibilities of the place where he finds himself. There was nothing slavelike or Trinidad-like about Tuskegee; nothing to be excused. However little one had known about it, it was real, and it was achievement on the American scale: scores and scores of dark-red Georgian brick buildings set about landscaped hilly grounds.

"You should understand," a very old lady said to me some days later, and she had spent almost all her working life at Tuskegee, "that until the 1930s Negroes in the United States simply did not have money."

And the effect on me of the first sight of the campus must have been like the effect on people who had seen it in the days of segregation, when it would have represented one of the few ways forward for a black person, and when to people who had little it would have appeared dreamlike.

Al Murray had booked me into the university guest house. It was called Dorothy Hall. It had been built in 1901 as an industrial school for girls. It was almost at the center of the campus now, across the road from the big bronze statue of Booker T. Washington lifting the veil of ignorance from his people.

It was a famous statue, and was the subject of Tuskegee postcards. I half knew it, but was nonetheless surprised by it. The sculptor had made concrete what was really only a turn of phrase, a metaphor.

Booker T. Washington, in a three-piece suit, was shown literally lifting a sheet off a crouching, muscular young black who had an old-fashioned folio book on his knees: figures and properties so unexpected when taken together that they made one wonder how long the muscular black fellow, naked except for the sheet that was now being pulled off him, had been hiding with his big book below the sheet, and why he had stayed there, and why he had needed Booker T. Washington to display him like a conjuror.

But a black man I had spoken to two or three weeks before had found the statue very affecting when he had been taken to Tuskegee as a schoolboy. "Perhaps you have to be black," he had said. And I was willing, at that moment of arrival, to see with his eyes of forty or so years before.

Still, there it was, rhetorical and a little nagging, ever so slightly working against the romance. *I will let no man drag me down so low as to make me hate him.* The engraved words of another age, the philosophy of helplessness—as were these other words, also engraved at the base of the statue: *We shall prosper in proportion as we learn to dignify and glorify labor and put brains and skill into the common occupations of life.* The philosophy of a man working against the odds, combining uplift with a wish not to offend. Yet—it had resulted in a great achievement.

I turned away from the statue and went to the entrance of Dorothy Hall. I saw that the windows were unrepaired and needed painting. One screen frame on an upper window was hanging loose. The beautiful dark-red brick of the old building was in need of repointing. These were bricks that the early students of Tuskegee had made with their own hands, after three heartbreaking failures with kilns.

The building faced west. It was late afternoon and very hot. I asked whether there was an elevator, to help me with my luggage to the upper floor. I was told that the building was old and the elevator no longer worked. By the time I had taken my luggage up, making three trips up and down the hot steps and through the very hot upstairs hall to my room, my lungs were inflamed again. And the constriction there was to be with me all the time I was at Tuskegee.

The colors in the hot paneled club upstairs were like the colors of a gentlemen's club. There was an oil portrait of a white military man; and on the landing wall there was a photograph of Teddy Roosevelt.

Dorothy Hall had been built in 1901; *Up from Slavery* had been published in 1901; and in that year Booker T. Washington had dined with Teddy Roosevelt at the White House. Old history, old dignities, old battles. And I was later told that many famous Americans had stayed at one time or another at Dorothy Hall.

Almost at the end of my time there, I found out where the elevator was. The person who showed me was one of the oldest men on the campus. He was, or had been, a musician. He had come to Tuskegee as a boy of fourteen in 1913, when Booker T. Washington was still alive; and he had taken part in the funeral procession of Booker T. Washington in 1915. The old musician was very famous locally, and many people I met thought I should see him. He was out of town when I arrived, but he sent word he was going to come to see me at Dorothy Hall on a certain day at twelve o'clock; and he was there absolutely at the time he had given. He was proud of keeping time. It was part of the Booker T. Washington tradition, he said. And his stories—he started on them immediately—were of that old, romantic time.

"It was like heaven when I got here in 1913. I'd never seen anything like it. I ran away from home and arrived here with a dollar and a half in my pocket. But Booker T. Washington didn't turn anybody away from this school."

The old musician was dressed artistically: pink shirt, blue tie, light-green check jacket. He was tall and straight and proud, at eighty-eight, of the erectness of his carriage. That was another part of the Booker T. Washington training. Clean clothes, erect posture, firm strides: no old-time shambling. That was the way Booker T. Washington wanted it. Everything had to be just so; everything had to be clean. Every day Booker T. Washington walked around the campus dictating notes to a secretary about things that were wrong.

The old musician came from a small town in Alabama, about 150 miles north of Tuskegee. "My father was a common laborer. My mother's family looked like white people and had some education." The old man opened his pink shirt to show the pale color of his skin. "Many white people up there referred to my mother's family as cousins. I came here just with my trousers and bag and no schooling. An old slave here, a Mr. Baker, he told me that if the people caught a slave learning how to write they would saw this"—the old man wiggled his right thumb—"they would saw that off, because if the slave could write he could write himself a pass to get off the plantation. Slaves weren't allowed to leave their plantation without permission. That was what Mr. Baker saw as a young man.

"All that my father could teach me as his oldest child—there was nothing wrong with it, but it didn't go far enough. This was what he taught me. Don't talk back to old people. Don't be sassy. Stay out of bad company. And help Papa take care of the family. All that was good, but it didn't go far enough. My mother's brother went to Talladega College. White people started that—the American Missionary Society, organized by white people to start schools in the South for freedmen. Tuskegee was different. After emancipation we could vote here. Black people. Some local politician wanted our vote, and Mr. Adams told him that 'If you could help us get a school, I think I can get all the colored people to vote for you.' So people in this county voted for this white man, and the state gave two thousand dollars to start this school.

"Up there in my hometown I paid a schoolteacher fifty cents a month to teach me reading and writing and arithmetic. Professor Moses had his school on the west side of town. Professor Carmichael had his school on the south side. I lived on the south side. My dad didn't know it, though—that I was paying fifty cents a month to Professor Carmichael. I was shining shoes. My father used to empty the coal out of the railroad train. Four o'clock in the morning. A dollar a day.

"When I came here and saw all these buildings, and the dining hall, and the tablecloths, fourteen students to a table, girls on one side, boys on the other, it was like heaven—I'd never seen anything like it. The old chapel! We had grown people coming here. They would walk here, wanting to learn how to read and write. Booker T. would get jobs for these old people, jobs from white people in the town, to work in the day, so that they could study at night and pay their board."

He loved the past, this dandified, good-natured man of eighty-eight. He was energetic and full of enthusiasm; he still drove his car. He drove me to see the site of the very first schoolhouse. "You mean no one has taken you to see that yet?" And then he was determined to get me back to Dorothy Hall at the time he had said. It was when we got back to Dorothy Hall that he showed me the little elevator there, and told me the story about it.

Henry Ford had come to Tuskegee in 1941, when the George

Washington Carver Museum was opened. Carver, the Tuskegee agricultural scientist, was then perhaps eighty. Henry Ford had been so shocked to see the old man tottering up the Dorothy Hall staircase that he had then and there made an offer of an elevator. Now the elevator was out of order and out of sight; and the old musician, older now than George Washington Carver had been in 1941, had to climb the difficult stairs.

THAT MENTION of George Washington Carver dislodged old memories, memories akin to those I had of the Booker T. Washington bed-making test.

Most of the teachers at the elementary school I went to in Trinidad were black. They were quiet people in the main, one or two fierce only with the whip; and at a time when the world offered them little they had their quiet ways of making racial gestures. A class question might be like this: Who is the world's greatest cricketer? If you said Bradman —the Australian—that might be wrong. A better answer, perhaps even the correct one, would have been Headley, the black Jamaican, or Constantine, the black Trinidadian.

The name of George Washington Carver was associated in my mind with that elementary school, and the subterranean racial pride of the black teachers. I remember a little film that must have been shown one day during class hours: a frightened black family in a hut, white horsemen outside. I wasn't sure what the story was: the memory of the film is faint. With this film there was a lesson about George Washington Carver, a black scientific genius, who had done wonderful things with the common peanut, and found uses for every part except the shell or hull.

The wonderful things he had done with the peanut I took on trust. But his inability to use the peanut shell had always interested me. Why —since bamboo pulp could be used for paper—hadn't the peanut shell been used for paper? It seemed to me to have the texture of bamboo pith (I was thinking of very rotten bamboo). And the question was there, the George Washington Carver association—why hadn't something been done with the shell?—every time I shelled a peanut. Just as the Booker T. Washington story was associated with the making up of beds.

But—no doubt because of the path my studies had taken—I had

never heard of George Washington Carver in the wider world. I had never heard of him outside that elementary school of mine; and I had grown to feel, not that he was a black fantasy figure, but that he was someone whose achievements had been exaggerated by local pride, just as the Trinidad *Guardian* exaggerated the doings of local people in metropolitan places.

I had never associated George Washington Carver with Booker T. Washington and Tuskegee. And now they were both there, both real, in a wonderful physical setting, with a whole museum named after George Washington Carver. It was in 1941 that the museum had been opened; in 1941 that Henry Ford had come and made the offer of the elevator; and that would almost certainly have been the year in which, in my elementary school in Trinidad, when I was eight or nine, I had seen the frightening film (probably provided by the American consul) about the black family in a hut and the white horsemen outside.

All now cleared up, as I read the leaflets of the U.S. National Park Service, which had taken over both the Carver Museum and the Booker T. Washington house as historical sites. He had been born a slave, this George, and he had belonged to a man called Carver. He had been born in 1861, perhaps, during the Civil War; and he had been kidnapped, together with his mother, by people who kidnapped slaves in one state and sold them in another. George had been recovered from the kidnappers and returned to the Carvers, but George's mother was never found. George educated himself. In 1897 he came to Tuskegee, and there he stayed for the rest of his life.

In addition to his agricultural research, he collected clays for paints; painted pictures; did needlework. He taught Sunday school. He had a high, feminine voice. In the museum there was a recording you could listen to of Carver reciting what was said to be his favorite poem:

> Figure it out for yourself, my lad.
> You've all that the greatest of men have had:
> Two arms, two hands, two legs, two eyes,
> And a brain to use if you would be wise.

Photographs showed him to be tall and thin, spare-faced, handsome, unusual.

Louis Harlan, in his biography of Booker T. Washington, has little to say about Carver, and that little is not always good. He was quarrelsome, according to Harlan, and deferential to white people. But perhaps the world picture of a not very masculine man, who had been kidnapped as a child and separated forever from his mother and had then had to depend on a kind and loving former owner, could only have been a slave's world picture. And perhaps, within that world picture, Tuskegee had been for him a kind of lifelong sanctuary.

SANCTUARY IN Alabama—this was how after a while I had grown to think of Tuskegee in the days of segregation. So many of the people I met had been in Tuskegee for much of their lives. And though this might have been fortuitous, many of the old residents were light-skinned people, some of them almost white, courtly, polished people, who would have been dreadfully wounded by the indignities of the world outside, and even now, in their old age, didn't wish to drop their guard.

But the idea of sanctuary—when I put it forward in connection with George Washington Carver—was rejected by an old campus man. He said that Booker T. Washington hadn't been concerned to offer anyone sanctuary. When he had asked Carver to come to Tuskegee, it was because, as always, he wanted the best for his school.

Not a sanctuary; the word this man preferred was "oasis."

"When I got here, in the twenties, there were no paved roads. The whole area, the Black Belt, is a poor area, and Tuskegee was really an oasis for blacks. In all kinds of ways. There was the academic atmosphere. The campus was pretty, comparatively. We weren't subjected to the sort of life black men were enduring in the rural areas, especially during the Depression. We had running water. We had food in the cafeteria. We had security. If I had been thrown out into the 'real world,' it might have been different. I might have become more aggressive—I can't tell what I may have done.

"It wasn't a conscious thing in my mind to seek safety. It was just the way my life developed. Though this environment did provide a lot of protection to the person against a lot of things that a person was subjected to in those days—I mean blacks. In the outside world we didn't have the same protection under the law that whites had. The moment you stepped off this campus you were subjected to all of the indignities. Everything was segregated.

"We were all aware of what the white attitude was, and we were unhappy about it. The most terrible thing was that you didn't know when it was ever going to end. But it wasn't something we dwelled on at the Institute."

And the elderly man who drove me round the campus, to show me the extent of it and to explain the stage-by-stage development of the place, and then drove me round the modest town, all black now—this man told me that in the old days a black man, even in a car, wouldn't have been wise to hang around the Lake Tuskegee area.

Indignity outside; within the campus, the erect posture, the military correctness. Yet always—and how the irrationality would have twisted people!—it was necessary to make signals to the people outside that you were not getting above yourself.

Mrs. Guzman, who came to Tuskegee in 1923, and worked for many years on *The Negro Yearbook,* recalled that the old school chapel was also a little cultural center for the town, with movies, concerts, speakers. "The white people in the town came. They were given the best sets in our chapel, the front seats. A lot of the students and faculty resented it. But that was the custom. Whites sat in front, and Negroes behind them. When a younger president came in and stopped that, the white people stopped coming."

But what would have looked like old-fashioned servility in the 1920s and 1930s would have been simple prudence in the days of Booker T. Washington. And perhaps some intuitive wisdom, some kind of peace offering to the people outside, who might so easily have crushed the black institute, lay at the back of Washington's insistence that everyone should learn a trade. It encouraged a misunderstanding of the school outside (and perhaps that didn't do any harm). Some people thought of Tuskegee only as an industrial, vocational institute. (Louis Harlan says that white people sometimes wrote to ask for trained servants; one man wrote in for "a full negro," very black, to take to France. All these letters were acknowledged.)

There was a good deal more to it, of course. Ruskinian or Tolstoyan ideas about manual skills, anti-industrial crafts, the training of the hands, were very much in the air in the latter part of the nineteenth century. Ruskin was certainly at the back of Gandhi's mind when, in South Africa in 1904, he established his Phoenix Farm (burned down by African rioters in 1986). And though the two men were so different —Washington the American with little time for Africans or Asiatics, Gandhi the spiritually adrift Hindu with little time for Africans—there was a remarkable coincidence in their aim and method: the inculcation of self-respect in a subject people through the idea of work and service.

And, interestingly, a number of the old people I spoke to in Tuskegee seemed to have found some kind of beauty and content and human completeness in the trades they were taught. The old musician who had come to Tuskegee as a boy in 1913 learned shoemaking. (Tolstoy liked to do a little cobbling in his study sometimes.) The old man said, "I could sew on a pair of soles in twenty minutes by hand. A lot of people don't know I know that trade. They know me only as a musician." Mr. Louis Rabb—who did business administration at Tuskegee and then went on with Tuskegee grants to do personnel administration at Columbia and hospital administration at Northwestern, and afterwards had a long and distinguished career at Tuskegee—Mr. Rabb did tailoring for four years at the Tuskegee high school when he came there as a boy from Mississippi. His father chose that trade for him, and Mr. Rabb told me with a certain amount of quiet pride that he still sewed for himself.

But outside the Tuskegee oasis the world was grim. On one rack in the library were the Booker T. Washington file boxes. On another rack were sixty-three file boxes labeled LYNCHING RECORDS.

To take down the Washington files for part of 1903 was to feel even greater admiration for the man. So many letters from simple people— letters in pencil, some of them, letters on scraps of paper, letters shot through with need and hope—so well kept, so fresh, after more than eighty years. Every one had been read, acknowledged; and many of the carbon replies had the initials "BTW." I noted a schoolteacher's letter from the island of Jamaica, many pages long, in a neat schoolteacher's hand (clearly a "fair copy"); another letter from a black woman on the island of Tobago. Perhaps these letters in the Tuskegee files were the only relics now of these people.

On narrow slips of pink paper there were initialed mauve carbon copies of Booker T. Washington's famous little notes to Tuskegee staff, dictated to his secretary during his walks about the campus or after his horse rides around the campus. And there were the more political letters to people in Washington, dealing with issues hard for the uninformed to understand. There are so many aspects to a life; so much gets lost.

How had such method and punctiliousness come to a man who had started so late and with so little? Perhaps one of his secrets was an absence of sentimentality. The letters from simple black people had moved me. Booker T. Washington might have been more hardheaded. He knew that people just freed from slavery hardly had an idea of education and often saw it as a means of avoiding physical work. He knew that many black people who could barely read had turned to preaching, for the easy life it offered. He had often ridiculed such people. In *Up from Slavery* he had had such a half-educated black say, "O Lawd, de cotton am so grassy, de work am so hard, and de sun am so hot dat I b'lieve dis darky am called to preach!" Extraordinary, this minstrel joke from the founder of Tuskegee. But the fact that he could make it, while never ceasing to fight for his cause, might have been part of his genius and toughness.

And there in the library was the reminder of the setting: the sixty-three boxes of lynching records. I dreaded to look at them. I thought they might have contained unofficial investigations or statements and would have been full of unbearable things. I was relieved, when I took down a box, to find that the records were mainly newspaper cuttings.

It was that kind of hostility that had given point to Tuskegee from its simplest beginnings. And as much as this hostility had frustrated some of the Institute's imaginative plans—for agricultural extension work among black farmers, for instance—so it had stimulated the Institute's growth, even after Booker T. Washington's death. Segregation and hostility, defining black needs, had also helped to define the Institute's goals, and given logic to the Institute's growth.

When segregation went, there was nothing to pull against; the function of the Institute could no longer be what it had been. When black men could join the air force, there was no longer any need for them to learn to fly at Tuskegee. When black people could be admitted to the hospital at Montgomery, one of the best in the United States, there was no longer the same need for the hospital at Tuskegee.

The town—where once black students had worn their Tuskegee uniform as a kind of protection—was now safe: when black people had won the vote, the white people of Tuskegee had moved away. So there had been a kind of victory here. But the town that had been taken over was small and poor, black-poor, with nothing of the life and money of the white university town of Auburn, just twenty miles away. And

Tuskegee Institute, now Tuskegee University, which could be said to have contributed to that local victory, was in decay.

The swiftly changing impressions I had had at the moment of arrival—the grandeur, the rhetoric, the decay—had endured and been amplified. President Reagan had visited the university not long before to inaugurate a new $18-million building for aerospace science and health education, named after General Daniel James, the first black four-star air-force general, who had graduated from Tuskegee in 1950. The campus roads of the presidential route had been asphalted for the occasion. But the roads elsewhere were not so good, and the broken glass globes of electric standards in other parts of the campus had remained broken. And no one I spoke to (though I spoke to no official) could assure me that the university could afford a faculty to match the splendor of its aerospace building.

Decay was melancholy enough to me, a visitor, a man passing through. It wasn't a subject I felt I could raise with older people who had given their lives to Tuskegee, who had received so much in return, and to whom the Booker T. Washington spirit of service and self-help had mattered so much. And the subject didn't come up. Were there tennis courts? Yes, there were: just at the back of the library. But grass was growing through the asphalt surfacing of two (or three) of the courts. A kind of silence was imposed on the visitor, as in a private house; certain things were not to be seen.

The subject of decay came up more easily in places where people felt more secure—in the veterinary department, for instance, which was said to be among the best in the country, and behaved as though it was. A department like that, successfully lobbying for federal funds (it had recently been granted $6 million for a new project), could survive on the basis of its own excellence. But for other departments it was not so easy. Now that good black students and faculty were in demand by universities all over the country, Tuskegee no longer had a special claim on government or foundation funds. The millionaire philanthropists of the North whom Booker T. Washington had charmed no longer existed; that way of doing things was over.

But there were people who thought that Tuskegee still had its special cause to serve. Black students didn't score as well as others in the standardized university-entry tests. Tuskegee had always been ready to take in such students, and its record showed that it could train such people for the world of work. One retired official said, "Tuskegee will take a student as it finds him academically and socially, and through individualized attention and concern will bring that student in four to five years to his full realization."

There was another, and perhaps more important reason why some people thought Tuskegee was still needed. Tuskegee was still in effect a black university, and it could provide a "black experience," which, with desegregation, more and more black people appeared to feel they needed.

In Florida Mr. Crockett, the Parole Board commissioner, had told me how he had felt he had to take his son out of a too-white setting; he had sent the boy first to a black high school and then to Tuskegee. And I heard now, from a pretty woman of twenty-three who came from a distant state where there were few black people, and who would have made her way in any university, why she had come to Tuskegee.

"The schools I went to in the other place were all-white. They don't concentrate on your being a black person. They give you some of your history, but not a lot. In the other place you try to push, thinking, 'If I can be like them I'd be all right.' You lose yourself a little bit. You're not really sure who you are."

"What was your very first impression when you came here?"

"My very first? 'Go back home.' After coming from a nice city, metropolitan, nice facilities, stores, shopping malls. After that, here, seeing little dirt roads—they're not *dirt* roads, but some places they don't have sidewalks. At home I was used to being able to go downtown a lot, used to going places. Here there was no bus service. When I got here I realized, 'There is nothing to do. Oh my God, I'm trapped here and there's nothing to do. And it's hot and humid.' I think people here are real *country*. They're closed. They're friendly, but they have their little country ways."

And the accommodation wasn't all that it could have been. "Some of the places are dangerous. There are things to be fixed, doors to be fixed. There are light switches upside down. I notice these things, being from where I come, a pretty place, where they do things prettily, nicely."

But clearly there was a reason why she had stayed on. "It was *my* idea to come here. My mother didn't want me to leave home. I wanted to be in an all-black town, to be not in a minority but a majority. And that is one thing I do like about being here. Sometimes in the other place you go into a place and you're the only black person there. But here, when you go into a business, the owner or the manager will be black, the workers will be black, and it helps you to feel you can progress after your goals and accomplish them.

"Here you are in competition with your own kind. And they can be hard on you, because they're trying and you're also trying. At home I used to be a C-D student. Here I'm an A-B student. I get encouraged seeing other people doing things. And here that happened. I'm ready to leave now. I would probably like to go to another black college, maybe in Atlanta. But it doesn't have to be black any longer. Tuskegee has served a purpose."

It was a version—a century on—of the Booker T. Washington idea. For this young woman (and there were others like her) the Tuskegee idea still held. Yet she said she had known almost nothing about Booker T. Washington before coming to Tuskegee. She had known only that he was a black man who had done something famous long ago. A month after she came she read *Up from Slavery*. "The teachers here encourage you to find out about the school, and you appreciate it."

Tuskegee was still a going concern. It had a devoted community; and it still had heart. Its financial predicament was the predicament of black schools generally; and it was better off than some. Its physical condition was very far from that of Fisk University in Nashville, Tennessee, where in parts the campus looked ruined. There was a melancholy bronze statue there too, at Fisk, meant to set the seal on glory, but now seeming to watch over the ruins. The statue was of W. E. B. Du Bois, the rival and critic of Washington.

Du Bois thought that Tuskegee's emphasis on vocational training was wrong; and that Washington's apparent acquiescence in segregation and black disenfranchisement could only lead to further humiliation. Was there an alternative, though? And mightn't it be said that Booker T. Washington's great achievement, his great service to black people at that time, was simply being very famous and admired? One can read books and documents, but it isn't easy imaginatively to re-enter that bitter time, and to have a sense of the weight for black people of day-to-day life.

The quarrel or debate between the two men, Du Bois and Washington, both mulattoes, is famous. Du Bois might seem closer to contemporary feeling. But his best-known book, *The Souls of Black Folk* (1903), a collection of essays and articles, is a little mysterious. The very title of the book is strange, even whimsical. The lyrical, mystical tone (mixed up with social and economic facts, and sometimes a little romantic fiction) calls to mind some of the essays of the late-nineteenth-century English country writer Richard Jefferies (1848–87). (This is the lyrical Du Bois: "I have seen a land right merry with the sun, where children sing, and rolling hills lie like passioned women wanton with harvest. And there in the King's Highway sat and sits a figure veiled and bowed. . . .")

I even have the impression that Du Bois might have been trying to do for Southern blacks what Jefferies had done for farm people in the south of England. There is an uncertainty in both writers about their relationship with the people they are writing about. Jefferies, in spite of hints that he might be socially all right, was the son of a small farmer, and almost a laborer; Du Bois was a mulatto. The Jefferies model would explain Du Bois's occasional evasiveness and too-pretty ways with words (using the poetic conceit of "the veil," for instance, for segregation). If Booker T. Washington can make a darky joke, Du Bois can speak of "the joyous abandon and playfulness which we are wont to associate with the plantation Negro"; can say, "Even today the mass of the Negro laborers need stricter guardianship than Northern laborers"; and he can ask, "What did slavery mean to the African savage?"

But we can read through both the Du Bois way of writing and the Booker T. Washington manliness to the facts of Negro life of the time, and see the difficulty both men would have had in defining themselves, and establishing their own dignity, against such an abject background. As if in resolution of that difficulty, Du Bois's book seems lyrical for the sake of the lyricism. It can appear to use blacks and ruined plantations as poetic properties. It deals in tears and rage; it offers no program.

In this beginning of Du Bois there was also his end. He lived very long, and towards the end of his life—facing irrationality with irrationality—he left the United States and went to live in West Africa, in Ghana, a former British colony that had in independence very quickly become an African despotism, and was soon to revert to bush and poverty, exporting labor to its neighbors.

At the very beginning of the century, in *Up from Slavery,* Booker T. Washington, in his late-Victorian man-of-the-world style, had cautioned against just that kind of sentimentality about Africa. "In the House of Commons, which we visited several times, we met Sir Henry

M. Stanley. I talked with him about Africa and its relation to the American Negro, and after my interview with him became more convinced than ever that there was no hope of the American Negro's improving his condition by emigrating to Africa."

On this journey I read *Up from Slavery* twice. On the second reading, after I had been nearly four months in the South, I found that the book had changed for me. It became more than the fabulous story of a disadvantaged man's rise. I began to see it as a painful coded work, making separate signals even in a single paragraph to Northerners, Southerners, and blacks.

I also began to see the book as the work of a man constantly concerned to raise funds for his school. That should have been obvious to me always, but it hadn't been; that had been swept away by the power of the fable. Below that primary appeal, however, there were others: the man of the world appealing knowledgeably to the very rich on behalf of the wretched, representing himself as honorable and worthy and manly and educated; yet at the same time taking care to do the contrary thing, and making it clear that as a black man he knew his place.

Hence his confident, socially knowing talk, like any solid late-nineteenth-century citizen, of the "best people" and the "vices" of "the lower class of people." But he is mortified when, on a train journey from Augusta to Atlanta in Georgia, in a Pullman car "full of Southern white men," two ladies from Boston, "ignorant, it seems, of the customs of the South," insist on inviting him to supper. The meal seems very long. As soon as he can, he breaks away from the ladies to go to the smoking room, where the men now are, "to see how the land lay." It is all right; the men know who he is and are anxious to introduce themselves to him.

In England he develops a high regard for the aristocracy and the time and money they devote to philanthropic works. He is impressed by the deference of servants, who are content to be servants all their working life and, unlike American servants, use the words "master" and "mistress" without any constraint. In that ambiguous observation there are consoling messages both for blacks and Southern whites. He becomes friendly, he says, with the Duchess of Sutherland. She is a famous beauty. But as a black man he will be out of place to say so directly. He writes, "I may add that I believe the Duchess of Sutherland is said to be the most beautiful woman in England."

So many snares; so many people to please; so many contradictions to resolve; so many possibilities of destruction. The achievement was great. But at what cost. He died at the age of fifty-nine.

To the west, on the road to Mississippi, were shabby small settlements, like an extension of the poverty of the town of Tuskegee. I spent the night on a timber plantation on the border. There was still something like presettlement desolation there: cypress trees, half stripped of leaves, their bald knees rising out of muddy water like a kind of humped aquatic animal; shifting swamps, with forest litter at their margins; great damp heat. The land was not old. Tuskegee had been settled only in 1830.

Two months later I entered Alabama again, but from the north, driving down from Nashville in Tennessee, down from the hills to the flat land around Huntsville. Huntsville was where space research and the industries it had attracted had created a whole new landscape in the South: wide boulevards, low, flat factories, spacious grounds meant only to please the eye. Huntsville was also near where, in 1873, the first State Normal and Industrial School for Negroes had been set up in Alabama. That past had been swallowed up—though cotton still grew at the very edge of the new industrial town.

From the NASA museum—full of Asian visitors, Indians, Chinese ("coming to look at the place where they intend to work," as the Southern businessman with me said)—Tuskegee seemed to belong to another age, to exist in a melancholy time warp. It made one think of the prisons of the spirit men create for themselves and for others—so overpowering, so much part of the way things appear to have to be, and then, abruptly, with a little shift, so insubstantial.

5

∎∎∎

The Frontier,
The Heartland

E VEN IN Alabama—the repeated vowel sound of which seems to be a mimicking of "ma mama" or "ma mammy" and (because of all the songs) carries suggestions of banjos and black men and plantations —even in Alabama I found that Mississippi had a reputation for poverty and racial hardness.

But the black (really brown) pharmacist at Tuskegee also told me that my asthma would abate the farther west I got. And, true enough, after the heat and humidity of Tallahassee (made worse for me by the glass tower in which I had been staying, the western wall radiating heat from early afternoon), and after the enclosed hot air of the upper corridor of Dorothy Hall in Tuskegee (where at times, after climbing the steps, I felt the heat catch in my throat, and I couldn't breathe until I got to the comparative coolness of my room), I began to revive in the air-conditioned air of the Ramada Renaissance hotel in Jackson, Mississippi.

The air-conditioning system was silent; the tinted glass of my window shut out glare as well as traffic noise. All around were great highways. To the east the city was green, trees hiding the better-off housing developments. To the northeast was a big new shopping area. Pleasing views: hardly the poverty I had been fearing. And I was grateful to the city for ridding me, as if by magic, of the constriction in my lungs.

But, of course, there was another side to Jackson, there, in its very center. And on Sunday afternoon it was easy to see, in the streets without business traffic. The inner city was black. There were streets of "shotgun" houses. It was the first time I had ever heard the expressive word: narrow wooden houses (like mobile homes or old-fashioned railway carriages) with the front room opening into the back room and with the front door and back door aligned. On Sunday afternoon the people were out on the streets, so that the effect of crowd and slum and blackness was immediate: as though outdoor life, life outside the houses, was an aspect of poverty.

At a street corner, on an open lot, in the hot midafternoon sun, there was a prayer meeting. It had no audience. Everyone there was a performer. The women were dressed for Sunday, and the men were in suits and ties, except for the pastor, who was in a white gown. This was the West Jackson Crusade of the Saint Paul Church of God in Christ. It was an occasion of music and dance. Many of the people in that dressed-up group were to have the chance to go to the pulpit or to hold the microphone and sing.

The songs seemed to be variations on a single line.

What would I do without Jesus?

That was all that a middle-aged man in a brown suit was singing, leaning on the pulpit and bending over the microphone in a confiding manner, as though he had a large audience, instead of no one at all (save the people in our car). What would that man have done for a living? What would have been his true—or his other—occupation?

The leader of the chorus was a big woman in a white dress. She stood a little way in front of the chorus. She was distinguished from them by the plain white of her dress, her size, and her voice. When her turn came to use the microphone she didn't go to the pulpit. She took the microphone on its cord and sang from where she stood:

Don't let nobody turn you round!

That was her line, and the variations on it seemed to come naturally.

Don't let—
Don't let nobody—
Don't let nobody turn you round!

And the group danced. Among the dancers were three small boys. One of them stood in front. He was very small, perhaps five or six, and he was in long trousers, with suspenders. The two other boys were bigger; they were at the back; and the dancing—all the intricate and inventive things they did with their legs—seemed to come to them in fits. At one moment they were like children at a grown-up occasion, indifferent and far away. And then suddenly they were possessed. The dance rippled through them. And then just as suddenly they came to the end of their dancing, even while the singing was going on, in the middle of a line of the song of the woman in white; and they returned to what they had been doing, their apparently childish concerns. The pastor, in his long white gown, danced while the woman sang, the disturbance of his gown, from his dancing on the spot, creating its own rhythm.

They were not the only religious group active in West Jackson that afternoon. The bus of another group passed by, a bus painted white with thin red markings. And after that bus had passed, I saw, a few house plots away from the dancing evangelical group, another boy dancing, this time with a black neighborhood dog, the boy holding the front paws of the dog.

When she had done with her singing, the young woman in white came across to where our car was. She was perspiring at the top of her forehead from her dancing in the afternoon heat, the heat added to here by its reflection from the streets and buildings. She asked, honey-voiced, whether we were witnessing the service, and she gave a tract.

In the tract there was a photograph of the pastor, not in his white gown and with his cross, not in a pose suggesting the rhythm of his own dance, but in a jacket and tie, studious, looking past the photographer. He was the Elder Jesse Kelly. In addition to being pastor of his church he was "founder of the West Jackson Crusade, local announcer of WOAD, graduate of JSU," and "presently working towards a Masters of Divinity at Wesley Biblical Seminary." Some story—like that of Danny or that of Reverend Clausell in Tallahassee—might have been behind this religious call, which included (according to the tract the woman in white had given) a Sunday school, a nightclub ministry, a radio ministry, a street ministry, and tent services.

The music and the singing held us; the dancing held us; we could marvel at the religious dedication. But we could only be witnesses; we couldn't participate. And the approach of the woman in white, in fact, made us think of leaving.

At the side of my grandmother's house in central Trinidad there was a tall gate, of corrugated iron on a timber-plank frame. This was the main entrance to the house and yard. One of my earliest ideas—when I was six or seven—was that there were two worlds: the world within, the world without. To go out of that gate was to be in a world quite different from the one in the house; to go back through that gate at the end of the school day was to shed the ideas of the world outside. Everyone lives with ideas like these; everyone has different sets of behavior. But in a racially mixed society, especially one where race is a big issue, the different worlds have racial attributes or overtones. Distinctions and differences can have the force of taboos—things sensed rather than consciously worked out. In such a society participation is different from witness; they engage different sides of the person. And it was with—old—relief that I put an end to my pleasure in the singing and dancing of the West Jackson Crusade, and returned to the silent healing of the air-conditioned room of the Ramada Renaissance in the north of the city.

IT WAS my wish, in Mississippi, to consider things from the white point of view, as far as that was possible for me. Someone in New York had told me that it wouldn't be easy. In Mississippi, though, I found that people were defensive about their reputation. This seemed to give me a start. But then I wasn't sure.

How quickly, for example, I appeared to get to the limit of Ellen's ideas and memories! She was sixty, of a good family. She had liberal attitudes; and it seemed hard for her to go beyond a statement of those attitudes.

She said: "I feel we've been through a revolution in Mississippi since the 1960s. It was like two separate societies here. Now black people have much better jobs than they had. Instead of everybody having to work in a home—I'm talking about women—now they're working in McDonald's or a bank or a store."

And there we stayed for some time, Ellen—perhaps because I wasn't being acute enough, or because I hadn't yet learned to talk to Mississippi people—not appearing to say more than that. I even put away my notebook. She was gentle, welcoming, anxious to talk. But I couldn't find questions to put to her. Her optimism, her idea of progress and change, covered nearly everything I could think about. We got finally to talking about her childhood. And that was when I took my notebook out again.

"I grew up in the Depression. But I didn't feel badly about myself. Everybody else was poor too. The reason I didn't feel badly was that I had a lot of aunts and uncles and cousins and all—a large extended family, but I didn't know you called it that. They loved me and had time for me. I would go out and spend summers with them. They always had time to talk to you and fix your favorite foods. They even made me dresses."

That idea of a small community, where everyone knew everyone else and people were related—I had found that for many people it was part of the beauty of the ways of the past.

I asked Ellen, "Where did those uncles and aunts live?"

"They lived in the most conservative town in Mississippi."

Happy summers in a small conservative town. What lay outside the family group? What did Ellen feel as a child about the rednecks? Was there really such a thing as a "redneck mentality"?

There was. She acted it out. " 'Don't mess with me.' " She raised her slender arms in a boxing posture. "A fighting mentality." But she had been protected from that. "I had an aunt who read a lot to me. She had a lot of books. Actually, she was the postmistress. She encouraged me to be my best self. I guess this sounds snobbish, but she would say, 'Ellen dear, there are some things we just don't do.' There were some *people* we just didn't go around."

She returned to the topic of the love she had experienced in her childhood, the love that had partly made her. "It helped me to have a positive self-image—though that wasn't the way we talked about it then. I think people still have scars from the Depression here. It seemed to me like it was very bad here. There just weren't any jobs. My sister was older than I and she suffered more than I, but that was because she had had more to begin with. She had things that were lost. I just grew up poor.

"I became more proud of being a Southerner when I got away from the South. My husband went to school in the East, and I worked. This was after World War II. At that time we had a politician, a senator called Bilbo. Bilbo was a racist, and he was advocating sending all the blacks back to Africa as a solution to the problem; and he was absolutely admired by the people of Mississippi, I guess. But he was absolutely hated by the people I worked with in Massachusetts. This was a psychology group I worked with. They were doing research in group dynamics—prejudice and so forth.

"That was when I began to look for things that were positive about the South and Mississippi. I thought about the people. And I thought about the hardships we had been through—and you can't expect people to act perfect when you think of all the things they've gone through. The people in Massachusetts—in 1946—they could act surprised that someone from Mississippi could read and write and we 'wore shoes.' It's still true in some places. People have a very, very bad impression of Mississippi. But it's changing."

"Is it because of the writers?"

"The writing grew out of the dirt and this love of talk, talk."

And, going back to her time in Massachusetts, Ellen said: "The people I worked with, they wanted to know if I would really do this. There was a black man visiting, and guess who they got to show him around? Well, I showed him around. He was a lovely person. I learned from him. I think they were surprised. They never did say it. I never gave them the opportunity. Do you see how far we've come?"

But there was Mississippi's reputation for violence.

"The rednecks to the south of the town were just mean. They had the reputation. They were very pugilistic. There were stories about them. Like, if a traveling salesman came through, they would hitch him to the plow and have him plow all night. I don't know if that was fact or fiction. They would get drunk on Saturday night and fight each other and kill each other off. That's really the worst part of Mississippi. It just had a bad reputation. But out of that group there grew some fine outstanding Mississippians, including some fine clergymen. It shows that there's hope, doesn't it?"

And there was also the racial issue, never to be forgotten in Mississippi and the South.

"I played with my cousins, and we played with black children, too. They were the children of the servants, the washerwomen and so on. That's why I think Southerners have a better feeling about black people than the Northerners. We called them Negroes—'black' is a new word. I've gotten used to it. We didn't use 'nigger' in my house." I didn't ask Ellen about the words, or prompt her; what she said came out naturally. "My relatives didn't call people niggers either. I guess they had a little more civility than that. Even though they lived out in the country."

For the third or fourth or fifth time Ellen said, "I grew up in a loving environment."

A memory came to her. She had been breaking off to say that our talk had begun to make her put things together, call up old things.

"My daddy liked to fish. He took me fishing. I don't think I have as harsh attitudes"—and she meant racial attitudes—"as some people, because of that." She broke off again and smiled. "My summers in the country are important, aren't they?"

"How many summers?"

"It's more like the first twelve years of my life. I know I feel differently from some other people, but I just don't know why."

"Religion?"

"I do think my religion makes the difference, and the feeling that we are all made in God's image. Probably not as a child. I'd have to have more understanding to think that." Then she said, "And these stories about people doing mean things."

Mean things, in a loving childhood?

Ellen said—memory working, unrelated pieces of the past fitting together, as she said they had begun to do while she talked, answering questions that had never been put to her before—"My mother told me about hiding her maid from the Ku Klux Klan. It shows just how far we've progressed. My mother had a maid. Her name was Mollie Wheeler, I think. And the Ku Klux Klan was trying to get her. I don't know why. My mother didn't talk very much about it. I think the Klan wanted to give the maid a good beating and send her away for some reason. My mother said she hid her in a laundry basket in her house to protect her. Of course they wouldn't come into my mother's house. This was really before I was born. They—the Klan—they were probably young men, OK people in the town."

"Didn't this frighten you?"

"I don't think it frightened me. It gave me a great sense of disgust for something like the Klan." She added, "The rednecks—that story I told you, it probably happened before I was born."

And I understood what Ellen was saying better than I said. No situation or circumstance is absolutely like any other; but in the Indian countryside of my childhood in Trinidad there were many murders and acts of violence, and these acts of violence gave the Trinidad Indians, already separated from the rest of the island by language, religion, and culture, a fearful reputation. But to us to whom the stories of murders and feuds were closer, other things were at stake. The family feuds or the village feuds often had to do with an idea of honor. Perhaps it was a peasant idea; perhaps this idea of honor is especially important to a society without recourse to law or without confidence in law.

Imagine this scene in a Trinidad Indian village of the 1920s or 1930s. A village big man, say, is murdered. The next morning, after the legal formalities, the body is displayed in a coffin, which is perhaps set out on two chairs on the road outside his house. This is a statement of defiance by the family of the murdered man. Among the people coming to pay their respects is the killer. He has to come; he cannot stay away; and he is almost certainly known. And now two men's lives are spoiled: the killer's, and that of the relation of the dead man who will have to kill the killer. The code demands no less; it isn't open to a man who wishes to be at peace with himself to walk away.

So deep, for me, was this idea of honor and the feud that the film of *Romeo and Juliet* (with Basil Rathbone) was one of my earliest true theatrical experiences, the story to me being not so much a story of love as of the family feud. What fear, what horror at all that was to follow, when the blood darkened the shirt of Mercutio! Honor—that was what I understood, or saw, in some of the murders around us. Not the barbarism that, as I understood later, outsiders attributed to us.

Some such way of feeling I attributed to Ellen, in her childhood in the small town where she had spent such happy summers with her extended family. Violence, where it existed, would not have appeared to her as naked as it would have done to absolute outsiders. Too many other things were attached.

Violence then; and there was violence now. The violence of her childhood had been white. The violence people spoke of now was black, and was of the cities.

She said: "I think it's just the frustration. So much of the violence is now in the black community. The black people don't like me to say this, but if you go to the penitentiaries you'll see it's true—a high population of young blacks."

How had she arrived at her civility, her calmness, her wish to be fair—in a state with the reputation that Mississippi had?

She said: "I went to college. I think that made an impression on me. I had a very good professor. They took a personal interest in you. And my father died when I was young. I was barely thirteen. That was when I started looking at myself and other people. I think I had to grow up too soon. I was living in a small town. My father didn't leave a lot of money for us to live on. And so my mother had to go to work. She was a nurse, and she went back to work. And I—I went back and lived with my aunts, to go to school, in that same little country town. My mother worked very hard to send me to college. She was very successful in her occupation. She was a strong woman, and she believed in fairness to all people. When she was in training she nursed everybody. She grew up with a great regard for all people."

Abruptly, then, out of random memories that were coming to her, Ellen said: "This story really did impress me. I was talking about it to one of my relations not long ago. This really happened, and I was there. I was eight. I was visiting my aunt, and she had a wonderful maid; and several of my cousins were there. Myrtle—the maid— played the piano. She could play anything by ear. She kept all us children entertained with her music and everything. One time she had a little roadster car and she took us riding. And we really loved her. She was a black maid. Maybe one of her boyfriends gave her the car. She was quite a girl. She wore bright lipstick and she had a big gold tooth in front.

"Anyway, she was missing one day. She lived in a house behind my aunt's house. And finally they went out to see about her. And they found her, and she was dead—in a wardrobe, upside down. She had been hit on the head with a pine knot. They called it a lighter knot—it was to start fires with. They thought it was one of her boyfriends, but we never knew. It was awful. I knew that was wrong. My aunt was grief-stricken. I think that if it had been a white woman killed like that, they would have found out who did it. But I think that's something I'm thinking now. I don't think I thought that when I was eight years old. To me Myrtle was Myrtle. I didn't think of her being black. She would snap her fingers and dance." And Ellen, remembering, sitting in her upholstered chair, made a gesture and snapped her fingers too. "She was just a lot of fun. She was the daughter of the woman who went from house to house doing the laundry. They did it in great big pots. This was before rural electrification, when they started having running water in most of the houses. My aunt had running water and a bathroom inside, because my daddy had built a water-tower when he had lived there—before I was born.

"I went back to her house." Myrtle's mother's house, at the back of Ellen's aunt's house. "They had removed her body. But I saw where it was. That was just nosy. My aunt didn't want me to go see it. But I wanted to, and she let me."

What a story, from a memory of twelve happy summers! And that story released another memory in Ellen.

"My mother and father used to tell me about when they would hang people in the courthouse square. Legal hangings, not lynchings. That was when my father and mother were children. And my daddy was born in 1897. And that was just abhorrent to me—and it was to them. These were stories that people would tell you as you were growing up. I think we've come a long way. It seems like people are becoming more civilized, I hope."

The stories told to Ellen as she was growing up were frontier stories; that was how I regarded them. They had echoes of any number of Western films; and it was remarkable to hear them from someone who had just turned sixty. In one lifetime, then, it seemed that she had moved from frontier culture, or the relics of a frontier culture, to late twentieth-century Jackson and the United States. It gave a new cast to my thoughts, and a new cast to my conversation with people.

There are some film directors who prefer to work in natural light, the light that's available, the light they find. And travel of the sort I was doing, travel on a theme, depends on accidents: the books read on a journey, the people met. To travel in the way I was doing was like painting in acrylic or fresco; things set quickly. The whole shape of a section of the narrative can be determined by some chance meeting, some phrase heard or devised. If I had met someone else my thoughts might have worked differently; though I might at the end have arrived at the same general feeling about the place I was in.

Ellen's thoughts, just before we separated, were of her father, who had died when she was thirteen. "My father told me you never got ahead by stepping on somebody's back. We all need to come up together."

That had been the great discovery of my travels so far in the South. In no other part of the world had I found people so driven by the idea of good behavior and the good religious life. And that was true for black and white.

M Y THOUGHTS were running on the frontier, the life at the ex-
tremity of a culture. And I went early one afternoon to see
Louise, nearly eighty and living alone in a big house in Jackson, in a
garden too much for her now, and dry after many weeks without rain.

In her old bookcase, American work from perhaps 1840, cherrywood that had taken on a lovely deep color after nearly a century and a
half, there were small, leather-bound volumes of an edition of *The
Spectator*—of Addison and Steele—issued by a Philadelphia firm in
1847. A reminder of the colonial past here, of an idea of civility
and education so at odds with the world around. A reissue in 1847 of
The Spectator—American publishers having in those days the camp-
following attitude to English books that English publishers today have
to American books. *The Spectator,* a hundred years out of date, at the
time when Parkman was making his journey on the Oregon trail and
coming across reminders, almost as terrible as bones, of the settlers
who had passed that way: abandoned furniture, pieces perhaps of the
early 1840s, like Louise's bookcase, which those settlers had loaded
onto their carts and wagons, hoping to take them to the West.

In a drawer of the cherrywood bookcase there were documents and
copies of documents connected with Louise's family history. Her family went back to colonial times.

Her husband's ancestor came from Pennsylvania. He came to Mississippi in about 1820. "All wilderness, you know." He was part of a
group, families who had intermarried. They hadn't come directly to
Mississippi. "They had traveled together in their migration through
Georgia, Tennessee, and Alabama." She gave this idea of the kinship
of the migrating group: "When the two young men"—her husband's
ancestor, and another man in the group—"were of an age to marry,
they went up to Oxford"—the Mississippi Oxford, in the hills to the
east of the Delta, the flat alluvial river plain—"and married two Tank-
ersley girls they had met." The Tankersleys were one of the families of
the migrating group. "The land hadn't been cleared and travel was
hard. And when they got there they stayed.

"My grandfather was a sixteen-year-old boy when he went to the
Civil War and fought at Shiloh in Tennessee. He survived it, and came
back to northeast Alabama and started his family. Things were hard
after the Civil War, and then my grandfather died. My father left home

at the age of fifteen and came and stayed with an uncle in the Delta in Mississippi. He had some education, and he paid a Baptist minister to teach him bookkeeping, and he opened a little store and began buying land in the Delta. *And it was beautiful country.* Now it's one big cotton patch—all cleared and drained. But then it was like William Faulkner's 'Bear,' one of his finest pieces of writing. It was just wilderness country —great oaks that had not been harvested. This was before the plantations. It was just gorgeous.

"It was a land of flowers, all kinds of wild iris and wild violets, water lilies and alligators. They were just beginning the plantations in the Delta. It was hard. You see, we had malaria. I had malaria every summer when I was a child. It took a little while to clear the Delta. It flooded every spring.

"When I was a little girl—say in 1915—they were still clearing it. They would go and chop around these mighty oaks and they would let them die and then they would cut them. When they were going to clear out a field they would kill the trees. I never paid any attention to it. It was what they did. I took it for granted. I played in the woods. If you were not at home for meals you were punished, because you had gone too far away and they had to go out and look for you seriously. Everybody had so many children then, you know. There was no birth control. We had so many. And many families lost lots of children."

Pioneer land, the Delta region of Mississippi. Yet Mississippi, for a frontier state, had the curious complication of slavery, from the days of the cotton plantations beside the river. The frontier, the pioneers, the solitude; but then, also, the cheap black labor. What did Louise think now? The black population was now very large in the country where as a child she had been delighted by the wildflowers and the big trees of the forest.

She said, "There is not much reason for being in the Delta unless you were a big landowner. You could hardly have cleared it yourself. Parts of it were just canebrake."

"I've read that word. What is it?"

"A wild type of cane, not anything you cultivate. We had plenty of help, servants. After they were freed they just stayed where they were, you know. They lived and multiplied everywhere. As many of the whites grew up, they left. But the blacks stayed. And one reason they stayed—it's interesting to read the obituaries even now—is that they are very gregarious people. They don't bother too much about lines of

marriage and that sort of thing, but they are very devoted families."
And black people liked to come back to the place they considered home.

That idea, about the importance of the family, I had heard about
in West Africa, in the Ivory Coast. It overrode the other idea—if it
existed at all among Africans—of marital fidelity. I had been told that
in the Ivory Coast it would be considered frivolous to give infidelity as
a cause for divorce. And that went with another, African idea: you
didn't marry a person, you allied yourself to a family.

Louise said, "I feel very concerned about the black thing, the black
problem. My maid told me this morning that up and down their street
they are out running and shooting guns in the air—these young
blacks." A twisted version of the frontier, here in the city of Jackson.
"I don't know how we are going to come out of it. Some of them are
very intelligent and ambitious. Some are primitive. Some white people
are too, but maybe not so many. We are not multiplying as fast as
they do."

She offered an unrelated memory, in which the ideas of the pioneer
life and black people ran together. "When I was growing up in the
Delta I had a nanny, I suppose. She even wet-nursed me. There were
no formulas. Doctors didn't know anything about babies. In fact, they
had only gotten a little beyond leeches, but not much further. They
did not have much skill."

The wonderful forests of the Delta, where a child could play among
the wildflowers, had been cut down. And her father had created a
plantation. What had happened to that plantation?

"My father died when he was fifty. He sold about a thousand acres
just before the Great Depression, and he had about seven hundred
acres left." But forest no longer. "Mud in winter, dust in summer. My
father bought a Chalmers automobile. This was even before the time
of radio. It was a diversion." Sometimes they just sat in the Chalmers,
for the pleasure, not going anywhere. "We lived quietly. If a town was
five miles away, that was a long way." But later, when the roads improved and the cars improved, people in the Delta became famous in
Mississippi for their willingness to travel long distances for dinner or
other entertainment.

And then Louise touched a topic that linked the Delta region to the
Trinidad of my own Indian community. Chinese had been brought in
to work the Delta; just as Chinese and Portuguese and, more endur-
ingly, Indians from India had been brought into Trinidad and other

colonies of the British Empire (including South Africa) to work the plantations, after the abolition of Negro slavery.

Chinese here, beside the Mississippi!

Louise said: "The Chinese lived strictly among themselves. And they still do. There was one at Vance, and the low-class whites would tease him unmercifully. My father looked after him if it got bad. After my father died the Chinese man left Vance too. They deviled him. The schoolchildren on their way home would pass his store and say:

> Chico Chinaman
> Eats dead rats.
> Chews them up
> Like ginger snaps.

And he would come out—it may have been his sense of humor—and shake his fist, and they would laugh and run away."

Still lodged in her memory, this meaningless children's rhyme, clearly from another country, and adapted to the Chinese of the Delta. As ineradicable as the rhyme lodged from childhood in my own head about Chinese in Trinidad, a rhyme sung by black children—and just as harmless:

> Chinee, Chinee, never die.
> Flat nose and chinkee-eye.

Who was the originator? An adult—or a child, speaking verse naturally, as certain children can do? There must have been an originator, for my Chinese rhyme as well as for Louise's.

It would have been pleasant to talk for a while about Mississippi children's rhymes. But Louise had other memories. She was getting tired now, and no longer as able to complete a train of thought as when we had started.

She said: "The blacks were so oppressed during that time that it was a peaceful place. They didn't do the sort of things they do now. We had very little trouble. They went their way; we went ours. We were used to having help. During the Depression my sister had a maid. She had a daughter the same age—" But this story was never finished. Perhaps it was too painful to recall; perhaps Louise wished to keep it buried. It led to this thought, unexpectedly: "I have a great respect for what the blacks call poor white trash. I think they have suffered. They too need opportunities." Then Louise said wearily, as if with the weight now of her illness and age, "But the needs of the world are so great that they are overwhelming."

The combination of thoughts about blacks, and poor white trash who needed help as much as anybody, and her sister and the Depression, led to the dredging up of this story:

"During the depth of the Depression—we have not had anything ever in the class of that Great Depression—we lived not far from a penal farm." Thinking of the story she was about to tell, she said: "But it was something terrible. One of the trusties up there worked in the homes of employees of the penal farm. Ah, it was something that electrified the Delta! This daughter of one of the warders there—they said she was having an affair with one of these black prisoners. Unheard of. But, anyway, the prisoner killed her father. And then they set out to capture him, and there was a reward of two thousand dollars. A big sum then. And this young planter's son just walked into a barn loft to bring him down. And of course the prisoner shot him and killed him. Twenty-three or twenty-four, the handsomest man you ever saw, and a fine young man; but he just walked to his death. And then of course they took the black man and killed him. This happened about ten miles away from where we lived. And it just really upset everybody. But now we have rapes here all the time. It was a very, very rare thing then. Now they don't seem to make much of it. I was a young woman, about twenty. It affected me very deeply. It was very tragic. But there were occasional instances of violence like that."

We talked about the Emmett Till murder in 1955. Emmett Till (how extraordinary the names of people become when they are associated with big and tragic events) was a black youth who had been accused of whistling at or molesting a white woman, and had been killed. It was something that had added to Mississippi's bad reputation.

Louise said: "Parts of my family were still living there in the Delta. And he did more than whistle at her. My brother had a drugstore in Sumner, where they had that trial. We are not that kind of people." Louise was talking of the social distinctions of the Delta. Earlier, speaking of her family's position as planters, she had said, "There are class divisions everywhere." And she meant now that the woman who worked as a store clerk—like the woman Emmett Till had allegedly whistled at or molested—was of a different class. "My mother and sisters never worked in that commissary. We always had hired help." "Commissary," a plantation word, meaning the plantation store, where workers bought goods on trust, against their wages. "My father didn't think it was a suitable place for the women of his family to be. All kinds of people came in there—sometimes drinking."

I had already been struck, in Ellen's account of her childhood, by the modest jobs that people of good family did. One of Ellen's aunts had been a postmistress; and now Louise was reporting that her brother ran a drugstore. It was as though, in the poverty of the South, class was something in the mind and consciousness of a family, related to an idea of good behavior and seemliness.

Louise said, "The civil-rights movement altered everything. It's good and it's bad." She added, the thought seeming to come to her by association, "I wouldn't like to live anywhere where there are not any blacks. I've lived among them all my life and I like them. And right now"—and she meant in spite of the crime in Jackson, and although the city was moving towards a black majority and might soon even have a black mayor—"they are warmhearted and humorous. I would miss them. But—we have such a mass of them here in Jackson. And wherever they are they are in a mass, because they like their own kind of people, and they are not going to settle where there are not other black people—they're lonely. This woman was in Iowa, and she was earning much more, but she came back here because it was lonely for her there. But they are forming gangs now in Jackson. If they could be scattered about the country, it would be better. But we are not Russia. We can't do that."

It was almost time for me to go. She half wanted to be free of the need to talk; but there was also a side of her that, having begun to talk, wished to go on. And once more she turned to her childhood in the Delta, when the land had been forest.

"We fed ourselves, but we lived below what would now be called the poverty line. It was a privilege to live in the Delta. At night we would hear animals in the forest. A panther. It sounded like a woman crying."

Close again to her now in old age, when she lived alone, was the loneliness of her childhood, the solitude of the Delta.

"My stepmother used to tell the story of a lady called Miss Sunshine Easterling—Sunshine Easterling!—who wanted to go to a party. But there was no transportation except down the railroad track. So—away they went, down the track, with a handcar. Pumping it up and down, you know."

I didn't know, really. I had seen the handcars she mentioned only in American serial-thriller films when I was a child in Trinidad.

"And," Louise said, "they were wrecked by a freight train, and Miss Sunshine Easterling was crippled for life. That story was to prevent us from yearning too much for a social life. We certainly were isolated in the Delta in those days.

"I remember one Christmas I got a most beautiful real beaver hat. It must have come from a store like Marshall Field, because there were no stores that had anything like that anywhere nearby. And there was nowhere for me to go with my beaver hat. So I put it on on Christmas afternoon and walked down the railroad track, hoping that someone would see me. But nobody did. I was twelve at the time."

Sixty-seven years later, alone again, in a Jackson developed beyond her imagining, widowed, nearly all the adventures of her life in the past, she recalled that earlier memory of solitude. Outside, her overgrown garden, full of trees, the ground dry, yellow, waiting for rain.

SOME DAYS later (when the rain had come) I went to call on Eudora Welty and mentioned this story of Louise's about the beaver hat. Miss Welty was only a year younger than Louise, and she knew the kind of hat Louise might have got for Christmas in 1920.

"Those hats were called Madge Evans hats. They were named after a child actress. They were sold only in one store in Jackson. Many years later I met the child actress. Of course she wasn't a child when I met her, but she had kept up with her acting career. I met her in New York. She was a little bit older than me. She said, 'I know your work, because in one story you had a Madge Evans hat. I'm Madge Evans.' She was a little girl like us when she wore the hat. The hat was wide-brimmed all around, with streamers that hung down your back as far as your waist. They were wonderful hats. And there were straw hats as well, for summer. In those days you wore hats all the time. You wore hats even to Sunday school."

THERE WAS no longer the forest Louise had known in the Delta; and an embankment along the Mississippi now kept the flat land from flooding every year.

The land was so flat that the trees looked low. And—from the car

—the fields of young cotton plants created long, hypnotic perspective lines zipping by: the green of the cotton plants alternating with the yellow or dark brown of the earth. But agriculture had fallen on hard times; and though there were still splendid plantations like the one called Egypt, the Delta was no longer the "one big cotton patch" of Louise's description.

Egypt, though, gave a glimpse of the past, and of the social graces and divisions of the plantation culture. At the back of the estate house and the plantation commissary was the Yazoo River, very muddy, down which the barges still go; the last river steamer called there in 1932. In the cool estate house, at lunch, there was a sense of space, of great distances separating one from one's neighbor. Books, the concern with history (Egypt had been in the possession of the same family for most of the century), and paintings (originals, mainly portraits, and reproductions), and even the small sculptured Negro head on the mantelpiece of the drawing room—all this suggested a culture far removed from the special Delta world of work.

Even during the lunch the pest-control people had been busy outside. And just beyond the gardens of the house were the level fields on which it all depended. A million dollars' worth of equipment tilled and harvested and fertilized those fields. There would have been much less equipment in the old days; there would have been many more workers.

In the flat land the single line of the widely spaced houses of the few black workers who were now needed stood out against the sky. In front of the houses, on the road—and seen very clearly, as though on a stage: the effect of the flatness of the land and the great height of the sky—the black children played, running about or cycling. In the estate house, at lunch, one might have been in Argentina, on an *estancia*. Outside, considering those workers' houses, one might have been in some country in Africa—Kenya perhaps, if there had been hills in the background.

But cotton, though the prices had improved recently, was no longer absolutely king of the Delta. What the flatness of the land concealed from the highways was that many thousands of acres of Delta land were now given over to catfish-farming, as complicated and big and American-ingenious, and mechanized and risky, as any of the ventures of the Delta.

I drove early one morning from Jackson to witness a "harvesting" of some catfish ponds. The "ponds"—each about fifteen to twenty acres—had been seined the previous evening. The seines were like the seines one knew. But the dragging had been done by two tractors, one on each embankment; and the embankments were strewn with dusty dead fish, now less like fish than like a kind of leathery material. There were snakes in the ponds sometimes; and goldfish, flashing red in the seine and in the wire-netted hopper that lifted the fish into the trucks from the pond. Goldfish, things of beauty when seen one or two at a time, had become "trash fish" here, to be separated from the catfish at the processing plant, and either thrown away with the other trash fish that a pond attracts (sometimes dropped by birds), or ground into fertilizer.

Nature, manipulated, had gone slightly haywire. The goldfish had been introduced to eat the algae that had been giving a bad flavor to the catfish. But when the goldfish had flourished far too well—rather like the kudzu vine, the other great plague of Mississippi, which, introduced from Japan or China to prevent erosion in the hillier parts of the state, had so liked what it had found that it had overrun many square miles, racing up electric poles and pulling them down, killing trees, creating great festoons and swags everywhere, blanketing woodland with a thick, even growth of—almost literally—ineradicable vines (the kudzu had been introduced for that very reason, because its marvelous roots held so fast to the soil). Like the water hyacinth in the Congo River, the kudzu had become a strangler.

Flavor—that was the great problem with catfish. And that had so far not been solved by all the research of the processing plant and the Catfish Institute. Catfish, especially in the summer, could develop strange flavors: mud, or burned wood, or something with a petroleum tang.

So the processing plant carried out five or six flavor tests on fish that were ready to be harvested. The tail of a live fish was cut off, cooked, and tasted. The purchasing manager of the processing plant said, "We cut the fish with the skin still on. We don't want to adulterate it in any way. It's right off the truck, the tail is cut, and it's into the microwave. It isn't skinned or anything."

The cooking and tasting was one man's job. "Our taster can easily do two hundred samples a day. It varies. I've known him do as many as 350 samples a day. He has his own kind of method of cleansing his palate. If a fish is very much off flavor he will turn on the fan in his kitchen—because the one that's off flavor will really smell up the test kitchen. Nowadays, in the summer, only two or three samples out of fifteen sent can be accepted. The rate of acceptance is higher in the winter." And the catfish farmer could only hope that the ponds with the rejected samples would become all right, and that the fish there would on a later occasion pass the flavor test.

So the fish being loaded that morning into the processing-plant trucks had passed all but one of their tests. There was to be a very last one at the processing plant. For two days before their trip to the processing plant, the fish had not been fed, so that nothing might interfere with their flavor. Now, on flavor, and weighing from one to one and a half pounds, the fish were almost at the end of their eighteen-month farm cycle.

In a hatchery, a small covered shed, they could be seen at the beginning: eggs in troughs, in water kept at a constant eighty degrees, an electrically driven paddle taking the place of the waving tail of the male catfish; without that disturbance of the water the eggs would die. In five days life—beginning as a black speck—comes to the eggs; and then the fingerlings are released into the ponds, to start their eighteen-month life.

The ponds are aerated constantly, because without oxygen the fish will die. The oxygen content of the ponds is tested every two hours, day and night; a catfish farmer cannot stay away for too long from his fish. The food or grain fed to the catfish is regulated by computer. It is dropped at fixed times at the deep end of the pond. The fish swim to the deep end at feeding time. They are creatures of habit. They do not eat if they are fed irregularly or fed too much. If there are too few catfish in a pond the fish do not eat enough to put on marketable weight, because (as it appears) the lessening of competition makes the creatures as "laid back" as the wild fish that feed at the bottom of rivers. How much, then—how much experimentation and accident and loss —had gone into the rearing of those fish being loaded that early morning into the trucks of the processing plant!

The plant was in the small town of Indianola. The workers from the processing rooms were sitting out in their lunch hour, in the broken shade of pine trees, across the paved road from the plant. They wore blood-stained white gowns and what looked like plastic shower caps. Most of these workers were black, and many of them were women. They sat on wooden stools at wooden tables and ate their lunch snacks. A number of them were eating hamburgers—workers in one food-processing industry eating the products of another food-processing industry: the give-and-take of industrial society.

When lunch was over the process resumed. The trucks of the processing plant released the fish they had brought—in well water, to keep the fish as clean as possible—into a metal cage. The fish were lifted in this cage and delivered into an electrical stunner, a box painted green. And they were passed down from there to the processing lines, inside the building, in a room noisy with machinery, to be de-headed, eviscerated, and skinned.

De-headed, eviscerated, and skinned—the purchasing manager, who was showing us around, spoke the difficult words as easily as, in another age, people would have spoken of criminals being hanged, drawn, and quartered. Something of that process was involved here. But the emphasis in the fish plant was on speed, speed to preserve the freshness of the fish, which were to be kept alive to the very last moment, then de-headed, eviscerated, and skinned in a flat three and a half minutes, and immediately afterwards put (at least, the fillets or steaks or strips or nuggets) into very cold water mixed with ice. The ice was important at that stage: every detail in this process had been worked out. The ice, the purchasing manager said, rubbed up against the cut or filleted fish and acted as yet another cleansing agent. The fish were completely processed, ready for market, in thirty minutes.

"And so," the purchasing manager said, "the customer can eat for dinner that evening a fish that was alive in the morning. This is a degree of freshness that cannot be equaled by any other aquaculture product. As far as seafood goes, forget it. Some of the seafood's been lying on a boat for four, five days before the boat gets back to dock."

"De-heading"—the word was new to me. But it was absolutely right. A man can be beheaded; a man is not de-headed any more than a fish is beheaded; and "de-headed" suggested the industrial process involved. Part of the speed of the operation depended on the skill of the de-header or, as the purchasing manager said, the head-sawyer. A good head-sawyer could cut fifty-five heads a minute. But the fish had to be well stunned, and not wriggling about; the stunner in the green box had to work. Men and women both did the head-sawing job. The woman I studied for a while wore yellow gloves and slid the stunned fish at a great rate against a vertical bandsaw. The evisceration was done by suction, by a machine such as I had seen, nearly twenty years before, in what had remained of John Steinbeck's Cannery Row in

Monterey, California. Outside, the entrails and other bloody matter of the processed fish poured down from two hoppers into red trucks, to be taken away somewhere, perhaps (but I didn't ask) to be turned into fertilizer.

In the office building there was order and silence; and the girls were white. In the waiting room there was a photograph in color of two pretty white girls who were Miss Catfish 1985 and Miss Catfish 1986.

In Cannery Row in 1969 I had been shown around silent, disused machinery by the man who had bought it and was hoping to sell it. He told me that machinery—even as involved and long-winded as the canning machinery appeared to be—wasn't difficult, once you "lived" it. And I felt that the president (and the purchasing manager) of this processing plant "lived" catfish in that way. But Cannery Row was a dead place, and Sam Hinote was building up a new industry.

He was forty-five. He had been born in Alabama and had gone to Auburn University. The name brought back my evening drives to that town and to the nearby town of Opelika, for dinner, when I was staying at Tuskegee. And, remembering something I had been told at Tuskegee about the comparative merits of the veterinary departments of the two universities, I said, "Auburn. But that's the rival of Tuskegee, the black university."

Sam Hinote smiled. I was a visitor; he was tolerant. He said, "Tuskegee is a black school. But Auburn is not its rival. Auburn's rival is Alabama State University."

He had started his professional life as an economist, a market analyst dealing with grain prices and other commodity prices. Then, as director of economic research for a big company in Omaha, Nebraska, it became his job to find new ventures for that company. That was how he got into catfish.

"We ended up in 1969 buying a small company that was involved in the catfish business. The company we bought had a hatchery and a processing plant. Their business was selling the baby fish to farmers, and buying back the market-size fish from farmers, and processing and selling the dressed fish. I thought it was very much like the early days of the chicken business."

His analysis was right. The fish-farming cooperative he began to run in Indianola in 1981 with fifty employees now provided employment for fourteen hundred people, and indirectly for many more, many of them black people who until then could only get seasonal jobs on cotton plantations, "chopping cotton" in the spring, getting rid of weeds that couldn't be poisoned, and working in the cotton gin in the autumn. Many farmers had been saved from having to leave their farms. "A lot of farmers didn't want to be involved in catfish, but they had few alternatives. It's hard for a farmer once they've become a farmer to ever give up. It's a way of life for them."

Sam Hinote had done a lot of useful advertising. "We're spending a lot of advertising dollars as a company and as an industry to upscale the image of catfish. We've hired professional chefs like this guy"—he held up a pamphlet with a photograph of a chef holding serious-looking dishes in both hands—"to help us change the image of catfish." Catfish, catfish—like the dedicated man he was, Sam Hinote appeared never to tire of speaking the word. The Catfish Institute, founded in 1986, had been publishing booklets. Sam Hinote gave me one: *Fishing for Compliments—Cooking with Catfish*. It had been an American-style campaign, and it had produced American results. The catfish business as a whole now had sales of $200 million; almost half of that came from the plant at Indianola. And Sam Hinote thought that within ten years the industry was going to have sales of $1 billion.

And though men cannot absolutely control other living creatures— Cannery Row itself died because the sardine vanished from that coast —and no one can be absolutely certain what will happen to catfish— what mutations, what debilities—as a result of this intensive farming, it is nevertheless an astonishing thing to have happened in a place that Louise knew as wilderness, malarial, liable to floods, but beautiful with wildflowers, and where now, within hours of leaving their ponds, the red entrails of fish pour into red trucks, their life cycle over.

THERE IS no landscape like the landscape of our childhood. For Louise, though her father had been a planter, the "big cotton patch" that the planters had created in the Delta was a disfiguring of the forest she had known as a child. And for Mary, born in the Delta forty years later, there would be no landscape like the flat, stripped land she had grown up in.

She said, "I think there is nothing more beautiful than the flat, flat land and the big, big sky."

She was showing me the small country town of Canton, fifteen miles or so north of Jackson, giving meaning to a shabbiness I had driven through once before without comprehension. I had taken in only the broken-down air of the main road through the town, and noticed the large number of black people in a town where there appeared to be little to do. All at once now, with Mary taking me through the streets around the main square, the layers of history became apparent, as they did in so many places in the South.

The town had been established in the mid-1830s. But most of the buildings on the square had been put up in the twenty years from 1890 to 1910. The Civil War had intervened; and in a street not far from the main square was the first reminder.

It was a street of pretty, old houses, but with black people. Some of them could be seen sitting on the porches. In the middle of this street was an open green space with a gray marble obelisk. It was inscribed on one side: *Erected by W. H. Howcott in memory of the good and loyal servants who followed the fortunes of Harvey Scouts during the Civil War.* On another side: *A tribute to my faithful Servant and Friend Willis Howcott, a Colored Boy of rare loyalty and faithfulness whose memory I cherish with deep gratitude. W. H. Howcott.* And on a third side: *Loyal, Faithful, True Were Each and All of Them.* The fourth side of the obelisk was bare.

The slave, Willis, had taken the name of the master. Had the "colored boy" who had gone to the war with his master really been a boy, or had he been a man who had remained a boy even in death? True feeling was there, but how much of defiance had there also been, in this obelisk put up after the war to celebrate the loyalty of slaves?

The obelisk was in a black street. The memorial to the Harvey Scouts was in the white cemetery, elsewhere. And the slave memorial was still tended. The grass around the gray obelisk was neatly cut; on the base there was a bouquet of artificial flowers. Black people sat on porches not far away. Black people walked past while we looked. Didn't they mind?

They didn't. But, Mary said, it was something that hadn't been put to them. Perhaps they would mind if someone came one day and put certain things to them.

In the white cemetery, some streets away, and centrally placed in it, was the memorial to the Harvey Scouts. It was also an obelisk, but not as plain as the one for the servants. It was carved with crossed flags, a star and crescent; and there was a metal plaque on the plinth. Some verse had also been carved:

> Long since has beat the last tattoo
> And peace Reigns now where Troopers Drew
> Their sabres Bright to Dare and Do
> Led Forward by Ad Harvey.

It was unsettling, that flawed last line; it made one think that the first three lines had been borrowed. Yet there had been sacrifice: CAPT ADDISON HARVEY BORN JUNE 1837 KILLED APRIL 19 1865 *Just as the Country's Flag was Furled forever Death saved him the pain of defeat.*

At the far end of the cemetery, not far from the corner with old Jewish graves, were small tombstones, in rows of five, running down the length of the cemetery, each stone marked UNKNOWN CONFEDER-ATE SOLDIER. It was shocking, in this small-town cemetery, the thought of all these unclaimed men. The bodies or the remains, Mary said, would have been gathered together some time after the war. The headstones might have been put up in the 1870s. The Harvey memorial, and the memorial to the black servants, would have been put up later.

The cemetery was still in use. Other people, with heavier needs, were driving about the lanes, as we had been doing. There were two new graves, below green awnings marked with the undertaker's name, Breeland. And not far away was the undertaker's own family plot, with a large stone marked *Breeland*. Mary said, "Some people think it's advertising."

Small as it was, Canton had its social and racial divisions. The railroad track divided the good side of the town from the bad. On the bad side, the black side, many of the houses were in disrepair; and many of them were shotgun houses, one room in front, one room at the back, the houses set close together. There were other, better black areas; but even new developments appeared to be going down. There didn't seem to be much doing in Canton. In an older part of the town were the settlements associated with the timber industry, when there had been one. Milltown was for the white workers. Next to it was the black area, with a designation that recalled the cabins of the slave plantations: Sawmill Quarters.

There was still a furniture factory in Canton, and there were two or three other factories outside the town. But the industrial area was in a mess. It looked like tropical slum. It was hard to think, when we got to the area of the country club—with a membership of professional people from Canton and from Jackson—that both areas shared the same climate and vegetation. In one area the sun seemed part of the blight and torpor. In the other, among the tall trees and well-cut driveways, the sunlight was like part of the general privilege of the place.

"Sun," "sunlight"—to me they had always been different words. "Sunlight" was a nice word. "Sun" was harsher; it was what the sunlight of early morning in Trinidad turned to at about eight, when it was time to go to school. The slogan on the label for Trinidad Grapefruit Juice, when I was a child, was "Fruit Ripened in Tropical Sunshine." I had always thought that the words were too pretty. "Fruit Ripened in Hot Sun" would have been truer to the climate I lived in; but then they might have been less of a slogan. "Tropical Sunshine"— they were tourist words, I always thought; and, indeed, they could have little meaning for someone who had known nothing else.

Agricultural and industrial depression now; civil-rights movement twenty to thirty years before; the Great Depression before that; and Reconstruction; and the Civil War—it seemed, considering the layers of history whose memorials or remains one could see in a place like Canton, that the South had moved from crisis to crisis. And at the back of it all was the institution that had seeded most of the crises, or aggravated them: slavery, which had led to this present superfluity of black people, people no longer needed in a machine age.

Mary said: "It's been frustrating to me because the enormity of the problem is something I know I'm not going to see solved. It's heartbreaking to see people living like that. And it will keep the area from progressing, economically and culturally. These people don't read books, or even newspapers. TV is the only thing. And in fact some of them probably can't read. Not in the way that you and I can read. They can read a sign, but not a thought or an idea."

During our drive through the town she had shown me a red-brick high school that had been turned into a furniture store after the schools had been desegregated.

"The enrollment in the public system made the building unnecessary." She meant that white people had withdrawn their children, and sent them instead to private and usually Christian academies. But now that was a financial strain on some people, and people were beginning to think again about the public system. "I've been encouraged recently because some of the people here who would not be considered liberal are realizing that so much of the future of the town is tied into the school system."

"Is there still bitterness about desegregation?"

"A lot of bitterness from the sixties has gone into the second generation. But now it's more of an economic resentment. People resent seeing the welfare programs like food stamps—and there is something that provides food and milk for babies. And of course people that have worked hard for their families are certainly going to resent seeing people being given for nothing the equivalent of what you've had to work hard to earn. Medicare is another thing. There are clinics for people who pay according to their income. Which means that they are supported by the federal government—that is, other people's income tax.

"I'm not a bleeding heart racially, believing in universal brotherhood. People are too different. I believe in God, but I'm not religious. This is the Bible Belt. For some reason Southern people have a tremendous capacity for faith—black and white. When I go to a church service where people are extremely devout I feel I'm missing something. But it doesn't last. Religion is very social here—fellowship, church suppers, things like that. And I suppose I'm not a particularly social person."

"When did you start thinking of yourself as a Southerner, somebody different?"

"I've always felt it. We're so proud of it. We are permeated by the feeling that the South is special. My family were always interested in the literary aspects. We were very proud of our writers here."

What about the other side? The bigotry, the violence? Was there one view that could hold it all?

"I was aware of the other side. The violence, the deprivation. There was a very ugly incident when I was growing up. That was the Emmett Till murder. He was a young black boy from Chicago visiting the area. He was shot supposedly for whistling at a white woman who worked in a little store in a rural area. And this all happened close to Greenwood, where I was living. This was in 1955. I was eleven. I remember reading it in the newspaper first. I had a friend and she knew the people in the store. And I remember people at school saying it wasn't true, that he was still living in Chicago, and that people were trying to make Mississippi look bad. But even at eleven I knew that was a sad way of thinking, and that people who thought like that were of the same social class as the woman at the store."

Here it was again, the emphasis on social distinctions. How did they operate in the Delta, where lives were so isolated and confined?

Mary said, "My grandmother would say of some people that they were not folks. That was probably her favorite phrase. She was very conscious of who were and were not folks."

"Who were folks?"

"Generally, folks were people who weren't transient, who'd lived here for some time. You knew their families. And if they'd moved in, say, from Lafayette County, you would know their families."

"But, apart from some people in Natchez, no one has been here for more than five generations."

"No. It simply meant that you knew they were the same kind of people. They knew how to behave. They didn't say 'nigger.' Nor did they say 'ain't.' People who said 'ain't' and 'niggers' were not folks—that would definitely put you beyond the pale then and there. She was a stickler for manners. If you put your elbows on the table, she would pick up those heavy silver knives and she would hit your elbows, if there wasn't company—in those days people had the heavy silverware, not the stainless steel. I think we behaved like this because we genuinely thought that this—the South—was the best place in the world. To be technical about it, my grandmother came from Alabama. She had lived in Mississippi since she was married. I can remember my parents talking to me and trying to explain the racial problem. And since nobody really understood it—"

I was interested in that idea. I said, "No one has put it like that to me."

"I don't think they did. Understand the race problem. I still don't think they do. I know that people of, like, my grandmother's generation —her generation and black people of the same generation had a closeness that doesn't exist any more. In those days no one had any money. You know, the Depression and things. A lot of the jobs the black people had depended on the white people—in the houses and yards and things. But the white people depended on the black people too. I think that at that time there was a better respect between the races."

"People outside didn't have that impression. There were the lynchings."

"There were, exactly. But the people I was talking about—and I'm sure that people are much more capable of violence than I realize—the people who carried out the inhumanities were not typical of everyone."

"What effect does the physical appearance of Canton have on you? The town you showed me."

"That kind of question makes us defensive."

"No, no. I don't want that."

"What did I show you? Buildings and fields."

"You showed me a lot that was run-down. It isn't worthy of the history." And I meant—though I didn't speak precisely—that if you took away the cemetery and the main square, there would be little in Canton that wasn't contemporary slum. The land and setting were hard to associate with a great and difficult history. How, in such a setting, did she support her sense of history?

Mary said, "It may not be worthy. But I don't think poverty and deprivation are limited to the South. I think we are addressing the economic problems more than we have ever done. People are addressing the problems of black and white as of one group."

"What do you like about the South?"

"It's a very nourishing place to live. I like the people, even though I'm not close to them. If there was some sort of tragedy people would rally round, even though they were not my family. And the sense of the past can be satisfying—even though my family is not from this area. What did Faulkner say? The past is more real than the present? I can't remember the exact words. But it's that the past is something we all live with. Possibly in larger places they don't put the importance on the past. We're preoccupied with the past. Some people think that's because we lost the war."

So we had circled back almost to where we had begun. I had asked, seeing some military-looking figure in a memorial in the cemetery, whether he was wearing a Confederate uniform. But the memorial wasn't what I had thought. And Mary had said, "There was no uniform. Towards the end they were lucky to have shoes."

WILLIAM SAID: "People up north think they know better than we about problems and people down here. They think they know how the black man thinks and the white man thinks. They have missed miserably on the black man." The North had disrupted the more economically active South in 1860; and they had done it again after World War II.

I wanted him to go beyond that.

He said, "Let's talk through certain things first, before you make notes."

I put away my notebook and we began to talk at random. He was a businessman, of a prominent Mississippi family. He was in his forties. He loved the outdoor life and was athletic and handsome. He appeared to be blessed in many ways. Yet what came out after a few minutes of conversation was that he was a man to whom religion was supremely important. His judgments, even the tough ones he had spoken at the beginning of our meeting, were contained within his idea of the religious life. And that was where we began again.

We sat on rocking chairs in front of his desk: the tradition of the porch, transferred here to an air-conditioned office.

William said, "The Bible says the Lord helps those who help themselves, and I really believe that. I feel there are not enough people trying to help themselves. And I don't think that the help these people need is a free check."

I asked about the development of his faith.

"Both sets of my grandparents were very strong workers in the Baptist church. My parents were and are strong members of the church. I don't remember us not praying or reading a Bible. I made my profession of faith when I was seven years old. I guess I went to my parents first—after hearing the Sunday-school teachers talk about Jesus and the Lord, and I believe that he did come out of heaven and walked among us and died for us, to give us an opportunity to be with him in heaven. And finally I said publicly, 'I want to accept Christ.' And they said, 'Fine, let's go to the preacher.' And he talked to me. And I guess they felt my feeling was strong enough, and I was baptized at seven. I grew up around it, I accepted it, and I made that profession of faith.

"I had a dream around that time—but it didn't cross my mind until many years later. I was spending the night with my grandmother. I was sleeping on the porch. I remember sitting up in bed—waking up real fast—and I thought I saw Jesus Christ walking through the back door. The door had a little knocker, a wooden ball on a string, and I remember hearing that knocker, and the door opening. And I just had that vision of Jesus Christ walking through that door. And I remember sitting up all night to see if he was going out through the back door. But he never did. I never thought much about that dream until six or seven years ago. I was riding down the highway, and it just flashed back in my mind. At that point I really realized that it was Jesus Christ entering my heart. And the reason I didn't see him leave that back door was that he didn't leave us. I just haven't discussed that story with my family. But I remember that dream and that whole night as if it was yesterday. I feel thát Jesus Christ entered my heart that day and he's never left."

"Did it change your attitude to other people?"

"I hope I have more patience with people. I hope I'm quicker to see the good than I am to see the shortcomings. I certainly try to have a short memory for bad experiences. I try to forgive and forget."

"What about irreligious people? What do you think of them?"

"I guess I feel that if I can set an example to them I can encourage them to be less irreligious. Nor do I think less of a person who has a different religion from mine."

"Do you feel you are in a religious community?"

"I think I am. I'm not sure that the religious part of the community is keeping up with the population growth. I'm not sure that the church *membership* is keeping up. But I realize that there are many Christians. I was encouraged by the short patience people had with the Gary Hart–Donna Rice situation. I am certainly encouraged about Christianity in this country and the work of the Lord."

"Why aren't you in the church?"

He misunderstood the question. "I was there until nine last night."

"No, no. I was asking why you aren't in the ministry."

"I believe the Lord has a will for every one of us, a plan for us. He knows what he wants us to do. If we were all architects, we would all have pretty buildings, but we wouldn't have farmers to grow food. I think that his plan for creation is that it takes a lot of people to make up this world. And he needs workers in all of these areas."

"Is this why you feel as you do about people who do no work?"

"I have never expressed it like that. But I think that is why I feel the way I do."

"Do you think men need to work?"

"No question about that. The Lord created the Garden of Eden and he put Adam and Eve there, and when they sinned he put them out of the Garden of Eden and told them to go to work."

"You feel that people are still working out that sin?"

"I don't think I'm still working out their sin. But I think that all of us have sins. The human race is a sinful race—and this is where we are, and that's what we have to deal with now. I feel strongly that we are required to work for six days and rest on the seventh. The Lord talks about giving each individual talents, and the Lord told us to use them. I think that working is an important part of using those talents. Some people are writers, farmers, architects. These are talents that the Lord gave them.

"Someone wrote to my father several months ago. In this letter he was saying: I enjoy my work; how does a successful businessman continue being a Christian? Should he stay with his business, or should he go back into the church? My father wrote a letter to explain why it's necessary for a Christian businessman to be in the world. Our own preacher here has said several times that with the TV pastors getting into such hot water and getting such bad attention, he's been seeing some doors closed against him; and the responsibility for leading people to Christianity is more on the shoulders of laymen."

I said, "Some people are saying that it's the work of the devil. that those TV pastors are in trouble."

William said, "When I fail at something I fail. I feel like I've got to take the consequences for my failure. I also know that I've got outside forces working against me. But I know that before I start. So I can't pass the buck. The devil might have made me do it, but it's still my problem, my responsibility. The ultimate accountability is mine."

I asked him to talk about accountability.

He sucked in his breath. "Whoo! It's difficult to go public about it. I guess it goes back to what I was taught by Mom and Dad: that if you have responsibility you have accountability. The more responsibility, the more people are affected. And I think the accountability to Christ is the ultimate responsibility I have. This also gives me a background to what Mom and Dad were teaching about responsibility and accountability. Perhaps the people dependent on me the most are my family. Then there are the people I'm tied into business with. They've given me a certain responsibility, and I've accountability. We are in business to serve customers. And that gives us another whole segment of people we're accountable to, people we'll never see.

"You've told me about your trip to the catfish farms. Those catfish are going to go all over the world. And the farmer has got to see that the fish is on flavor—for that person who is going to eat that catfish, for where that catfish is going to end up. If we do it right they'll come back. If we do it wrong they won't come back."

So the religious ideas of the God-given talent, work, and account-ability coincided with sound business practice. It was true of other religious groups as well, this coincidence of religious devotion and business sense: one kind of dedication encouraging, and even becoming, another kind of dedication. It was true of certain Hindu caste groups and certain minority or heretical sects in Islam. But religions and cultures have their own identities. One isn't just like another. The idea of the God-given talent is contained in the Hindu idea of *dharma*; but the Hindu religious-business dedication is different from the dedication William was talking about. However much his business practices appear to contain the idea of service, the Hindu businessman has a contract with God alone, and not with men.

And it was of his contract with men that William went on to talk. He said: "To me, without religion there wouldn't be any purpose. It's religion that gives us purpose in being here. The purpose is to serve the Lord. And the only way we have of serving him is to serve mankind. We can't give him anything he doesn't already have. We can't touch that. Nothing he doesn't already have, unless it's our heart."

William spent a certain amount of his spare time on church work. He gave "devotions" sometimes; he taught Sunday school sometimes; he worked with the boy scouts. Did he, so full of his church, judge people according to the degree of their faith?

He read the question as half a political one, connected with "equal opportunity" and the racial issue. He said—puzzlingly, unless you understood the semipolitical question he felt he was answering—"I try not to judge an individual as an individual. I don't have the facts to judge on. But I try to judge and weigh his actions against the work that has to be done—to weigh his strengths and weaknesses as I can interpret them. Though that's what I used to be *told*—that this person fits this particular job. Maybe they did, maybe they didn't. But what that does is that the individual knows intuitively: 'I'm here because you've been told to put me here. It doesn't matter about my job performance. Therefore it doesn't matter what I do here.' And at that point the person loses incentives and a proper motivation."

But William talked about this wearily, as though he had talked about it many times before and had no faith now that the plain and obvious things he was saying would ever be heeded.

Then, rocking, leaving the subject of equal opportunity aside, he said, "I have such a wholesome respect for the early-American natives.

I really feel like they believed that the Lord lived in everything on earth, the rocks, the trees, the bush, the animals—the Lord lived in everything—and they were part of it. And what I think of the early-American natives is that they had an almost reverent respect for nature. For them the life of a blade of grass was as important as a great buffalo. They didn't make any distinction. And they probably realized, more than the greatest scientist on earth now, that everything on this earth is totally related. They understood the chain reaction that comes from getting one thing in nature out of balance with the others. And I think that, because of the reverence they had for all living things, they had a reverence for mankind that I'm not sure we'll ever see again."

"How did you find out about the Indians?"

"I've read a few books. I've made a few trips out west and talked with a few Indians by the roadside. And I was impressed with the minuteness of the attention to small details that they had. For every action there is a reaction. And what worries me the most now is that where I see a new highway or subdivision, where they're clearing land, there's a major destruction of plant life, animal life that can't be replaced. The thing that disturbs me about that is that it's not done with any consciousness or concern. It's only done with concern for the dollar.

"Go down on your stomach on the ground. Look at a square foot of grass for about forty-five minutes. See the life, the insects. And magnify that to the size of a project."

"But Mississippi needs investment."

"I don't know how it can be worked out. The more concerns you have for these little things, and that side of life, the more concern you're going to have for your neighbor."

The contract with other men, serving God by serving mankind— they were themes to which William returned.

"I feel that man and nature have to go together. The Lord put us here to be caretaker of things. A lot of my thoughts are tied back with religion and the Lord's creation."

It seemed to me that we could now go back to what he had said at the beginning, about the North's historical wish to disrupt the economy of the South. But he didn't want to go back just then to that side of things. He wanted to stay a little longer with his more mystical thoughts.

I felt I had begun to understand how his fundamentalist faith—

from the outside so constricting—was in fact complete and flexible. The mixture of the Old Testament and the New, the life of Jesus and the Book of Genesis, made a whole. The sanctity of the created world, the good life of conscience, the loving of one's neighbor as oneself— they ran together, and they appeared to fit the Mississippi character and history: the love of nature and the outdoor life, an admiration for the pantheism of the Indians, the love of family and community, the resentment of outside interference, which could feel almost like inter- ference with a religious code.

William said, of his religion, "I don't wear it on my sleeve. I hope I don't flash it around. It's just part of me. I don't want to be a goody- goody or better-than-thou, because I don't feel that way. I just want to be part of God's creation. His handiwork is in everything. And the more respect we have for his creation, the more respect we have for our fellow man."

A FTER TALLAHASSEE and Tuskegee, I wanted in Mississippi to look at things from the white point of view, as far as that was possible. But it was put to me not long after I had arrived that, with the high percentage of black people in the state, and with the possibility that Jackson might soon have a black mayor, I should meet some black politicians.

Andrew, a young Mississippian politician, put this to me at lunch one day, and he thought the man I should meet was Willard. Andrew himself was going to meet Willard for the first time that day, after lunch, and he thought I should come with him. "If the meeting goes well," Andrew said, "I can leave and you can talk to him. I can always talk to him some other time."

Andrew was not looking for black votes. It was his ambition as a politician to rewrite the Mississippi state constitution of 1890, and to do that he needed all the political support he could get. For this first meeting with Willard he had dressed with some formality, in a pale- blue seersucker suit.

The meeting was to take place in a hotel not far away. We left the cool of the restaurant and went down into the glare of the parking lot. The car was hot. The air conditioning, turned on to "high fan," roared; and it became hotter in the car than it had been outside. The air had just begun to cool when we arrived at the hotel and had to get out, into the glare of another parking lot. Always these reminders of the discomfort of earlier generations; and wonder at the energy they had shown; and more wonder that a great war should have been fought in temperatures like this.

We sat in the lobby and waited for Willard. Conversation was easy up to the time at which Willard was due to come. After that it became awkward, with both of us waiting for Willard. Andrew said, "I've never met him." He said that two or three times. Once he got up and walked across the lobby to greet someone he knew: impeccable his manners, his charm unfailing, his politician's role now apparently second nature to him.

And then, when we had given him up, fifteen minutes having passed beyond the appointed time, Willard came. He was in shirt and trousers; no tie; and he was unexpectedly ordinary, not at all the black leader or would-be leader I had imagined someone like Andrew treating with. I had expected a black man of disturbing charm. There was no charm to Willard. He was in his forties, plumpish, strong, no mark of physical hardship on him. He had prepared a serious face for the meeting. If one didn't know he was regarded as a politician one would have missed the rage in his eyes, or one might have read that deliberateness of gaze as sensuality.

Willard was very much a local politician. In Mississippi, because of the 1890 constitution, the most modest of public offices are elected offices. This provision, intended to prevent any government from having too much power, and intended also to keep blacks out of even small jobs, now worked in favor of blacks, and politicized posts that elsewhere would have been purely professional or technical. Willard looked after the roads of a particular district of a particular county: a very small post indeed.

I left almost as soon as I had met Willard. And, partly through Andrew's good offices (the meeting must have gone well), a meeting with Willard was arranged for me some days later.

It was an early-morning meeting. I had assumed from the directions I had been given that the place was in Jackson. I hadn't asked what the distance was. But after twenty minutes or so on an interstate highway I began to feel that I was driving back to Alabama.

At last, the time now past the time fixed for the meeting, the exit appeared. Only then did I realize that I had been given nothing like a house or office address, that I had driven all this way with only the number of a county district for destination. However, I pressed on, thinking I might make inquiries when I crossed the county border. I passed a board. It gave the name of the county and the number of the district. It was not the number I had been given, but I thought I would stop to ask at the building at the back. There were cars parked around it. When I got to the building I saw that among the parked cars there was a space, and the space was reserved for Willard. This was the address I had been meant to come to. But he wasn't there.

I pushed the door open and found myself in a shed divided into offices. The shed was full of black people. In the front office or cubicle there was a black girl with a telephone, with other black people around her.

This girl asked brightly for my name. I gave it. She said that she had been trying all morning, and Mr. Willard had been trying all the day before, to get to me, to tell me that Mr. Willard couldn't be at this address, but that he would be free to see me at an hour later than the one he had given, at Jackson. He would meet me in Jackson at my hotel. They had telephoned all the hotels in Jackson to locate me. But they hadn't succeeded. They had telephoned the Sheraton, the Holiday Inn. Where was I staying? I told her. She said that Mr. Willard would be there in an hour. How would she get a message to him? By the radio, she said; and I felt that the radio was important, a badge of office.

I asked her to radio him while I was there, so that I would know he had got the message. She said I was not to worry. So I drove back to Jackson, along the route that had seemed so long and unlikely earlier that morning, and which towards the end had made me a little frantic because I had thought I was going to be late for Willard.

When I got back to the Ramada Renaissance there was no Willard. Not then, and not in the afternoon. When I telephoned his office the girl said that Mr. Willard had spoken to her on the radio and that he intended to keep the appointment. He even knew my room number, she said. But Willard didn't come; and the next day there was no message from him or his office.

Later I told Andrew of Willard's little—or big—joke. Andrew said, "I don't really know him. I met him for the first time that day with you." And when I asked whether the politics of cooperation such as he envisaged were really possible, Andrew said he had to be an optimist. The black problems were bad, and there were many blacks in Mississippi. If he wasn't optimistic, he said, it would be better for him to move to Oregon, where only 10 percent of the population was black.

Andrew said, "It's been dawning on everybody that a disaster is occurring in the black community, and we do have to talk about it. The attitude of the polite press won't do any longer." Yet Andrew knew only what he knew. "I regurgitate more of what I've read about the society than what I've experienced. I get it from TV documentaries and specials. I haven't really experienced it. I haven't talked to black folks or rednecks. I've got to go over the top of some of these basic problems. If we can't get together we are lost."

Optimism in the foreground; irrationality in the background.

THE STORY about my adventure with Willard must have got around, because one day I had a telephone call from a man called Lewis. He said he was black and he wanted to introduce me to the real black culture. He worked in the stores section of a county department (like the one Willard oversaw). He began to give me directions to get to his house. But then he said he would come over to the hotel to pick me up. He said he would be there within the hour.

He was as good as his word. I recognized him as soon as he came into the Ramada. He was easy, light, friendly. His manner was so easy that I was prepared for general or neutral conversation, at least in the beginning. But as soon as we were in the privacy of his car, and even before we drove out of the Ramada parking lot, he said that in the old days he wouldn't have been able to live where he now lived. He had helped "integrate" his neighborhood. It turned out to be a modest neighborhood. The houses were small and close together. The surprise, after what he had said, was his yard. It was overgrown, and noticeable among its better-kept neighbors.

Inside, the house was cluttered, close, unaired. He made no reference to the clutter (even a few unwashed cups and plates in the sitting room), saying only that his wife had gone with the children to her mother's for a few days; and there was a kind of order below the clutter.

On the sitting-room wall were framed enlargements of two old black-and-white studio photographs. They were of his grandparents. The period clothes, the choking up of the neck in collar and ruff, and the stare of the long-held expressions were oddly moving. In the enlargement or the printing the tones of the photographs had been bleached away, so that both the people looked white, with black eyes. The photographs carried the stamp of a studio in Memphis.

Lewis said: "Mississippi people. They went to Memphis. Everybody went to Memphis. My father came back to Mississippi after the war. Do you know what they did? The people in the photographs. Do you want me to tell you? They were servants. Those two people made me. No hate developed in me because they taught me never to hate. The word was never used in their house. 'Be a good boy.' That was the motto. 'Treat everybody nice.' You heard it every day. I was taught that—to be good, and to be good to everybody."

It was hot in the sitting room because the air-conditioning unit had broken down. I asked him if he could open a window. He said he couldn't; the insects would come in. So we sat in the high, warm, musty smell.

He said, "When my grandfather died my grandmother sent some of my grandfather's clothes to my father. Servant clothes, suits. They were still good clothes, you see. Still some wear in them. And my father left one to me. I put it on one day. Just cloth, but I felt it burn my skin."

"Do you still have that suit?"

"I don't know where it is."

"All this is such a long time ago, though."

"But the past is always interesting. Knowing the past, I can do a better job. It's an awakening for me, to think of the past. Sometimes it's a rude awakening. To think of some of the things that happened— that I couldn't live where I'm living now, and didn't even think of it. That I sat at the back of the bus. That my grandmother washed clothes for white people at fifty cents a basket. Why didn't they pay her more? But I didn't question it when I heard. It's a rude awakening now. Still, they shielded me from the hate. It was there. I lived in my black section. They lived in their white section. That hatred was there, all around me, and I didn't feel it. They saved me from it, my grandparents, and my father after them. I'd hear about killing black men. But my father never allowed us to talk too much of it. And I'll tell you. Up to the day he died he said to whites, my father, 'Yes, sir!' 'No, sir!' No matter how young they were."

"What do you think of that now?"

"It doesn't bother me. He was my father. He did well for us, his family. So I didn't say to him, 'Don't say it.' " He went on, "I myself fight daily to be happy. Every day. It's the one thing I strive for. To be content, to be happy with myself."

What did he mean by that?

"I can't change my surroundings, but I can respect myself. I'll tell you a story. I went one time to my mother's sister's house. Black soldiers used to come to the house across the road, and they would be entertained by the young lady who lived there. One day one of the soldiers complained he had lost his billfold. The policeman who came to deal with this came to my mother's sister's house, because the young lady was sitting on the porch there when he came. He walked up to her and said, 'Gal, did you take that boy's billfold?' She said, 'No, sir.' He said, 'Get in the car.' And when she bent down to get in the car he kicked her hard on her behind. That never, *never* got away from me."

"What did you feel about that?"

I wanted to know, because I was no longer certain of the point of some of the things he was saying, the memories he was playing with. It was getting dark, too, in the little choked house—he seemed as indifferent to this as to the airlessness and the clutter—and it was becoming harder to see the expression on his face when he spoke. He was running a number of ideas together. He wished to be happy, content; he had been shielded from pain; and threaded into this was something like admiration for the grandparents who had founded his line and taught him to keep out of trouble in an irrational world.

"What do I think of the policeman and the woman? I don't know. I was so young. I didn't talk to anybody about it. I just saw it. It was cruel. But I don't know what I really felt about the cruelty. Every now and then the incident crosses my mind. Even today. I see it. But I don't know what I think about it."

Wasn't it a little self-indulgent, living so much in the past, especially now that times had changed?

"Yes. I'm enjoying the harvest now. But I don't think I've done much as a fighter, a marcher for freedom."

"That worries you?"

He didn't say anything. Then he laughed. "I don't know how I feel about it. I suppose I am in my own little world. And I suppose I'm selfish, being in my own world. I ought to be mad and angry and fighting. But I don't get mad."

"Is this something from religion? Did your grandparents teach you that?"

"I'm not religious. I'm not like many people who go to church every Sunday and want to be deacons."

"Why do you look back at the past if you don't know what you think about it?"

"I love to talk about the past."

How far back did that past go? Did it go back to the days of slavery? It didn't, of course. The past he liked to talk about was the past he could remember, that curiously sheltered past.

He said, "If my grandmother made fifty cents a day I ought to be happy with what I make now."

What was it about his grandparents that he now especially remembered and liked?

"Pride. Pride. My grandmother used to sit up in church with her corset on. Very proud, very cultured-like. Very classy lady. I don't know where she, and the others, got it from. Probably from the whites. Today I don't see it. They're nice people, but they don't have that something. I suppose I don't have it either. But you must know that I truly respect my past, be it segregated, be it filled with racism, be it whatever. Because I feel I have a place in the world, and I'm going to get it."

The telephone rang. He took it up in the darkness. He listened more than he talked. He was being rebuked by someone he knew for not keeping an appointment.

He said, when he put the phone down, "I'll drive you back to the Ramada." That was where he had told the man on the phone to meet him. "We'll talk again tomorrow. I'll come for you at six."

It was a relief to be out of the house and in the open, warm though the air was.

And now, driving to North Jackson, Lewis appeared to qualify some of the things he had said in his house. In the house he seemed not to have put together his thoughts about the civil-rights movement. Now he spoke with reverence of Martin Luther King.

He said, "If he hadn't turned it the nonviolent way, they would have killed *every* black in Mississippi. Every black in the South."

I heard real panic in the words.

I asked him again about his "little world." Had it really protected him?

He said, "I suppose I was aware of everything outside. I was frightened of it—I suppose."

And then, without prompting from me, he began to talk about God. In the house he had said he was not religious in the way most people were. Now he said that without God he would have done nothing; without God he would have been nothing; without God he didn't know how he would have endured.

In the parking lot of the Ramada Renaissance he drove to the edge of one of the parking rows. There was a black man in a parked car. Lewis introduced me. The man in the car shrank from me.

Lewis didn't come at six the next day, or at half past six. No one answered when I telephoned. About eight o'clock he answered. He sounded tired, distant.

"I've been ill. I've been to the doctor. I didn't go to work today."

"I telephoned very often and got no reply."

"I was a long time at the doctor."

He asked me to come to see him right away. I took a taxi. The ventilation in his house was better, but the clutter was as bad. He looked extraordinary. He was barefooted, with a dressing gown open over a bare chest and a black net over his hair. The getup was like a black version of the shower cap and white gown of the workers in the catfish plant.

He said, "The net's to keep my hair curly."

I began to say polite things about his illness. He brushed the subject aside. He walked barefoot about the sitting room. "I'll tell you about my grandfather. I think he was the kind of man who knew how to handle people, especially Southern whites. 'Yes, sir!' 'No, sir!' And tip your hat to them and grin. But he was successful, in his day. Regardless of how mediocre it might seem today or yesterday, it happened. And that's it."

"It bothers you that you didn't do more for the civil-rights movement?"

"The dogs never bit me. Does it bother me? I don't know. You must decide for me."

The telephone rang.

It was his friend again, the one of the night before.

Lewis said into the phone, "He's here. We want your input." He laughed, and seemed to be getting out of control, laughing into the phone, stamping with his bare feet, and acting a little for me.

He said, when he put the phone down, "My friend is scared of you." He laughed in his new way. "You must take off that jacket. Take off that jacket, and let me show you how the blacks really live. I will take you to certain places. You will get the smell of corruption."

He made a gesture with his hand, like a cook suggesting an appealing aroma. And I understood then, putting things together, that he wasn't speaking metaphorically. The line of development that had begun with his grandfather was ending with him: his own little world, different now from the one he had grown up in.

He began to dress to meet his friend. He said—and I'd hardly arrived—"I'll take you back to your hotel."

He put on his trousers and shirt, and we went outside. He left the door unlatched. I pointed this out to him. He said, "I have to do something. I'll go back inside."

I waited for him for some time. When he came out there was a white cream on his chin, the white glowing in the dusk and against his blackness.

He said, "Blacks have kinky hair. Do you know about that? That hair grows under the skin. It is very hard to shave. This cream I've put on softens it. By the time I come back here I will be ready to shave, and I will get a very smooth shave."

And that was how he drove me back to the alien white part of the city, with the net on his hair and the white cream on his chin and upper lip.

He gave me another day to meet him. But he couldn't make it; I wasn't surprised. He sounded very tired and slow and far away when I telephoned. He asked me to telephone later in the evening. When I did there was no answer.

JUST AS it is hard to comprehend American distances and the heat of the Southern summer until one has experienced them, so in Mississippi and in the city of Jackson it was hard to understand that people of seventy would have lived through many different worlds; that the childhoods of solid citizens would have left memories of frontier life, primitive conditions, and closed communities, things hard now to recapture.

The town of Eupora, in the hills to the east of the Delta, is now on Highway 82. But someone like Judge Sugg, who was born in 1916 and retired from the state Supreme Court in 1983, carries memories from his childhood in Eupora of the time when the Big Black River had no bridge, only a ford. So that when the river was high there was no means of crossing it, and people stayed where they were, in their little communities, until the water subsided.

"We had dirt roads. No electricity. I've seen all sorts of wonderful things happen in the world. I enjoy the luxury of modern civilization. Instant television, instant entertainment. Instant everything. I enjoy it all. Life was hard for us in the early days. At the end of the Civil War we were destitute. And the slaves who had been freed had no training. It has taken us a hundred years to rebuild our capital base. Our slaves had no capital. We were an agricultural state."

Dates are relative. To me 1890, if I apply it to a place like Trinidad, and apply it therefore to the time when my Indian ancestors were just migrating to the New World—to me that date belongs to a period of darkness, something mythical, very far away. Apply it to England, and I think of the modern world: Oscar Wilde, the young Kipling, Gandhi (four years younger than Kipling) studying law in London. In the South dates became relative in this way. And I understood that many of the people of a certain age whom one saw had a special kind of success story to tell. Many of them had started with very little, had started in the wilderness perhaps with only an idea of civilization. (Many of them would have started with as little as my grandparents in Trinidad; but—a further relativity—they had found themselves in a place of greater potential.)

"Everybody was poor. I was fortunate. My father was a merchant. He was also sheriff for one term. He ran a general merchandise store. Merchants lent to farmers. They furnished the merchandise to the farmers, and at the end of the year, when the farmers sold their crops, mainly cotton, they settled. If there was a bad year the merchants suffered with the farmers, because if the farmers couldn't pay the merchants couldn't collect. There was nothing in writing, no promissory notes or anything. The saying was, 'My word is my bond.' "

A success story for the judge. But in the seventy or eighty years before his birth it had been a life with little movement forward for his ancestors. That too is worth contemplating.

"My family on both sides came to Mississippi between 1830 and 1840. My Sugg grandfather lost his leg in the Civil War. He could barely read and write. When he came out he saw that a one-legged man couldn't make a living as a farmer. He went to school for three years, and then taught school for three years. Then he became treasurer of

Calhoun County for four years and chancery clerk of Webster County for four years. He bought a farm. He had seven children who grew to adulthood, and some tenant families. The tenants were black, former slaves. I was up there about ten years ago, and I met some old people who were descendants of the tenants my grandfather had. When I left Webster County about a third of the people were black. I'm a country boy, you know. I haven't become accustomed to living in the city yet.

"Once a year a tent would come. They called them 'chautauquas.' They would stay about a week in the town. They would have musical programs; sometimes a man would lecture; and you would have plays, dramas. That was our outside entertainment. They came in by train. That was the only way they could come. On Sunday afternoon a passenger train came through. We had four a day. But on Sunday at two-thirty we had a passenger train that went east. A third of the town would go down to the station to see the train, to see who was on the train and who was getting off, and who was leaving town. Everybody just had a big time—that was something to look forward to.

"I remember when I was real young we received word that the Ringling Brothers Circus was going to come through some time after midnight. About half the town got up to get to see the circus train go through. You could see we were hurting for entertainment. It was over a hundred cars—that's what it seemed like at the time."

Unlike the Delta, where there were rich and poor and caste or class distinctions, in the hills there were no social distinctions, except between black and white.

"We didn't have private schools. Everybody went to church. We didn't have a society section. We didn't have a social register. We were just people. We had lots of illiterate whites. In the Depression we had only six months of school for one year; at other times we had eight months. There just wasn't the money to pay the teachers. Formal education suffered. But many of the older people were self-educated, like my father. He wrote a beautiful hand. He used good English.

"I had a desire to look at the things I had read about. New York to me was just on the map. I just never dreamed I would go there. I knew that China was across the Pacific and Europe across the Atlantic. I never dreamed I would go to these places. Yes, I dreamed of it, but I didn't think it would become a reality.

"But most people were content to remain where they were. We were a close-knit group of people. We had only about thirteen, fourteen hundred people in the town. The only way you could go anywhere was by rail, and you couldn't keep a secret in a place like that.

"I believe that closeness is responsible for some of the Mississippi character. When you live that close to people you have to get on with them, or you'd be ostracized. You learn to accept people as they are. We had many eccentrics, rugged individualists. A friend of mine said the other day, 'We don't seem to produce characters like we used to.' I said, 'We're the characters now.' "

The closeness of that community, deprived and ill-educated, led to violence. People mightn't feel the need for promissory notes, and mightn't lock their doors, mightn't even have keys for some of the doors. But tempers could be quick. There were homicides, crimes of passion.

"They would just get angry, get into an argument, lose their temper. Some of them would be drunk. They would maybe be quarreling and have a fight, and somebody would get killed. They were slow to arouse, but when you get somebody like that angry somebody would get hurt. Otherwise, helpful people, lovely people."

Self-reliance was another aspect of that Mississippi country character. "We had two and a half acres of land behind the house. To work that requires hard work. It makes you recognize the fact that anything you want you have to work for it. And it's tied into the religion, because we are taught in the churches that work was honorable and you were not to be lazy and you shouldn't be reliant on other people for a livelihood. In the Book of Proverbs there are many references to work and discipline and reward."

So there again it was, the idea of religion threaded into the idea of the pioneer past.

"I guess I was about the third or fourth generation from the pioneers. I guess some of it still remained. But I wasn't too conscious of it. When I think back to my childhood it reminds me of what I read about countries that are emerging. They are just beginning, some of them, to realize they can have a better life, but they will have to begin with what they have, and that takes education and training. This country was built on hard work.

"The other day I went on a trip, my wife and I, to Arizona. I had been there before. The desert country has an appeal, with the openness of the space. We drove around for four days. And I got to thinking about the first people who went and settled Arizona, and the difficult times they had crossing canyons, rivers, finding water, and protecting themselves from the Indians who were unfriendly—not all were, but some were. And I'm just thankful that I live in a country that has a heritage of people who are willing to look beyond the horizon and catch a vision of opening up new country for others to enjoy a better life.

"I think religion had a great part to play in the pioneer spirit. Because, in the pioneer spirit, at the back of the mind you know you are going to make things better for the generations to follow. Part of the motivation for that would come from religion. I think they are so closely intertwined you couldn't separate them."

The frontier, nature, faith, work, the contract with other men—in Judge Sugg's world picture the ideas were as knitted together as they were in the world picture of William, the businessman. The Baptist faith made both men complete, each in his own way. But Judge Sugg had also been led by his faith and his past (the two things almost one) to an unlikely compassion—for black people, who had formed 30 percent of the population of his little home town.

"I grew up with blacks that I knew intimately, played with—many blacks my own age. And I thought that they were for the most part a deeply spiritual people. After our church was over we used to go to the black churches on Sunday night and stand outside to listen to them sing, and also to see. We enjoyed hearing and seeing them. I remember an old black man we called Uncle Steve. I don't remember his last name. He played a tambourine. And many times it was the only accompaniment—but it was enough. They had rhythm. You could hardly stand still hearing the songs. Many of the songs they made up. Those songs have a great message."

So it must make him unhappy, what had happened to the blacks in the cities, and in Jackson?

He said: "Being black is not the reason. There are also many whites in that position. The reason is they don't have any spiritual values. Somebody asked Jesus one time what the greatest commandment was. The first one was: Love God. The second was: Love your neighbor as yourself. And that to me is the effect of Christian principles applied daily."

Mississippi's reputation for violence towards blacks was deserved. "Especially in the 1960s, many people were unwilling to acknowledge that black people had the same rights and privileges as people of other colors. I think this was a holdover from the days of slavery, when the blacks were servants and were looked upon as property, not people. And we white people have got to recognize the fact that God loves *everybody*."

I told him about my conversation with Alex Sanders, the Court of Appeals judge in South Carolina. Judge Sanders had said that the change of heart in the South, the acceptance by white people of black people's rights, might have had a divine cause.

Judge Sugg said: "I believe that God has to create a change of heart —from our adhering to the principles I have mentioned. He has set up the principles there, and I have to accept it. He didn't strike me with a bolt of lightning and say, 'Hey, son, love that black man.' Remember that I grew up in a society where black people were not permitted to enter your front door. They were servants. I had to do some soul-searching."

"When did you start doing that?"

"Early. Before the sixties. And I finally came to the conclusion that when he said love your neighbor as yourself—I came to the conclusion that the black man was your neighbor too. And I believe I've overcome 99.9 percent of the attitudes someone would have, growing up in a society of white supremists.

"Well, here again I haven't had any bolt of lightning. It's been a slow, steady acceptance of the truth that's been with us since the world began. For example, I am now teaching a black man to read and write. He's thirty-nine years old. I count him as one of my friends. We go fishing together. He went to school through the eighth grade, but he lived in a rural community. His father was a farmer. So when school started in September he had to stay at home and pick cotton, gather the corn and other crops. So that by the time he finally entered the school in November all the books had been given out, and he just sat in class. From time to time he had to miss school to cut firewood. Had to drop out in the spring to prepare the land for planting. The result was he didn't go to school for half the school year. He could read a little, write a little, but not enough to function in our society. He is a good man; he has a good job; he works hard. He is deeply religious, married, with three children. Illiterate people are not dumb. Most of them have real good minds."

This was how Judge Sugg touched on the work that had been

occupying his retirement: the teaching of English to illiterate people and to "internationals."

"I regard it as religious work. It gives me an opportunity to share my faith with the people I teach. The Christian faith is built on the great principle that we have to help our fellow man."

When he was sixty, and while he was still a judge, he had taken a Baptist workshop in the teaching of English as a second language. He had done so with his wife's encouragement.

"Two months after I took the workshop this young man appeared before me charged with burglary. He was fifteen years old. I sentenced him to the training school. The next day one of his sisters appeared and told me that he had got into trouble because his older brother led him to assist in the crime. The older brother was an ex-convict. The father and mother of the young man were both alcoholics, and he had gone to school for only part of one year—that was all the school he had gone to in his life. The sister told me that if I would give him a chance she would provide him with a home and get him a job. I told her that if she provided him with a home I would teach him to read and write. So I did. At the end of little more than a year he could read and write. His father was no longer an alcoholic. So I permitted him to return to Texas with his mother and father."

There was a moving symmetry to the judge's career. The man who had grown up in an isolated, inward-looking community had now, in his busy retirement, found a mission. His faith had seen him through all the changes of his circumstances. At every moment his faith had been part of the completeness of his world.

I HAD the vaguest idea of what a redneck was. Someone intolerant and uneducated—that was what the word suggested. And it fitted in with what I had been told in New York: that some motoring organizations gave their members maps of safe routes through the South, to steer them away from areas infested with rednecks. Then I also became aware that the word had been turned by some middle-class people into a romantic word; and that in this extension it stood for the unintellectual, physical, virile man, someone who (for instance) wouldn't mind saying "shit" in company.

It wasn't until I met Campbell that I was given a full and beautiful and lyrical account, an account that ran it all together, by a man who half looked down on and half loved the redneck, and who, when he began to speak of redneck pleasures, was moved to confess that he was half a redneck himself.

It wasn't for his redneck side, strictly speaking, that I had been introduced to Campbell. I had been told that he was the new kind of young conservative, with strong views on race and welfare. (Judge Sugg had told me that people of that type were still coming up, but that his own way, of understanding and help, was the way ahead and was the way most people would eventually go.) Campbell was also the man who represented the other side of the religious South: the authoritarian side. And it was of family and values and authority that we spoke, all quite predictably, until it occurred to me to ask, "Campbell, what do you understand by the word 'redneck'?"

And—as though it had been prepared—a great Theophrastan "character," something almost in the style of the seventeenth-century character-writers, poured out of Campbell. It might have been an updated version of something from Elizabethan low-life writing, or John Earle's *Microcosmography,* or something from Sir Thomas Overbury. (Sir Thomas Overbury, on the English country gentleman, 1616: "His travel is seldom farther than the next market town, and his inquisition is about the price of corn. When he travelleth, he will go ten mile out of the way to a cousin's house of his to save charges; and rewards the servants by taking them by the hand when he departs.")

Campbell said, "A redneck is a lower blue-collar construction worker who definitely doesn't like blacks. He likes to drink beer. He's going to wear cowboy boots. . . ."

That was the concrete, lyrical way Campbell spoke. But it would be better at this point to go back and hear a little of what he said about himself.

"My father was born in Alabama, and his family picked themselves up, left the farm they owned, 360 acres, left it and came to Mississippi to get an education. His father, my father's father, and his mother said, 'We got to get you guys over there to get you a good education.' They obviously had some money saved to do that, pick up and leave. They kept the farm. Daddy sold it all five or six years ago. And when they came to Mississippi all the brothers got jobs when they weren't in school. My father left Alabama in 1923–24. Graduated in 1928. Wound up having a garage and gas station. But they were happy. I never heard my father say a curse word in his life, and that's the truth. He worked all the damn time. We weren't ever real close. He didn't have time to be close.

"My mother was a schoolteacher. I grew up in the Baptist church. I was pretty force-fed. We went to church as soon as the doors opened. We went there on Wednesdays for the prayer meeting. We would go for the big summer revivals. Go every night, bored to death."

Then, without a pause, Campbell said: "In the long run it was the best thing I've ever had. My mom and dad gave me values that came back to me when I was twenty years old. But I'd rebelled out. Most of the children conformed. I really wanted to act crazy. I drank more, ran around more. I started working in a grocery store when I was twelve, and that's the damned truth. I loved it. You met all the characters. You got all the black trade. They sat on the feed bags; Mama came to town with four or five kids, and she had to nurse a couple. I liked working there. Always somebody coming in there. Hee-hawing all the time. You knew everybody who came in. It was a good store. This was Saturdays. I liked the money. When I started I made four dollars a day. When I left I was making about seven.

"I cut right away. I drove a damn dumper in the summertime. They were constructing this interstate and they needed somebody who could read and write, to count the sacks of fertilizer that went into the airplane. They were fertilizing the sides of the road to get the grass to grow. It was boring as hell. These are days long gone. It's funny how you change and mature. I wanted to be crazy. I had a good time being crazy."

"You wanted to be one of the boys?"

"It's important in Northeast Jackson, as we call it, to be well liked, to be well thought of. But I wasn't relating to the church. I'd go with my mama at Christmastime, but I was bored to death. But the values of the church—do good, do right, don't drink, don't kill anybody, no stealing, the Ten Commandments, don't covet your neighbor's wife—I don't believe in some parts of this culture those values are being instilled. Those kids running up and down—I used to work in mobile-home parks, and we've got some unsavory characters there—they need their butts worn out, like I've gotten mine worn out.

"I think the reason for that is the breakdown of the family. Where the father and mother are not both there doing their job. I bring up my children to respect me. And I think he fears me, and I think that's good, because he knows I'm not going to put up with everything. I hug him and kiss him every day. Some people say I'm right; some people say I'm wrong. I was afraid of my father. I was afraid I was going to get my behind worn out. I don't like it any other way. People saying 'Yah,' 'Nah'—smart-mouth children—I think they'd do so much better if they worked hard for just ten more minutes every day, and if they said 'Yes, sir,' 'No, sir,' and you whipped their ass until they said it right.

"I think it all goes back to being brought up right. Get some values back in the homes. We're talking about blacks now. Get them to stay in the school, keep their damn butts quiet. I'd be a dictator and have this place shaped up. I'm just a law-and-order, blood-and-guts guy."

Campbell was in his early forties or late thirties. He was short and chunky, a strong man. He wore bright colors. He talked like a man with a character to keep up, but there was no touch of humor in his voice or face.

He had seen the black area of Jackson spread. And he had made money out of that, buying from fleeing whites and selling at a profit to the blacks moving in. There was one year when he had sold ten houses like that, and had made $60,000.

"That wasn't bad. I was profiteering. I ought to be shot."

I wasn't sure what was "character," and what was real. And then I said, "Campbell, what do you understand by the word 'redneck'?"

And the man was transformed.

He said: "A redneck is a lower blue-collar construction worker who definitely doesn't like blacks. He likes to drink beer. He's going to wear cowboy boots; he is not necessarily going to have a cowboy hat. He is going to live in a trailer someplace out in Rankin County, and he's going to smoke about two and a half packs of cigarettes a day and drink about ten cans of beer at night, and he's going to be mad as hell if he doesn't have some cornbread and peas and fried okra and some fried pork chops to eat—I've never seen one of those bitches yet who doesn't like fried pork chops. And he'll be late on his trailer payment.

"He's been raised that way. His father was just like him. And the son of a bitch loves country music. They love to hunt and fish. They go out all night to the Pearl River. They put out a trot line—a long line running across the river, hooks on it every four or five feet. They bait them with damn old crawfish, and that line'll sink to the bottom, and they'll go to the bank and shit and drink all night long, and they'll get a big fire going. They'll check it two or three times in the night, to see if they're getting a catfish. It'll be good catfish. These redneck sons of bitches say that they'll rather have one of these river catfish than one of those pond catfish. They say it's got a better taste.

"You know, I like those rednecks. They're so laid back. They don't give a shit. They don't give a shit."

"Is that because they're descendants of pioneers?"

"There's no question about it. They're descendants of pioneers. They're satisified to live in those mobile homes. I never knew how my father was so cultured. If you saw the place he came from—he came from the most absolute, the most desolate place in the woods on the Mississippi-Alabama border. The rednecks have the pioneer attitude, all right. They don't want to go to the damn country club and play golf. They ain't got fifteen damn cents, and they're just tickled to death.

"They're Scotch-Irish in origin. A lot of them intermarried, interbred. I'm talking about the good old rednecks now. He's going to have an old eight-to-five job. But there's an upscale redneck, and he's going to want it cleaned up. Yard mowed, a little garden in the back. Old Mama, she's gonna wear designer jeans and they're gonna go to Shoney's to eat once every three weeks."

I had seen any number of those restaurants beside the highways, but had never gone into one. Were they like McDonald's?

Campbell said, "At Shoney's you'll get the gravy all over it. That's going to be a big deal. They'll love it. I know those sons of bitches.

"If he or she moves to North Jackson, he'd be upscale. He wouldn't be having that twang so much. But the good old fellow, he's just going to work six or eight months a year. He's going to tell his old lady, 'I'm going to work.' And he ain't going. If it rains, he ain't going to work—shit, no. He's going to go to the crummiest dump he can find, and he's going to start drinking beer and shooting pool. When he gets home there'll be a little quarrel with his wife, and he'll be half drunk and eat a little cornbread and pass out, and that's the damn truth. And she'll understand, because she's so used to it.

"She doesn't drink. It's normally the redneck guys who drink—whiskey or beer. She's got some little piddling job. She's probably the basis of the income. She's going to try to work every day. But he's always waiting for that big job at fifteen dollars an hour, which is never going to come around. One time he had a union job at twelve dollars an hour. And he thinks that's going to come back. He'll be waiting fifteen years for another twelve-dollar job. And he won't get it unless he gets off his ass and goes to Atlanta, Georgia, or Nashville—someplace that's hot. It's sure not hot around here. But he's so damn satisfied. The son of a bitch's so damn satisfied. When he gets the four-dollar job: 'No, I got something else to do.' I could give five guys a job today, minimum wage. Three-thirty-five an hour. But I wouldn't find five sons of bitches if I looked all damn day long. 'You want to work for three-thirty-five?' 'No. Not going to work for no three-thirty-five son of a bitch.'

"So he's going to be making six dollars on an average, six to six and a half an hour. And just for six, eight months a year. You see, he doesn't want to work all day long. He's satisfied by getting by. They don't like to be told what to do. It's the independent spirit. It's the old pioneer attitude. 'I've got enough to eat, drink, and a little shelter. What more do I want?'

"Religion? They'll go to church when the wife beats the hell out of him. But he's not going to put on a coat and tie or anything. He won't do it. He'll kick her ass.

"They're not too sexual. They'd rather drink a bunch of old beer. And hang around with other males and go hunting, fishing. We're talking about the good old rednecks now. Not the upscale ones. They've got the dick still hard. That's damn true.

"The rednecks are about sixty to sixty-five percent of the white population. I'm running the good old rednecks and the upscale rednecks and a whole bunch of lower-middle-class rednecks. They have the same old attitude as the black people. Daddy is home a little more often. But they're tickled pink that they ain't got nothing. You wouldn't believe."

I asked about the dress, and especially the cowboy boots. Why were they so important?

"It's the image they have to project. They'll have an old baseball hat with the bill turned down just so. They won't have the cowboy hat. They want that particular redneck style. They want people to know that they don't give a damn. They want people to know: 'I'm a redneck and proud of it.'

"What you must put in, and make sure you do, is them sons of bitches *love* country-and-Western music. It's down-home music. It's crying music. Somebody got killed in a truck. Or a train ran over somebody. Or somebody ran away with somebody's wife.

"Presley is a redneck like you wouldn't believe. He's a double red-neck. Some of the women here would whip your ass for saying it. I'm probably a redneck myself."

And when he said that, Campbell won me over.

He said, "I just dress differently. Polo shirt and Corbin slacks."

I liked the concreteness of Campbell's details, the brand names, the revelation of a fashion code where I had just seen bright colors.

Abruptly, then, he went off on another track. "If my father hadn't worked so hard—and I know that was important, to work hard and try to do good—"

I got him back to the subject of redneck sex.

"If they're young they got it hard. But the older they get they drink more, and then they don't care about it any more. And she's just there, getting some clothes washed down in the laundromat once a week. Sit down and watch it and smoke some cigarettes—that's right, that's what she will do.

"I'll tell you. My son ain't gonna fool with a redneck girl in Rankin County. Can't hide it. Everybody knows everybody else. And I'll tell you something else. They talk different. And I want my children to stay in their social strata, and that's where they'll stay. I would say, 'Keith, you weren't brought up like that. You get your ass out of that. You're way above that, and we're going to stay way above that.' But Keith's all right. He wants to dress nice; he wants to look good; he wants to make money. We run in the Northeast Jackson crowd. That's supposed to be upscale."

I said, "But beauty is beauty. A beautiful woman is going to win admirers anywhere."

"Beauty is beauty. But when she opens her mouth and starts talking and says she lives in Rankin County—uh-*uh*—that's the end of any charm. But that case will probably never happen with me. It will never happen with my son, because he already knows what a redneck is. You know what the word comes from? The back of the man's neck is red from the sun—"

But something happened—somebody came into the room, someone asked a question—and Campbell didn't finish the thought. It was fin-ished for me some days later when I heard from an old Mississippian that the word "redneck," when he was a child, was not a pejorative; was the opposite, in fact, and meant a man who lived by the sweat of his brow; and that it was only in the 1950s, when the frontier or pioneer life was changing, that the word began to have unflattering associations.

Campbell said: "I admire them for their independence. But it's not right for the society now. No question about it. It was great a long time ago. But not now. You can't get business done in a modern city with that kind of mentality. We got to change that redneck society and that black society, or the wealth is going to be just in the few hands that it's always been in. As far as I'm concerned, I hope it stays like that. I ought to be shot."

He came back from that political pitch. He said: "Rednecks like four-wheel-drives. Four-wheel drive pickup trucks. They can run down everywhere through the swamps. And some of them like an old beat-up van, half-painted. Half-painted, because he's going to fix this side but he's never going to get around to the other side. He'll drive that son of a bitch forever, until it falls apart or gets a flat tire, and he'll just leave it then. He won't have a spare, you see. And he'll come back that afternoon and get it fixed. He'll get one of his buddies to get an old tire, and they'll go and fix it. The sons of bitches can fix anything on a car. Them bastards can do anything. They can drag the car to the side of the highway and jack it up and fix it on the spot."

The morning was over. Campbell had a business lunch. He was going just as he was, in his bright, horizontally striped green-and-yellow jersey, the stripes of varying width. But he had so enjoyed talking of redneck life; it had brought back so many memories of his own "crazy" youth, and prompted so many yearnings, that he wanted to talk a little more, and he promised to come again, in the afternoon, after his lunch and before a business trip to Florida.

He telephoned after his lunch. I asked how it had gone.

"I'm smelling like hell. A whole load of garlic at lunch. But made money. Unusual, a business lunch where I actually made money."

We met later, in a hotel bar. He had been drinking to celebrate his deal. His eyes were moist, a little bloodshot. He had spoken deadpan in the morning; and he spoke deadpan now. But the drink had made his speech chaste. He spoke no swear word, no unnecessary or blaspheming intensive.

I said I had been thinking over what he had said about the rednecks. From the way he had described them, I thought of them as a tribe, almost an Indian tribe, free spirits wandering freely over empty spaces. But weren't they now a little cramped, even in Mississippi?

Campbell said: "It's a nice life, but it depends on a natural life being available. I would say that if those rednecks didn't have these natural surroundings in Mississippi—because the outdoor thing's their favorite pastime—they would be very bored. And hunting rights are becoming so valuable now, they're going to be forced out of the market within five years. We've got a lot of people coming up this far north now from Louisiana, because we have a lot of deer, big deer, and they're paying big prices for hunting rights. I bet you couldn't drive forty-five minutes out of Jackson without finding land that wasn't leased. It's going to have a 'Posted' sign: 'This land is leased by So-and-So Hunting Club. Don't Trespass.' One day there's going to be a killing about it, I tell you. They've already had a couple of killings in the state. Duck-hunting especially—it's so competitive in the Delta, so valuable, so expensive to get a lease up there. You've got to have a lot of money. It will cost you about three thousand dollars a year to hunt duck. Though duck-hunting is more of a gentleman's sport. Those rednecks are more meat-hunters.

"Still, there's a lot of land in Mississippi. They'll poach on somebody. Otherwise they'll just be beer-drinkers and have no place to go and nothing to do. It's what's worrying me about rednecks. They're not adapting, and they're being left behind. As the population grows, it's going to be more and more expensive for them to go out hunting, and they're not going to be able to afford it.

"At the moment they have some dog clubs. They get in real cheap somewhere and they'll do some deal, some deal with somebody's family —fifteen, twenty, thirty guys in a family deal; cousins, all of them on family land. All getting together ten or twelve times a year. And they'll have a ball."

"What about the women? Do they go out on those trips?"

"They just sit at home. They're worrying about where the next sack of potatoes is coming from. But they can live on a hundred dollars a week. Cheaper than you and I. And they're not skinny. Some of them are big and fat. What am I saying? They're *all* big and fat.

"After lunch, you know, I went back to the office. The secretary's a redneck woman. I told her about our talk this morning. About the rednecks and the frontier mentality. Telling her it's not so great these days, you know. Different times. And she said, 'You know, Mr. Campbell, at one time I used to be envious of you. I wanted what you had. But now I feel I'm just different. I'm just born into it. I ain't got nothing, and I know now I ain't going to have nothing.' I said, 'It's because you ain't got the right kind of husband. Why don't you kick your husband's ass?' And she said, 'Oh, Mr. Campbell, I can't do that. He's just an old redneck.' And her children are just like him.

"Presley, he was the all-time neck. And that fellow there, that fellow at the desk with the long hair and beard."

He was talking about a man with a red plaid shirt hanging out of his trousers. This man was walking delicately on the floor, as though nervous of slipping on it with the leather soles of his cowboy boots.

Campbell said, "He's probably thinking, with that hair and beard, that he's God's gift to the world. But he's just a neck. He's as lost as a goose. He's never been on a tiled floor in his life. He's come in here thinking it was another motel. He doesn't know what to do. He's just moping around here: 'Oh shit, where am I?' "

ART HALLOWS, creates, makes one see. And though other people said other things about rednecks—though one man said that the best way of dealing with them was to have nothing to do with them, that their tempers were too close to the surface, that they were too little educated to cope with what they saw as slights, too little educated to understand human behavior, or to understand people who were not like themselves; that their exaggerated sense of slight and honor could make them talk with you and smile even while they were planning to blow your head off—though this was the received wisdom, Campbell's description of their mode of living made me see pride and style and a fashion code where I had seen nothing, made me notice what so far I hadn't sufficiently noticed: the pickup trucks dashingly driven, the baseball caps marked with the name of some company.

The next day, a Saturday, there was a crowd in the hotel and the restaurant across the parking area from the hotel. And, as if in fulfillment of Campbell's description of the redneck style, three men got out of a dented and dusty car and opened the trunk to take out their redneck boots. They had arrived in gym shoes. They took off their gym shoes and put on their cowboy boots before going into the hotel.

One among them was opening a bottle of beer with his teeth. I felt now, after Campbell, that the man doing that very redneck thing perhaps needed a little courage. Perhaps, entering the hotel and walking on the tiled floor, he was going to feel "as lost as a goose."

For some days Campbell's words and phrases sang in my head, and I spoke them to others. One afternoon I went to a farm just outside Jackson. Someone there, knowing of my new craze, came to me and said, "There are three of your rednecks fishing in the pond." And I hurried to see them, as I might have hurried to see an unusual bird or a deer. And there, indeed, they were, bare-backed, but with the wonderful baseball hats, in a boat among the reeds, on a weekday afternoon —people who, before Campbell had spoken, I might have seen flatly, but now saw as people with a certain past, living out a certain code, a threatened species.

It gave a new poetry to what one saw on the highway: the baseball caps with the bill "turned down just so," the bandeaux or sweat bands on the forehead of women drivers of redneck-style pickup trucks. Even the advertisements in the newspapers for those trucks—and the price: about $8,000—had a new meaning.

AND IT was of the redneck, the unlikely descendant of the frontiersman, that I talked to Eudora Welty when I went to call on her. I had arrived early, and waited on the street below the dripping trees. She was ready early, and could clearly be seen through her uncurtained front window. But I was nervous of knocking too soon.

So for a while we waited below the big, dripping trees in the gloom after rain, she behind her window at the end of her wet front garden, I in the car. And when I felt the time was suitable I walked up the wet path to her front door. On the door, in her strong writing, was a note asking people not to bring any more books for her to sign. She wanted to save as much of her energy as possible now for her work. I knocked; and she opened, like someone waiting to do just that. She was extraordinarily familiar from her photographs.

The frontier was so much in her stories: a fact I had only just begun to appreciate. And she was willing to talk of the frontiersman character.

"He's not a villain. But there's a whole side of him that's *cunning.* Sometimes it goes over the line and he becomes an outright scoundrel. The blacks never lived in that part of the state. They came over to work on the plantations. Most of the rednecks grew up without black people, and yet they hate them. That's where all the bad things originate—that's the appeal they make. Rednecks worked in sawmills and things like that. And they had small farms. They are all fiercely proud. They dictate the politics of the state. They take their excitement—in those small towns—when the politicians and evangelists come. Scare everybody, outwit everybody, beat everybody, kill everybody—that's the frontiersman's mentality."

I told her the story Ellen had heard as a child about the rednecks to the south of the town where she had spent her summers: the story of traveling salesmen who had been roughed up and hitched to a plow and made to plow a field. Ellen had said that this story had come down from the past; and I had thought of it as a romantic story of the wickedness of times past, an exaggerated story about people living without law. But Eudora Welty took the story seriously. She said, "I can believe the story about the salesmen. I've heard about punishing people by making them plow farms."

We talked about Mississippi and its reputation.

"At the time of the troubles many people passed through and called on me. They wanted me to confirm what they thought. And all of them thought I lived in a state of terror. 'Aren't you scared of them all the time?' A young man came and said that he had been told that a Mr. So-and-So, who was a terrible racist, owned all of Jackson, all the banks and hotels, and that he was doing terrible things to black people. It was a fantasy. It wasn't true. The violence here is not nearly as frightening as the Northern—urban—brand."

A frontier state, limited culturally—had that been hard for her as a writer, and as a woman writer? The richness of a writer depends to some extent on the society he or she writes about.

She said: "There is a lot behind it, the life of the state. There is the great variety of the peoples who came and settled the different sections. There is a great awareness of that as you get older—you see what things have stemmed from. The great thing taught me here as a writer is a sense of continuity. In a place that hasn't changed much you get to know the generations. You can see the whole narrative of a town's history or a family's history."

I HAD been hearing more and more about the unusual constitution of the state of Mississippi, the constitution drafted in 1890, after the Civil War and Reconstruction. I had heard that this constitution was responsible for a good deal of what one saw still; and I went to see former Governor William Winter about it. He had a high reputation in the state, both as a governor and as a man knowledgeable about the state's history.

Mr. Winter saw me in his office late one afternoon, at the end of a busy day; that morning he had flown to Little Rock, Arkansas. The former governor was now a partner in a Jackson law firm. He spoke precisely and legally; he had books and a map ready; and all the time we spoke he was looking up references in books.

On the wall of his office—and among color photographs of his family—was a large, old map of the state. When he went to get me a cold diet-cola drink I got up and looked at it. It was linen-mounted and framed, and had been a gift to Mr. Winter. It was a French map, of 1830 perhaps. It showed only the southern counties of the state as settled. A large central area had been marked out for further white settlement. Though this area was almost as large as all the settled counties put together, on the map it was just called Hinds County (and part of that area was to become the Rankin County of which Campbell had spoken with so much feeling). The areas to the east and north were still, in 1830, Indian country: Choctaws and Chickasaws.

Half the state Indian country in 1830; in 1860, the Civil War about to come; in 1890, after the Civil War and Reconstruction, a new constitution. History here seemed to come in thirty-year segments. Add the yellow-fever epidemics of 1873, 1874, 1878, 1903; add the Great Depression. There was nothing settled, stable.

The former governor said: "The atmosphere in which the 1890 constitution was written was dominated by the need for whites to provide a means for the restoration of white control of the political processes of the state. The constitution of 1861 did not afford a vehicle for the elimination of black voters and black officeholders. There were many black officeholders when the 1890 constitution was written." There were two black senators, a black congressman, a black lieutenant governor, and a black superintendent of education. "The 1890 constitution of Mississippi became a model for other Southern states—in its resourceful provisions for the discouragement of black voting."

Almost as important as the racial provisions were the antibusiness provisions. The people who wrote the constitution wanted the state to remain "a pastoral state, an agricultural state." They didn't want big business or the corporations coming in, encouraging "unfavorable competition for jobs with the agricultural community."

"We threw various roadblocks in the path of corporate development. It had the effect of discouraging investment in industrial plants in the state. A major paper-manufacturing company, the Gaylord Corporation, desired to locate in Pearl River, Mississippi. Because of the constitutional limitations here, that plant located across the river, in Louisiana, within sight of Pearl River County, and virtually created a new town in Louisiana, Bogalusa. There was a limit in Mississippi on the amount of property a corporation could own, a limit on the capital structure of a corporation. Even in 1890 that constitution singled us out as being noncompetitive for capital.

"There is an archaic tone to the whole document. We need the psychological benefit now of a late-twentieth-century document. And, the second thing, we need the restructuring of the manner in which we govern the state. We have to eliminate many of the processes designed to decentralize and fragment power. In 1890 there was a distrust of any concentration of power in any one individual. With the result that there's not a single law that's passed by the Mississippi legislature that is in strict accordance with the constitution of 1890."

He handled a mighty law book and showed me Section 59 of the 1890 constitution.

"Bills may originate in either house, and be amended or rejected in the other; and every bill shall be read on three different days in each house, unless two-thirds of the house where the same is pending shall dispense with the rule; and every bill shall be read in full immediately before the vote on its final passage; and every bill, having passed both houses, shall be signed by the president of the senate and the speaker of the house of representatives, in open session; but before either shall sign any bill, he shall give notice thereof, suspend business in the house over which he presides, have the bill read by its title, and, on the demand of any member, have it read in full; and all such proceedings shall be entered on the journal."

There was a provision in the section for amendment, so that laws could be passed. But an awkward member could still cause delay. "I have seen it happen. I have seen one member stand up and demand that the bill be read."

Was there an element of madness in the framers of the constitution?

"It was an anti-government legislation. It was intended to make it as difficult as possible to pass legislation. The attitude being: The fewer bills we have, the better off we are going to be. The less government the better—that is a fair way to put it."

"What sort of men were they in 1890?"

"They represented the ultraconservative, planter, agricultural interests. Many of them were veterans of the Civil War. There was a strong racial bias which ran through the membership. They were committed to eliminating the black presence in the political process."

"Do you think there was anything like a romantic feeling for the land?"

"It was a feeling for the land of the landowner, not the worker. The yeoman farmer was not the dominant feature of the convention. The constitution spoke to the economic interests of those who drafted it. For instance, it spoke of the maintenance of a levee system along the Mississippi River—which really has no place in a constitution.

"The story about that is like this. In the spring of 1890 the levees gave way and parts of the Delta were inundated. To cope with that, the constitution-framers later that year, 1890, wrote into the constitution a whole article designed to cope with such disasters. Article 11."

He showed it to me. It ran to eight pages. It dealt in great detail, technical and fiscal, with the way the levees were to be maintained; it outlined taxation to meet the expenses; it mentioned the names of vanished railroad companies.

"An article like this really has no place in the constitution of a state. But you can see the preoccupation of the drafters. They were looking after their farms up in the Delta."

There might have been no romantic feeling for the land. But how did the former governor explain the anti-government tone of the constitution?

"It reflected the basic frontier aspect of the state. They were saying: 'We're going to use government to solve those problems that appear to us important, but we're not going to use government to interfere with our lives.' As it was used, the constitution worked against the powerless in the state. But that is no longer a valid objection. Corrections have been made."

And the constitution has left its mark. "The Carolinas and Georgia had tobacco-processing plants and textile plants. Alabama has a well-established industrial base going back to the nineteenth century. Mississippi never developed this kind of base."

On the former governor's desk, and got out for our meeting, was a map of the United States showing, for 1984, the "economically competitive" counties and the "distressed" counties. The competitive counties were colored blue, the distressed counties pink. The map showed three concentrated areas of distressed counties: on the Mexican border; the Indian areas in the West; and, making almost one pink area, the Southern Black Belt of Alabama and almost all of Mississippi. Only the area around Jackson was colored blue.

AND YET, though there was distress—comparatively speaking: American distress was not like the distress in other countries—and though many people would agree with what the former governor said about the archaic nature of the constitution, there was also in some people a nervousness about change. The frontier constitution had grown to represent something true about the state. Many people now grieved for the past which that constitution had secured, when life was "easier," more countrylike; when communities were small and everyone knew everyone else; when time was not money.

In the 1830 map in the former governor's office Hinds County had been marked out for settlement by people whose descendants were to become the rednecks of Campbell's poetry. Now the rednecks, like the Indians before them, found their hunting grounds shrinking.

IT HAD been a frontier state, but always with this contradictory component of slavery. It was of slavery that the old plantation land around Natchez, on the river, spoke. That land, as flat and warm and soft as the ricelands of South Carolina, spoke of wealth and the need for black men, by the thousands. But Natchez also had its plantation houses, nowadays the object twice a year of "pilgrimages": the old sentimentality of the South, the divided mind, the beauty and sorrow of the past containing the unmentionable, ragged, black thing of slavery.

It was a wretched little town, steaming after rain on its "bluff"—not very high—beside the muddy river. Rain dripped from the heavy branches of the red and white crape-myrtle trees. It had had an oil boom. That boom, like so many other Southern booms, had abated.

Louisiana lay across the river. I drove there, hoping to find some solid, real place—rather than something connected with the tourist trade—to have lunch in. It was flat, delta country. The air that came through the car's air conditioning smelled of onions. It was this high smell, as much as the flatness of the land and the apparent hopelessness of my quest—just fast-food places beside the highway: tall, beckoning signs above, simple structures below, bright colors against the flat green—that drove me back to Natchez.

The Louisiana town was called Vidalia. Vidalia was also the name of a kind of onion. It must have been a delicacy in the South; in many places I had seen home-painted signs at the roadside offering Vidalia onions. So I smelled onions until I got back to Natchez, where I had the jungle-sewer smell, the smell of the river, which was almost exactly like the jungle-sewer smell of Manaus, on the Amazon, in Brazil. Just as the rusting corrugated-iron roofs and the relaxed black people sitting in old wooden houses or standing or rocking and staring gave a touch of the West Indies—as disturbing to one's sense of place as the overgrown tennis courts of Tuskegee had been: those courts one afternoon, with African students at play, had absolutely suggested Africa.

And I was wrong about the Louisiana town of Vidalia. A woman in a souvenir shop with a little view of the river told me so. The Vidalia of the onions was in Georgia, however much I might have smelled onions in Vidalia, Louisiana.

The woman, suffering—trade wasn't so good—said: "My husband loves Vidalia onions. On Sundays"—they lived on the other side of the river—"when we are going to the club, he will say, 'Susan, get a couple of Vidalia onions.' I will say, 'To take to the club? On Sunday?' And he will say, '*Bring* me the onions.' He has a black girl up there in the club who spoils him. He loves bread, butter, ketchup, and slices and slices of Vidalia onions. She fixes it for him."

There was a cloudburst. I looked over her stock. She was selling a big black mammy in a long red dress over a white blouse.

She said, "The day I bought them I said to Pearlene—she's the cook—'Pearlene, do you know what I've done this morning? I've bought two of you.' It broke her up, and she said, 'Well, at least you could buy me the dress to go with it.' "

It cleared up. But as soon as I went outside it began to rain again. I went back into the shop.

I said, "I don't want to get a cold."

She said, "The first year I ran this place I got bronchitis every day. If it wasn't for my husband, I wouldn't have stuck it out. But then somehow I developed an immunity. Silver tarnishes in three days in this kind of weather. Polishing silver every three days can't be good for the silver."

The rain fell harder, big, splashing drops. She talked on, pleased to have the company, in the middle of her Natchez souvenirs. The Mississippi was hazed with mist and rain; the bridge was indistinct; the Louisiana bank couldn't be seen.

And when I got back to Jackson—driving along the Indian Natchez Trace Parkway—I found that the rain, and the great heat, and my own ignorance of the beauties to look for, had kept me from the other wonder of Natchez. The river was altering its course; the bank at some place was being washed away; and some of the pretty old houses of planter days were collapsing into the river.

> And every gal on Natchez bluff
> Will cry as we go by, oh.

They were lines brought back to me by the weather, and the heat, and the thought of plantation labor: lines, perhaps mangled by memory, from a long narrative poem about the Civil War by Stephen Vincent Benét, which I had looked at forty years before.

6

◪◪◪

Sanctities

DRIVING BACK one stormy afternoon in Mississippi from the Delta to Jackson, and excited by the dark sky, the rain, the lightning, the lights of cars and trucks, the spray that rose window-high from heavy wheels, I began to be aware of the great pleasure I had taken in traveling in the South. Romance, a glow of hopefulness and freedom, had already begun to touch the earlier stages of the journey: my arrival at Atlanta, the drive from there to Charleston. I had all but forgotten the writing anxieties I had had on both those occasions.

And I thought that afternoon that it would have completed my pleasure if I didn't have to write anything; if I didn't have to worry about what to do next and who to see; if I could simply be with the experience. But if I wasn't writing, if I didn't have a purpose and at times a feeling of urgency, if the writing hadn't given me a schedule, places to go to, how would I have passed the days at the Ramada Renaissance hotel in Jackson, beside the freeways? Would I have even come to Mississippi?

The land was big and varied, in parts wild. But it had nearly everywhere been made uniform and easy for the traveler. One result was that no travel book (unless the writer was writing about himself) could be only about the roads and the hotels. Such a book could have been written a hundred years ago. (Fanny Kemble's account of traveling in

1838 from Philadelphia to the Georgia Sea Islands, by rail and stage-coach, partly on a road covered with logs, is a proper adventure.)

Such a book can still be written about certain countries in Africa, say. It is often enough for a traveler in that kind of country to say, more or less, "This is me here. This is me getting off the old native bus and being led by strange boys, making improper proposals, to some squalid lodging. This is me having a drink in a bar with some local characters. This is me getting lost later that night."

This kind of traveler is not really a discoverer. He is more a man defining himself against a foreign background; and, depending on who he is, the book he writes can be attractive. A book like that can be written about the United States only if the writer, taking the reader into his confidence, sets himself up as alien or outlandish in some way. Generally, though, this approach cannot work in the United States. The place is not and cannot be alien in the simple way an African country is alien. It is too well known, too photographed, too written about; and, being more organized and less informal, it is not so open to casual inspection.

I had been concerned, from the start of my own journey, to establish some lines of inquiry, to define a theme. The approach had its difficulties. At the back of my mind was always a worry that I would come to a place and all contacts would break down and I would not get beyond the uniformity of highway and chain hotel (the very romance I was surrendering to that afternoon in the Delta). If you travel on a theme, the theme has to develop with the travel. At the beginning your interests can be broad and scattered. But then they must be more focused; the different stages of a journey cannot simply be versions of one another. And, more than the other kind of travel, this traveling on a theme depended on luck. It depended on the people you met, the little illuminations you had. As with the next day's issue of a fast-moving daily newspaper, the shape of the chapter in hand was continually being changed by accidents on the way.

Pure luck—our conversation had begun so tamely—had given me Campbell's lyrical account of the rednecks of Rankin County: the outdoor life, relic of frontier self-sufficiency, mixed up with a dislike of black people, and oddly meshed with the love of country music, "down-home music, crying music," and the cult of Elvis Presley.

That meeting with Campbell (putting to flight ideas about Faulkner and Oxford, Mississippi) had suggested to me how I might move.

Though I knew little about music; and the achievement of Presley, while he lived, had passed me by.

P RESLEY'S BIRTHPLACE was in the small town of Tupelo in northern Mississippi.

The businessman who was taking me there said, "He was the lowest of the low." He spoke gravely, without compassion; and with a very slight toss of the head. His distaste for the lowness he had in mind was touched with something like awe.

I remembered Campbell's words, and quoted them: " 'The all-time neck'?"

"Lower than that."

In a magazine in the Jackson hotel I had seen a photograph of the narrow, two-roomed "shotgun" house, front porch opening into bedroom opening into back kitchen. I had expected, from the photograph, to find a preserved building in an urban wasteland. But Tupelo was a busy little town, one of the busier business places in Mississippi, and the area around the Presley birthplace had become suburban, with the house itself like somebody's ancillary cabin (or "dependency") in the shade of a tree, with lawn all around.

On the front porch was a swing seat for two, hung on chains fixed to the ceiling. The front room was the bedroom. It was freshly papered, with a simple floral design; and on one wall was a framed printed copy of the "If" poem.

I asked the woman in attendance whether the poem had been there in the Presley days—in the days of Presley's father, that is, who was said to have built the house. It was a foolish question; the woman didn't answer. The businessman said that the paper on the walls in the old days would have been newspaper.

And of course the house had been made to look as pretty as possible, with the swing seat and the bedstead and the period stuff in the kitchen—like something from the Mississippi Agriculture and Forestry Museum in Jackson, where the artifacts, the household tools, of only a few years before had been put on reverential display because, though so recent, they were part of a special country past which many people had shared and which had now vanished. (In England the 1920s are within reach, like the day before yesterday. In Mississippi the 1920s are long ago, closer to the beginning of things.)

In the Mississippi museum the past on display could be felt as a kind of religion, a bonding. And there was something of that feeling in the prettied-up little shotgun house. (Imagine people living in that cramped space, though: imagine the crush, the disorder.) The very lowness of the man's origins had made him that much more sacred, to the—fattish—people who sat on the swing seat and had their photographs taken.

At the back of the house was a hall where cards and souvenirs and copies of Memphis newspapers printed the day after Presley's death in 1977 were on sale; and there was a new small chapel, with stained glass. At the side of the house was a park. Presley money had worked that magic. It was like the stories one heard—and these stories were always moving, the fulfillment of so many kinds of fantasies—of nurses in hospitals and other simple people whom Presley had surprised with the gift of a Cadillac.

In the souvenir shop the businessman said, "Did you get that woman's accent? Listen." He spoke with the awe with which he had spoken of Presley's origins. But my ears didn't have the fine local tuning. They didn't pick up what the businessman heard.

The businessman's attitude was historical. It had precedents almost as old as the state. Even Fanny Kemble, faced with the "pinelanders" of Georgia in 1839, is moved to rage and contempt, rejecting as unspeakable the people of her own race whom she sees as degenerate. One thinks of Fanny Kemble as gentle, hating injustice. But as a former actress, from a very great English acting family, she was also concerned with the way people looked. She hated slavery; but she didn't care for the physical appearance of the blacks on the American plantations (she thought the West Indian blacks were better-looking). And the passage about the pinelanders should be quoted in full. Its very repetitiveness catches the writer's confused emotion and shame:

"These are the so-called pinelanders of Georgia, I suppose the most degraded race of human beings claiming an Anglo-Saxon origin that can be found on the face of the earth—filthy, lazy, ignorant, brutal, proud, penniless savages, without one of the nobler attributes which have been found occasionally allied to the vices of savage nature. They own no slaves, for they are almost without exception abjectly poor; they will not work, for that, as they conceive, would reduce them to an equality with the abhorred Negroes; they squat, and steal, and starve, on the outskirts of this lowest of all civilized societies, and their countenances bear witness to the squalor of their condition and the utter degradation of their natures. To the crime of slavery, though they have no profitable part or lot in it, they are fiercely accessory, because it is the barrier that divides the black and white races, at the foot of which they lie wallowing in unspeakable degradation, but immensely proud of the base freedom which still separates them from the lash-driven tillers of the soil."

Georgia had been established in 1733 as a colony for free men. But within sixteen years the slave-owners had changed that; and communities of poor whites like the pinelanders, migrants from other states, had been created. There were no poor-white groups of comparable size in the West Indian slave colonies. There were only planters and slaves, in the main. So that after emancipation the islands became in effect black; and, without rednecks, there was on the islands no post-Reconstruction, "Southern"-style history. In the settling of the New World, and other new places in other continents, there were immense cruelties, not only to the local populations but also to the people transported. Long after any group can be held responsible, succeeding generations live on as victims or inheritors of old history.

I began to get some new feeling about the Presley cult at Tupelo: the birthplace of the man of the people, the saint of the people, made pretty and suitable, a shrine. And I was half prepared for what I later saw in Charles Wilson's informal Presley collection when I went to the Center for the Study of Southern Culture at Oxford, Mississippi.

The most striking item was a poster that showed a tight-trousered, full-bottomed Presley playing a guitar in the lower left-hand corner, with a staircase leading up to his mother and Graceland—the Presley house in Memphis—in the sky. Redneck fulfillment—socially pathetic at one level; at another, religious art of a kind, with Christian borrowings: the beatification of the central figure, with all his sexuality, Graceland like a version of the New Jerusalem in a medieval Doomsday painting.

On the outskirts of Memphis was Graceland. Highway direction signs proclaimed the name. A public road separated the house and grounds from the Graceland parking lot, the ticket hall, and the place where the two Presley airplanes were now parked: emblems of majesty.

The tours of the house and grounds were organized. Visitors couldn't wander around; they had to be taken from the ticket hall in special tour buses. On the afternoon I went the tours had been booked up an hour and a half ahead. So I didn't see the house, and had to be content with the stories of television sets everywhere, the decorations derived from the decorations of Las Vegas hotel rooms, the petty extravagances of a man whose pleasures and palate were simple, who didn't know how to spend the money he made and got into trouble when, thinking he owed himself more, he looked beyond the simple things he liked best.

And it was easy in the busy ticket hall—Presley songs on the speakers, disturbingly alive: the saint's immortality—to sense the glamour, the magic of the voice, and the incomprehensible wealth it had brought. The wealth—spent in the way it was known to have been spent: simplicity magnified, and then magnified again—was like wealth for everyone, for all the fat people of the people who—acting on a similar Presley-like principle of expenditure, but restricting it to what was available to them, the fast foods they found eternally tempting, luxurious and within easy reach, like a real-life version of manna or a modern version of something in a classical legend—had turned fulfillment and the glory of abundance to personal fat, fat as a personal possession.

Ever since the Charleston hotel (and especially after the busy business people of the hotel in Atlanta) I had been aware of very fat people, people who had risen (like dough) to special spheres of obesity. Not one or two; they were almost a class. Charleston was a resort town. They had appeared there, in the hotel, in gay holiday clothes that were on them doubly and trebly exaggerated; and they had, bizarrely, also appeared in couples. At one time there were at least four such couples in the hotel—gargantuan, corridor-blocking, and (no doubt the effect of numbers) not without aggression.

I had noticed them in other places after that. But it was Campbell who first spoke to me about the fatness of redneck women, and made it appear a regional or group characteristic. It was at times a pleasure and an excitement to see them, to see the individual way each human frame organized or arranged its excess poundage: a swag here, a bag there, a slab there, a roll there. A kind of suicide, it might have seemed; but I also began to wonder—in the Graceland ticket hall, among all those proud and excited folk—whether for these descendants of frontier people and pinelanders there wasn't, in their fatness, some simple element of self-assertion.

How was this adoration of the singer to be understood? These people had political leaders; they had sportsmen, film stars; they had any number of heroes. But these heroes were observed from a distance; this singer was a person like his admirers. He was a person his admirers felt they could live through: the singer experienced for them, on their behalf.

In colonial days in the British West Indies—for about a hundred years after the abolition of slavery—the black people had no heroes. They began to get heroes very late, and these heroes were sportsmen, cricketers mainly. No other kind of hero was possible in that limited society. But then, when a political life developed, towards the end of the colonial period, West Indian blacks acquired leaders, union men in many cases, who then became political leaders and later, in independence, prime ministers. For these early leaders who were their very own, West Indian blacks had more than adulation. They wished these leaders to represent them, and more than in a parliamentary way. They wished their leaders (who had started as poor as everybody else) to be rich (by whatever means) and powerful and glorious. The glory of the black leader became the glory of his people. The leader lived (or lived it up) on behalf of his people; and the people lived through their leader. Ordinary ideas of morality and propriety didn't apply. A leader wasn't required to be modest and correct; those were the virtues of another world. A leader was invested as a black man with a responsibility: to be grand, larger than life, for the sake of all blacks. This idea of the leader—which has caused such havoc in the West Indies—has changed in recent times, but it is still there.

Something like this black political adulation seemed to be at the back of the Presley cult. It was strange—to me—that music should have carried so much of a people's emotional needs. And when, in Nashville, Tennessee, I went to a performance of the "Grand Ole Opry," the long-running country-music radio program, I felt quite apart from what I was witnessing. It was like a tribal rite; it might all have been in a foreign language.

How much talent was there on display? But did talent matter in this setting? It was enough for the famous and the greatly loved simply to show themselves to the audience. The auditorium was full; the aisles were full of people with cameras. The cowboy hats and overalls—working clothes—of some of the performers gave a clue: country music created a community, and was the expression of a community.

Nashville was the center of the country-music industry. It was an industry, but the streets of the music area were full of tourists in holiday clothes.

An elderly black man, driving me back to the hotel one day, said of the visitors, "They're all white. Do you see? Blacks hate country music. It's redneck music to them. It symbolizes all that oppressed them and all that they hate."

I asked whether Presley had that attitude to blacks.

The old man said, "To talk to Presley about blacks was like talking to Adolf Hitler about the Jews. You know what he said? 'All I want from blacks is for them to buy my records and shine my shoes.' That's in the record."

W HEN I MENTIONED this to Allen Reynolds, a producer, he said, *"Oh no! Oh no!"*

Allen was from Arkansas. He was forty-nine, and I felt he might have been a little weary of defending the South against racial charges.

He said, "I was at the Baptist Hospital in Memphis, and Elvis was there. Not as a patient perhaps—his wife may have been there. I was in a gathering near the elevator. Two black nurses came sailing by in a state of possession. They were saying, 'He's here, he's here.' Holding their hearts, and flying off to see Elvis. I tell this story because it makes me question that theory that blacks hated Elvis."

Allen had been educated in Memphis. He loved the city, "musically and otherwise," until the killing of Martin Luther King in 1968. That killing spoiled relationships with black musicians and other black people. Nothing might have been said, but the killing was there, a barrier and an embarrassment, a cause for silence. (And I was aware, during my own time in Memphis, of the sourness of things there, with the black city an extensive, irretrievable desolation, and with the white people, under siege, living far to the east.)

Allen still had friends in the music business in Memphis. "One of them is Sam Phillips, an independent label-creator. He's a kind of idol of mine. His achievements still impress me. He did Presley in the late 1950s. He grew up in Mississippi or Louisiana. A big influence on him when he was a boy was black music. We had this blending of music in Memphis. Sam loved black music and he was consciously looking for a white man with a black"—he searched for the word—"attitude. Black energy."

I asked Allen what country music meant to him.

"I grew up very close to country music, and I can't find anyone who can define country music. But to me it's real people's music, lyrically and melodically. And it's directly out of daily life.

"My grandparents listened every Sunday night to the 'Grand Ole Opry.' My grandmother was one of fourteen children. And there was a guy called Little Jimmy Dickens who would sing a song called 'Sleeping at the Foot of the Bed.' And my grandmother would say, 'That's how it was.' When people would come visiting there would be no question of getting a new bed. The adults would sleep side by side, and the children would be placed at the foot of the bed. Country music at its best comes from the emotions of everyday life."

In country music, the music itself was not important. What mattered were the words. But the words were few and simple, and the themes were so stylized. Was it hard to judge the quality of a song? Could one be taken in by trash?

Allen said: "I can tell pretty quickly. For instance, I am now working on an album with a singer called Kathy Mattea. She's a new singer; this is only her fourth album. The way the business works is, there are a number of publishing companies with writers who make it their daily job to go into the office and write songs. I don't think that's always a very satisfactory system. It results in a lot of greeting-card stuff. When I announced that we were looking for material for this album of Kathy's, I got a huge volume of songs—almost all of which is not acceptable—from the publishers and the writers."

That explained the typewritten notice I had seen on the front door, asking people just to drop their cassettes through the mail slot, and not to come in and talk.

"I must listen to a grocery-bagful of cassettes every week. Nashville is like a Mecca for a lot of dreamers. But at the same time I keep on meeting publishers and writers, because I'm looking for material, and the real struggle is finding the real songs. So the sign on the front door is only partially operative."

"Are you looking for a song, or for a writer?"

"Both. I am always looking for the real writers. We have some who are very fine. Most of those I know are from simple backgrounds, rural backgrounds. It doesn't mean they are not educated. They are from all over the country. But generally they come from a background that is only partially urban. They have a good strong connection to the small towns and the people."

I thought about other forms of stylized writing—Restoration comedy, the P.G. Wodehouse upper-class fantasy—where a witty manipulation of the form could be art enough.

Allen said, "I know someone from the other end of the country. This person writes a wide variety of music. He has had some success in country with some pieces that I know are just imaginative, and based on the feel this person has for the stylized elements. And yet some of these pieces are very good pieces."

"But you would say that some of the best work comes from true knowledge."

"And originality."

"Is that still possible?"

"Yes. But the industry doesn't encourage originality much. As with other writing, there's ten percent that's original, and a lot that's quickly here and gone."

We went up to listen to some of the tapes that had been sent in for the new Kathy Mattea album. In the listening room there were, literally, the grocery bags he had talked about.

Allen said, "The first thing I notice in most of these tapes is how little originality there is in them. Even the titles can be the same. Any number of songs about the fire of love, the flames of love. Many titles like that. The fire of love that can't be quenched."

The song we listened to was about love, sentimental, generalized, with no concrete detail to attach it to a setting or a person.

Allen said, "It's a commercial ditty. Greeting card. Three writers worked on that one, and you can tell they had no purpose except to make some bucks. The music too. It's a hybrid. A little bit of pop, a little bit of country, a little bit of schmaltz. And not any soul. And back into the grocery bag it goes."

There were tapes on the shelves of the listening room. And on top of the shelves were clown figures in china.

We listened to one of the songs Allen was going to use in the album.

"It's called 'Eighteen Wheels and a Dozen Roses.' He—the truck-driver—is on his last run home with a dozen roses for her. Now they're going to do a lot of catching up. It's not a heavy song. I'm humored by it. There've been a number of songs in country related to the trucking business. A lot of the country audience relates to cars and trucks."

I picked up separate lines of the song, saw the play on the numbers in some of them: "Eighteen wheels and a dozen roses"; "A few more songs on the all-night radio"; "Ten more miles on his four-day run."

Allen said, "Eighteen wheels. Everyone knows that's a big road rig."

He played another song he had chosen. It was called "Late in the Day."

He said, "It's reflective, sad. Dealing with lost affection, lost love." He quoted a line: " 'You don't know it's a good thing till it goes slipping through your fingers.' "

And we listened again:

> Now I pour whiskey, break the ice,
> Put my feet up, close my eyes,
> And try hard to listen to what my heart might say,
> Try to find the rhyme to take me back in time,
> To be with you here, late in the day.

Allen said, "I love that song, because the mood and imagery are evocative to me. And the melody alone is dear, is beautiful to my ears."

We talked about his discovery of music.

"In my life it has been a natural thing to have instruments in the house and to make music for your own entertainment and the entertainment of your friends. When I was a child—in Arkansas—neighbors would come over in the evening with guitars, fiddles, harmonicas, mandolins, and they would sit and sing for hours. They loved it. In my grandmother's day, during the summer they had teachers who would travel from community to community. They would have singing schools, and children and adults would go every day and learn singing and harmonies. And they would have 'a big all-day sing,' as they called it, at the end of that week.

"Part of the attraction of the church in the South was the music. It was the music and the singing and the harmonizing that they enjoyed. For the whites and the blacks, the influence of the church and the gospel music is real apparent to me in the secular music. Some of Elvis's favorite songs—to sing—were for the church. He personifies the interrelation of secular and gospel, white and black."

Kathy Mattea, whose new album Allen was producing, belonged to what Allen called "the folksy side" of country music. There was another side. "One of our great singers and writers is Loretta Lynn, and she is one of the real earthy writers, and a legend. Her music is more connected to barroom and domestic storms. She began singing when she had a house full of babies. It was a manifestation of something natural in her—a natural way of entertaining herself, expressing herself. And she was poor. All she had was a radio and a guitar. A hard life, a poor life."

Although singers were for the most part religious people—religion a natural part of people of the South—and although audiences, equally religious, expected their singers to represent family values, there was at the same time a contrary current. Allen said, "Audiences see the singers struggling with their own *demons*. And they identify with the struggles." This made audiences humane and receptive and loyal, and gave an element of the passion play to the life and songs of some performers.

Reverend K. C. Ptomey, the Presbyterian pastor of Westminster Church, in one of the more prosperous parts of Nashville, said of country music: "It's white soul music. It's comparable to the role that music played for slaves in the last century. It creates community among oppressed people. I like it. I listen to it because in the words I hear protest against the oppressive aspects of life as a poor white person experiences it." About the much-publicized religious faith of some of the singers, he said, "They're religious in a special way. Religion is to them a shared emotional experience rather than a shared doctrine."

A ND SOMETIMES the emotions could be extravagant. While I was in Nashville there was published a book called *Sunshine and Shadow*, the autobiography of a "Grand Ole Opry" singer called Jan Howard. She was about to start on a sixteen-city promotional tour, and the Arts and Leisure section of the Nashville paper, *The Tennessean*, carried a review of her book:

"One of 11 children born into desperate poverty in rural Missouri, she was raped at age eight by one of her father's friends. At 15 she married. She bore three sons in four years, then became a battered wife who eventually collapsed in a nervous breakdown.

"When her husband tried to kill her, she fled with 10 dollars in her pocket and her sons in tow. She knocked on the doors of strangers and begged for shelter. Her second husband, an Air Force sergeant, turned out to be a bigamist. Both of her children by him died."

After this her luck changed for a while. She met a songwriter in California, married him, moved to Nashville, and became a star. Then the marriage ended, messily.

"While she was recovering from the bitter divorce her oldest son Jimmy was killed in Vietnam. Soon after, actor/singer son David became a drug-induced suicide. . . . "

It was hard to believe that anyone could live through all that and come up singing. But there she was on the stage of the "Grand Ole Opry," a slender, slight figure, dressed up and smiling, although her terrible story had taken up much space in that morning's paper. And the Opry audience, running up the aisle to the stage with their cameras, were photographing her and willing her on, wishing her well.

"Down-home music, crying music"—that was how Campbell had described it. But that was only the beginning. White soul music; the singer as star and victim, in both roles representing the community; and in and out of the simple music, through the echoes of ancient Scottish and Irish reels and jigs, there was a feeling of melancholy and loss, the melancholy of a transported people faintly remembering, or perhaps just having a community sense of, "old, unhappy, far-off things, and battles long ago." Inseparable from this were the fundamentalist frontier religions, which had preserved for these people the idea of a complete, created world and a complete, divinely sanctioned code.

Jan Howard told *The Tennessean* about the difficulties of writing her autobiography. "It was horrible reliving some of the bad parts. Sometimes I'd be sitting at the typewriter and find myself shaking so hard I literally couldn't touch the keys. Or I would cry. And sometimes I would literally pray for the strength to do it."

Music and community, and tears and faith: I felt that I had been taken, through country music, to an understanding of a whole distinctive culture, something I had never imagined existing in the United States.

THE MAGAZINE in my hotel room, mixing its metaphors, said that Nashville was "the buckle of the Bible Belt." Churches took up twelve pages of the Yellow Pages directory. *The Tennessean* had a "religion news" editor, and there was a weekly page of "religion news," with many advertisements for churches (especially Church of Christ churches), some with a photograph of the stylish-looking pastor or preacher. Most of the Protestants in Nashville belonged to the fundamentalist frontier faiths; the predominant denomination was the Southern Baptist.

The classier churches, the Presbyterian and the Episcopalian, looked at this Baptist predominance from a certain social distance, without rancor or competitiveness.

Dr. Tom Ward, the Episcopalian pastor of Christ Church, said that the Southern Baptists who sometimes came to his church found it too quiet: " 'Y'all don't preach.' The Baptist ethos is the preached word. Which is the ethos of the Christian church in the South. Preaching meaning the emotional speech rather than the learned essay of the Church of England—preaching the word and counting the number of saved souls. But I have to say this. To say, 'I'm a Southern Baptist,' is another way of saying, 'I'm a Southerner.' What I mean is that that is the ethos, religiously. What is buried in their psyches is the fear of hellfire and damnation. My father was read out of the United Methodist Church in Meridian, Mississippi, in 1931—when he was seventeen—because he went to a dance. That's the Methodist Church. A lot of the Ku Klux Klan literature is Christian. Revivalism—why? To rekindle the spirit. What spirit? One bad step; many bad steps; and you have the Ku Klux Klan."

The Presbyterian pastor of Westminster, K. C. Ptomey, agreed that the Southern Baptist identity was in part the Southern identity. "That's very accurate. You see, a Southern Baptist distinguishes himself from an American Baptist. American Baptists are much more openminded; they are not so rigid. I would add about the Southern Baptists: it has to do with sharing biblical literalism; it has to do with morality. For example, to be a Southern Baptist is to be a teetotaler. Morality, dancing, drinking—it encompasses the whole of life."

I asked him about the revivalism.

"The revivalist mind-set is 'to get back to God.' You often hear the words used."

" 'Back'?"

" 'Lost' is the word they use. And what they mean by that is 'damned.' And therefore they need to be revived."

T HE SECOND-largest denomination in Nashville was the Church of
  Christ. It was also fundamentalist, and also originally a frontier
faith. It had started (K. C. Ptomey told me) as a breakaway from the
Presbyterians; and in some ways it aimed at a greater purity than the
Baptists.

"They have developed into a sect or denomination that believes
they are the only true Christian denomination. The Baptists wouldn't
say that. But the Church of Christ people would say, 'You are not a
Christian. You have to be in the Church of Christ, because it is the
only true church.' "

There were more Church of Christ churches in Nashville than in
any other city. Reverend James Vandiver, who was of the church, told
me why.

"The mid-South is at a pivotal point. It is so near the place of
American origins. People came here from the seaboard, and they migrated from here to Texas, Oklahoma, and the prairies—and in all
these places you will find the numerical strength of the Church of
Christ. From a cultural and socioeconomic point of view, the people in
this area have common value systems and basically an agrarian economy. And basically people of that niche tend to be a bit more religious."

Reverend Vandiver gave me much of his time. He was happy to
talk about his church and anxious to help with my inquiry. I found
him absolutely fair. I wanted to meet someone from the church who
had developed doubts about it. He promised to arrange that, and he
did. Later he even put me in touch with someone who had left the
church.

He was the pastor of the Harpeth Hills Church of Christ, a good
way to the south of downtown Nashville. When he was giving me
directions on the telephone he referred to his church as a "facility."
When I came to a certain boulevard or ring road I would turn left; a
hundred yards on I would see "the facility." I liked the word. I had
first heard it used in a comparable way in Grenada in 1983, at the time
of the American invasion: at a morning briefing the military press
officer had referred to the temporary barbed-wire compound for prisoners as a "facility."

The Church of Christ facility at Harpeth Hills was of clean red brick: a prosperous church of a prosperous community. Reverend Vandiver was perhaps in his forties, sturdily built, with glasses. He asked me to call him James or Jim.

"That informality suits me and suits our theology. We try in every way possible to erase the distinction between clergy and laity."

Music was playing in the office.

Jim said, "A soft-music station. I had it on while I was doing some work this afternoon. The younger generation would call it elevator music." He smiled.

He was in shirtsleeves, but he was wearing a tie. He sat on a three-seater settee against the paneled wall. Above him was a painting of an arbor; to one side of the settee was a ficus tree. One whole wall was of bookshelves.

Jim said: "Let me explain the Church of Christ in the simplest way historically. We are seeking to do two things in religion. One is to accept the Bible as our sole rule of faith and practice. We believe in the inerrancy of the Scriptures." The other thing the church was trying to do was to go back to the very earliest Christian faith. "Within three centuries of Christianity's foundation Romanism was predominant, until Luther, Calvin, and the great reformers, the people who said, 'Let's give the Bible to the common man, and reform the Roman church. Let's lay aside the abuses, the corruption that's developed.'

"There's always a thread that looks back to the Scriptures and says, 'Let's duplicate.' In the early 1800s here, with the westward expansion, there arose these frontiersmen—as well as people of the seaboard—and I think the frontier spirit had a lot to do with it. These people represented a broad mainstream of Protestantism—especially the Methodists, the Baptists. The Church of Christ represented an abandoning of Protestantism, and did not represent a return to Rome, but to the very beginning of the faith, all the way back to Pentecost, the first Biblical dating of the Christian culture.

"That was the frontier spirit. 'We're on the frontier now. Let's lay aside differences. Let's be brothers in Christ.' I'm not trying to be coy, but I think the church of which I'm a member was established in A.D. 30. I'm just saying that the restoration movement here is a historical tracking of that movement on American soil."

"When was that?"

"Early to mid-1800s. That was the period we refer to as the American restoration."

"What was the need, you think?"

"Every great religious renewal has been sparked by a return to the Scriptures."

"You are so close to the Baptists. And yet you are so opposed to them."

"We are close to the Baptists in many things. Bible, Trinity, a church, evangelism, personal conversion to Christ. But we are different in other things. We sing without music. We observe the Lord's Supper weekly. We teach that baptism is *essential* to salvation. The Baptists teach baptism only as a requirement for admission to the church. And we're autonomous; every church is independent."

But, important as the church was in Nashville, it was in decline. The church that had suited the needs of frontiersmen was less suited to city-dwellers. Jim was aware of the difficulties; he was clearsighted and frank.

"We are in a time of great change, and that's a real challenge for us. Change? From agrarian to business and industry, from rural to urban, from blue-collar to white-collar, from lower to middle and upper class."

In *The Tennessean* I had read an item by the "religion news editor" that six Nashville Church of Christ churches were thinking of a merger, "to overcome high overhead . . . flagging membership and to rekindle enthusiasm for fellowship and missions." The six churches had a total membership of twelve hundred: six small churches, of an earlier, more rural time.

Henry came into Jim's office. That had been the arrangement: that Jim and I would talk alone for a while, and that Henry would then join us. Henry was twenty-six. He was of middle size, with well-brushed-back hair, white jeans, and a short-sleeved blue Polo shirt. He had been a student all his life, and though his doctoral studies were in an inconclusive, suspended state, he still had academic ambitions. He had just been to Uganda on behalf of the church, prospecting that country for mission work. At the moment, for money, he was working as a carpenter, just breaking even on his $8.00 an hour.

I asked what he thought about the church's chances in Uganda.

He said, "Very good. But the situation could be evolving into a situation ripe for another coup." (And yet, within a few minutes, he was to make me understand that his ideas about Africa and mission work were not so straightforward.)

In southeastern Uganda he had seen terrible things. He had seen hundreds of people tied up and sitting in circles. That had made an impression on him, but he didn't appear to know what to do with the knowledge and experience.

I wanted to know about the development of his faith—this young man in jeans and a Polo shirt. Had he had some kind of spiritual illumination? Had he made a confession of faith? I had been told that it was necessary.

He said, "There is a loophole. An irony. My parents were both pillars of the faith. There was a strong bonding between father, mother, and child. But—what this is to say—I knew what the necessary steps were to salvation in Christ. As early as five or six, I knew what those steps were. That's not uncommon at all."

"It's like part of your identity."

"Sure. I followed those steps of faith at the age of eight. I was baptized, fully covered in water, at the age of eight. But, going back to your question about spiritual experience, the answer is, candidly, no. In retrospect, I question whether those actions at the age of eight mean anything." He broke off and said, "I'm in a whirlwind at the moment. I've experienced a split with my family."

I was surprised. Jim had promised to arrange a meeting with someone with doubts, but I had been expecting to meet that person on another day.

Jim said, "As a mentor, let me say first of all I think Henry is typical of a person who grows up in a religious setting in which he makes a profession of faith."

Henry said, "As a doctoral student I have come to question the objectivity—the rational processes—which the Church of Christ—"

I had noticed at the beginning how he qualified his words. Now he appeared to be having trouble completing a train of thought: many new things were breaking into the original idea.

He said, "I feel compelled to throw this. My African experience has reinforced a suspicion I've had that there might be something amiss— what I want to say—a Westerner's thought processes or thought form —I believe I can broaden this, and include not only the Church of Christ but other conservative Protestant churches as well—our misuse of reason—the Western mind—the conservative evangelicals—"

I noticed that he was wearing an Yves Saint Laurent belt.

Jim said, "I see you headed to the reduction of a lot of concepts."

"I got to Africa and I was repulsed by what the missionaries had done. Instead of teaching the Africans first-century Christianity, they had taught them a Western, white-man's Christianity. Of all things—many of the young African ministers did not see themselves as carrying out their ministry in the most proper way without, for example, wearing a sports coat and tie, something that's totally un-African."

That appeared to make a whole: the ideas of the Church of Christ fusing with a rejection of colonial mimicry.

And Henry went on along that line. "Christianity was born out of an Eastern framework—"

A thought, unexpressed, came to me: an Eastern religion for the Wild West? Had the early Church of Christ really been presented to its followers like that? Or was the Easternness of the religion a more recent idea?

"—and we need to know when to separate the true essence of Christianity from Western cultural baggage."

That made a whole, but then Henry said, "My parents' mentality is very exclusivistic, in terms of who is going to get to heaven. It's as basic as saying who are really—with a capital 'R'—Christians. The real tension began when I went to the university. They were not happy at all about that. I've been questioning parts of the body of church knowledge. And the idea seems to be that, if I don't have the same set of beliefs as my parents, I am rejecting the right belief." Abruptly he said, "I feel so desensitized to what's going on."

He said that with relief, as though glad to give up the juggling with so many new and unrelated ideas.

Jim said, "That's typical of questioning people of conservative churches."

I said, "Somebody told me that I should study the Southern churches well. Because in fifteen years it's all going to change."

Jim said, "I agree."

Henry said, "I agree." He added, "The whole package of Christianity is bothering me. The point is, Jim, that is what is going on in my mind intellectually. But emotionally I have a very strong attachment to this *fellowship*."

An experience of Africa, the shock of a tribal civil war, a new vision of missionary effort, leading to a wider questioning: what had once been the complete, satisfying faith of a complete, clear, enclosed world no longer answered. And he was "in a whirlwind."

B UT BEN—whom I met on another afternoon in Jim's office—was serene. He came from a Church of Christ family. His grandparents on both sides were of the church, and his father was a professional man. Ben was eighteen. He hadn't come from the country; he had been born in Nashville, but his faith was pure. He had preached for the first time when he was sixteen.

He said, "The youth leader of the church encouraged us to get to know God—"

I asked about the youth leader.

Jim said, "He's a full-time staff person."

Ben said, "The youth leader encouraged us to get to know God and to share him with others. He tried to instill in us a zeal and a fervor that would radiate. So naturally, when my knowledge of God grew, I wanted to share that."

"Were there certain exercises that you were made to do?"

"In worship and in church we would go to class and we would study and interact with each other. But then outside the church we would go and do things together—have a devotional at someone's house and eat together. And then, just being with the people you share the faith with, you would be uplifted. A lot of the time we would talk about what was going on in our lives. If you weren't getting on with your parents, for example, we would sit down and talk about that—both as a personal problem and a general issue or topic."

Jim said to Ben, "A lesson in helping others." And to me, "A great amount of peer pressure which the adolescent faces. We believe that Christians live in the real world and should not withdraw from the real world."

Ben said: "Occasionally we would—thirty or forty of us—go out of town, to a camp area, where we would be away from a lot of the distractions, the TV and radio, the outside influences, where we would all be together and break down into groups of four or five people. In the smaller groups you can always get more personal. It's easier to share with each other in the smaller group than in the group of thirty."

I said, "Like the early Christians going into the desert."

Jim said, "It's comparable."

Ben said, "That re-creation of our spiritual lives—that's where the comparison with the early Christians holds good."

"How long were those camps?"

"Friday afternoon, all of Saturday, and much of Sunday. A weekend."

"Fun? Or solemn?"

"Not solemn," Ben said. "Meaningful."

"Joyful occasions?"

"Joyful. An inner joy, that we were re-creating, and growing. We knew that we were always stronger people, closer to God, and closer to the people around us as well as to ourselves, when we left. And that's the idea of the whole weekend."

"How many weekends have you been on?"

"I've been on eight."

Jim said, "Twice a year."

I asked him about his knowledge of God, and how that had come.

"Oh, not miraculous. Nothing that happened last Wednesday or last Thursday. But all through the day I have a constant feeling of his presence and I know that he's with me. It's really developed in the last couple of years, when I have started to search the Scriptures. We're encouraged to search the Scriptures. You don't have to. It's a personal decision."

"What of the future now?"

"I hope to become a lawyer. I think it fits hand in hand. The type of religion that we have is a people religion. Just as Mr. Vandiver can be an influence from the pulpit, just as easily I can be a light in my community as a lawyer, and have people see me as a kindhearted, moral individual."

"But the Church of Christ brotherhood is shrinking."

"Numerically we might decrease. But the people who will be falling by the wayside will be those people who were halfhearted in their faith anyway."

HENRY, in all his turmoil, had spoken—and Jim Vandiver had pointed it out to me—of his emotional attachment to the fellowship within the church. And Ben loved the idea of the brotherhood. But Melvin, who was in his early forties, and had drifted away from the Church of Christ in the last five years, made a face when I mentioned the subject of fellowship.

He said, "*No, no*. The fellowship would *irritate* me. I've never enjoyed the fellowship, *ever*."

And it was hard, indeed, to see someone so elegant and accomplished, playing down his profession and his skill in that profession—it was hard to see someone with those manners drawing sustenance from the kind of weekend Ben had described.

He said, "It's boring."

And at once the objection, so simple, appeared unanswerable. But Melvin had been in the church for much of his life. There was much knowledge behind that snappy word.

"I don't think it was always boring. Going back seventy-five years, I think it would have been entertaining, a form of entertainment, the fellowship. Now I would agree that it's an extension of the evangelical movement. To keep you involved, to keep the numbers up.

"The South was almost entirely agrarian. Tent revivals were an opportunity for almost the entire community to meet in one place—as well as Sunday services. You'll find that revivals played a very large part in the growth of the Church of Christ up till ten years ago—and they are *the* most boring, dull experiences you can have."

I said, "America being a fun civilization."

"Agree. They're fighting a losing battle. And that's a very large factor, the fun civilization. Most of the people that attend these large evangelical events are young people. Eventually they don't go back. They get bored. And that's unfortunate. The church should never attempt to provide entertainment. It's boring when they try. It doesn't stimulate you emotionally or intellectually. All you have to do is to turn your TV on to be entertained.

"I think I could defend this point easily. The whole American evangelical movement was based on these *shows,* these circuses. The best example now is Oral Roberts. Those days are gone. There's movies, TV, traveling. But if all you did in the old days was sit on your farm, that provided a break in your life.

"It will completely die, the church. Or let's say it will not exist in twenty-five years as it exists today. If it were to exist at all, it must go *back* to its teachings. No, that's wrong. I think it probably was an error from the beginning. To keep it alive, it must offer answers of a redemptive nature. By which I mean that's really all it can do. It can only address people's questions about what life is. It's got to stop trying to be a judge, the entertainer, the meeting place. In the old days it was even the town hall. You didn't take your problem to a lawyer. You went to the church. The Church of Christ will tell you today that you shouldn't bring a lawsuit against anyone, that you should take your problems to the church and allow the church to arbitrate. This was a very efficient way of handling problems in a small agrarian community. Very effective. Though the church being judge and jury imposed on people moral guilt—they felt condemned by God for civil offenses."

A rising professional man, he had grown to reject the completeness of the culture of his childhood. Religion, the frontier faith, had created this completeness; now it was a burden he could do without. In a new world, he wished religion to have its place, like everything else. Yet he knew that he was rejecting a part of his identity.

"The Church of Christ does an excellent job in meshing traditional values with Christian principles, universal Christian principles. The result is that when one begins to doubt the traditions he is unable to separate his doubt about tradition from his belief in Christian principles. It becomes very confusing. The confusion is at times unbearable. I can understand why Henry has trouble finding words for certain things. There's guilt and alienation, the idea of abandoning your heritage. I went through a lot of guilt. Guilt is the most critical. The Church of Christ deliberately instills guilt in people. It is extremely judgmental. There is almost the circle-of-wagons sense that if you attack certain traditions it's blasphemy. I think I should tell you that I think of myself as a spiritual person. Actually, I think I am more spiritual now than I was. In a literal sense."

And in Melvin there was something like grief at the necessary break with the South he had known.

"The South is losing its identity, and that's a lamentable thing. Being Southern is a state of mind. I know that's a trite thing to say. It's a way of looking at your place in the world, a place that's more defined than many other places. Have you been to California? It's everything the South isn't. And an odd thing about that is that many business ideas begin in California. The fast food, the interstate highways, clothing styles. The reason is that creative people are stifled in the South. They move from the South and other places to California. Creative people have to get away from the South. It will be a very long time before that stifling will disappear. It will be my generation that will break the link. It's not something I say with any pride. Nor shame. No judgment. I say it purely as fact."

Wasn't there the possibility of a new kind of intellectual life, a new kind of strength, from that breaking of the link?

Melvin wasn't having any of that. He went back to his original point. "The link is broken by people of my generation because they don't want the boredom deal. As opposed to soul-searching experiencing. 'I just don't need this.' The church are genuinely perplexed by what's happening."

There was confirmation of what Melvin had said from another distinguished man. This man told me that his neighbors, professional people, successful people, originally from small towns where they had been Baptist or Church of Christ, were now all Presbyterians. One reason (as Reverend Ptomey had hinted) was that the Presbyterian religion was more socially acceptable. The other reason was that it was more lenient, less demanding, less intrusive or encompassing. Religion now had to have its compartment, almost its social place.

The frontier had ceased to exist. And the religions it had bred were beginning slowly to die. In the old days, when men, often of little education, had needed only to declare themselves ministers, people would have seen themselves reflected in the expounders of the Word. This quality of homespun would have made the religions appear creations of a community, personal and close and inviolable. Now a certain distance was needed.

O NE OF the most successful country-music songwriters is Bob McDill. The South is his best subject: redneck celebration, against a background of the hard years middle-aged men have lived through and have spoken to their children about. McDill's best songs have the feel of folk songs.

> Cotton on the roadside, cotton in the ditch.
> We all picked the cotton, but we never got rich.

He had an office in a music publisher's in Nashville, and he had a certain fame for going to his office every working day to write his songs. It was there that I went to see him. On his desk was a lined yellow pad with what looked like a fair copy in pencil of a finished song. There were no other papers on his desk. But there were curious ornaments:

London mementoes—a toy red double-decker bus, a guardsman, beef-eaters, a London taxi.

He was forty-three. He was tall and slender. He liked the outdoor life, and went out duck-shooting. (That was the gentleman's sport here, as Campbell had told me; real rednecks were meat-hunters.) He had been born in East Texas, and had been writing songs since he was fifteen or sixteen. He had always been interested in poetry, music, guitars, drums, banjos, pianos. "Not that I play them all, or play them well."

He said that the early songs he had written were self-indulgent. "I didn't learn to write commercially until I was in my late twenties." The professional attitude was necessary. The songwriter writes for singers, and has a special relationship with singers.

He went to Memphis in 1967 and spent a year there. "In Memphis I tried to write songs for black artists, black singers. I was on the staff of a publisher as a writer, and was also working in a studio as an assistant engineer." That attempt to write black songs didn't work. "I could have succeeded if I had had time enough to learn that black mentality, that black approach to music. I was beginning to learn it when I left. You've got to say something that the singer wants to say and can identify with. It was the same thing when I moved here. I had to learn this mind-set. I learned this subculture, which wasn't my own. The vocabulary is very limited. You have to learn to do big things with little words. In both black music and country music, and more so in country music."

It was such a special art, songwriting, so far from my own. I wanted to be taken into it a little way, and I asked him to talk about the problems he had had with a song.

He chose "Somebody's Always Saying Goodbye."

> Railroad stations, midnight trains,
> Lonely airports in the rain,
> And somebody stands there with tears in their eyes.
> It's the same old scene, time after time.
> That's the trouble with all mankind.
> Somebody's always saying goodbye.
>
> Taxicabs that leave in the night,
> Greyhound buses with red taillights.
> Someone's leaving and someone's left behind.

Well, I don't know how things got that way,
But every place you look these days
Somebody's always saying goodbye.

Take two people like me and you.
We could've made it. We just quit too soon.
Oh, the two of us, we could've had it all,
If we'd only tried.

But that's the way love is, it seems.
Just when you've got a real good thing,
Somebody's always saying goodbye.

Bob McDill said: "The bridge—between the images of the first two stanzas, the detachment, and the personal thing—that gave me a lot of trouble. Until I hit on the idea of just conversation. It eases the listener into it. There was another problem—I still hadn't defined the situation between the two people, the lover and the lost one. I had to do that in four lines. It seems so obvious now. But you know how long the obvious takes. I saw that there was no need to make a judgment on the behavior of either party. 'Somebody is always leaving.' It sounds almost as if it could be her, the singer. But, for whatever reason, she knows now it was a terrible thing—he threw away a great thing. Two verses of images, and then in seven lines you have to create all that personal thing.

"I also had trouble with it musically. Two long pieces of melody that are complete once, twice. You need relief—and then I hit on the idea of repeating just the second half of the A-section melody."

When he began to talk about the writing he stood up and looked away.

"Sometimes you begin with an emotion, a feeling about something. Sometimes a title, sometimes a line of the lyric. But then the hard part comes. You take that little thing, that little bit of idea, and build on it and build on it. That's the tough part. The problem then is not to mess it. Your text is so small that every word has to count. From the very first word you are working towards that center.

"You write line by line. The couple of parts we have to deal with which serious poets don't have to deal with is the tonality and also the singability. You can't do complex things and things that are hard to say. It has to be so easy to say and sing. It has to fall out of the singer's mouth."

I asked him for an example of a line that had to be put right. He couldn't think of anything like that in his own work.

"The computer in the brain is rejecting all the time. It rejects everything that is clumsy, hard to sing."

And at the end there was no way of defining what a good song was going to be. It was all a matter of feeling.

"If it feels good, if it does something to you, it's good."

No amount of questioning, no amount of explaining, even from someone as willing to talk as Bob McDill was, could take one to the magic: the calling up and recognition of impulses that on the surface were simple, but which, put together with music, made rich with a chorus, seemed to catch undefined places in the heart and memory.

> Mama said, don't go near that river.
> Don't go hangin' round ole Catfish John.
> But come the mornin' I'd always be there
> Walkin' in his footsteps in the sweet delta dawn.

Almost nothing at first. But then the images and the associations come: Mama, river, catfish, footsteps, delta, dawn.

Bob McDill said he had had to learn the subculture. But the Southern images and words of his best songs are far from the stylized motifs of a good deal of country music. And though he makes much of writing in an office in a matter-of-fact, day-to-day way—and perhaps because he talks in a matter-of-fact way, since the mystery cannot be described —it is probably true that, when moved, he writes with that most private part of the self with which Proust said serious writers write.

He says that his best song is "Good Ole Boys like Me."

> When I was a kid Uncle Remus he put me to bed,
> With a picture of Stonewall Jackson above my head.
> Then Daddy came in to kiss his little man
> With gin on his breath and a Bible in his hand.
> And he talked about honor and things I should know.
> Then he staggered a little as he went out the door. . . .
> I guess we're all gonna be what we're gonna be.
> So what do you do with good ole boys like me?

Every detail there was considered. His aim, he said, was to get as much of the South as he could in a few lines. And the song has become very famous; many people I spoke to referred to it; the mood of the song spoke for them. A "good ole boy" (as I had gathered from Campbell in Jackson) was a redneck; but it was also a more general word for an old Southerner, someone made by the old ways. The song might seem ironical, then celebratory. But below that it is an elegy for the South, old history and myth, old community, old faith.

T HE SOUTHERN Baptist convention, meeting two weeks or so before in Saint Louis, had voted itself—over strong moderate opposition—into an extreme fundamentalist position. Baptist seminaries were to be purged of people who didn't believe in biblical literalism. Sunday-school literature was to reflect this new strictness.

Reverend Tom Ward, the pastor of Christ Episcopal Church, said, "The more the Baptist religion is threatened, the more fervent it becomes." Reverend Ptomey, the Presbyterian, thought that the new moves represented the negative side of Baptist fervor. He said, "They've manipulated the political processes within their denomination to appoint people to the boards of their schools who share their perspective on biblical literalism."

Reverend Will Campbell, more involved than either of these men, was outraged. Will Campbell was a famous local Baptist pastor or counselor. He had no church of his own. He operated informally, from his forty-acre farm just outside Nashville; the informality was part of his fame. In spite of the Thoreau-like setting and his frontiersman style, he had had a formal theological education, including three years at Yale Divinity School. He was in his early sixties.

He had been to the convention. He said: "I cannot analyze why I came out with a near-clinical state of depression. I never was a steeple pastor—I walked away from that thirty years ago—but the Baptist notion historically is a glorious one. This little band of left-wingers, truly radicals, they believed in separation of church and state. No one believes in that any more. They would not go to war; they would not take an oath or serve on juries; they would not baptize their babies; they practiced community of goods. None of this holds good today.

"Moderates and fundamentalists—neither party is historically Baptist. They claim to believe the Bible literally. No one believes the Bible literally. Ask the man who tells you he does, 'Shall we start dismantling the penitentiary?'

"I never know if the true Baptist notion ever made it across the Atlantic Ocean. The frontier spirit, the culture, so dominated the religion that what you had was a civil religion, a cultural religion, a melding into one."

I said, "But it served the people well."

"It did indeed. But it betrayed the faith."

Will Campbell had a special idea of the faith. "Religion should not be credal. The great church of Christ came into being by ignoring the life of Christ. What I heard in Saint Louis—what depressed me—was doctrine, doctrine, and its defense. I heard little about discipleship. The churches offer a theology of certainty. And that worries me. Jeremiah said, 'It is not good to be too sure of God.' And even Christ, when he was about to be crucified, cried in great agony, and the agony comes over in the translation, 'If it be possible, let this cup pass from me.' No great religion can give all the answers to everything. Jesus didn't tell people what to think. He didn't prescribe a confession of faith. Christ offered no creed or special theology."

He seemed to be saying that faith was something that had to be constantly looked for and struggled towards. When I put that to him, he said it was fair. But Will Campbell's ideas were difficult; and I wasn't sure whether he wasn't being polite.

It occurred to me afterwards that only a very devout man, and someone raised within the Southern Baptist church, could ask so much of people. His setting—the forty-acre farm, the log-cabin study where he met visitors—represented something about the man. He gave one an idea of the power of the frontier preacher, and the strength of the old faith.

But it wasn't only for this that Will Campbell was famous and almost, as someone said, a Southern monument. He was famous for the political positions to which he had been led by his faith. He had done brave things in the civil-rights movement. But he hadn't stopped there. Religion and a wish to come to terms with Southern history had taken him beyond the black cause to the cause of the rednecks, the haters of the blacks. He had seen both these Southern groups as tragic. And something like a religious conversion (within his already fervent faith) had led him to offer spiritual succor to members of the Ku Klux Klan.

The conversion had come about like this. A mocker had asked one day what the Christian message was. Will Campbell had said that the message was: "We are all bastards, but God loves us anyway." (It was a version of the illumination he had had at Yale—"God cares about the suffering of his people"—that had taken him beyond the rigidities of his upbringing and had led him to the civil-rights movement.) Some time later a Klansman shot and killed one of Will Campbell's friends. The mocker then asked Will Campbell, who was full of grief and raging about rednecks and Kluxers and crackers, "Which bastard does God love the most?" The bastard who had been killed, or the bastard who had done the killing and was alive? Will Campbell had no doubt about the answer: he had a mission to the living Klansman as well.

The story of the conversion is told in Will Campbell's autobiography, *Brother to a Dragonfly*. Things are not always clear in that book. The main narrative is broken into by many little stories and is at times too fragmented. But it seems that with that conversion there came to Will Campbell a fuller and special comprehension of Southern history.

The poor whites, many of them descendants of indentured servants, and to that extent sharing an ancestry of servitude with the blacks, were of no account in the South until the Civil War. Then, because they were needed to fight that war, they were evangelized and given their cause; and afterwards, as rednecks and Klansmen, still poor, still victims, they were held responsible and derided for what was really the racism of the entire society.

The Klan religion, of piety and hate, derived from that war, Will Campbell compares to Old Testament Judaism. And he finds a resemblance to the 137th Psalm ("If I forget you, O Jerusalem") in a "spirited" Klan song like:

> You niggers listen now,
> I'm gonna tell you how
> To keep from getting tortured
> When the Klan is on the prowl.
> Stay at home at night,
> Lock your doors up tight.
> Don't go outside or you will find
> Them crosses a-burning bright.

And he explains the resemblance to "If I forget you, O Jerusalem" by means of this paraphrase or transposition: "If I forget you, O Atlanta,

Vicksburg, Oxford, Donelson, remember, O Lord, against the Yankees the night they drove old Dixie down! When Sherman said, 'Raze
it, raze it, burn it down to the ground!' Happy shall he be who takes
your little Yankee babies and slams them against Stone Mountain."

Will Campbell didn't talk about the Klan when we met. He gave
me a copy of an article he had written, "The World of the Redneck,"
which outlined his views and gave the text and analysis of the Klan
song. He didn't refer me to his book, *Brother to a Dragonfly*; that I
turned to on my own. We talked of religion and the Southern Baptist
convention; and the "liberal wilderness" he said he had walked in for
many years. We talked, above all, of the immense Southern past, which
—though born in 1924—he carried in himself, and which his setting
—a log cabin at the back of his house on his farm—appeared to pay
tribute to.

He was from Mississippi. "I was a fourth-generation Mississippian.
My family homesteaded in Mississippi about 1790, I'm thinking. In
the frontier, Mississippi was a territory. It was part of the Louisiana
Purchase. A territory, not a state. And citizens from states like Georgia
could migrate there and stake a claim to a section of land if they intended to live there. The land belonged to the federal government.
Pretty soon it was cotton. The whole economy in Mississippi was cotton for a long time. Six hundred and forty acres of land—that's a lot of
land for a family. But say a family had ten children. You divided that.
Sixty acres. Still, in the nineteenth century a family could make a living
on that. But divide it again—that's how the families separated and
scattered."

Will Campbell was chewing tobacco while he spoke. It was something he was known for; and from time to time he spat into a spittoon.
I had never actually seen anyone use a spittoon. In various places in
the South I had seen big billboard advertisements for Granger Select
chewing tobacco: "Meet Up with a Cleaner Chew." The Granger slogan had been puzzling until someone had told me it was really redneck
language, "meet up with" meaning "get to know," "become friendly
with." I asked to see Will Campbell's tobacco. It was Beech Nut,
licorice-flavored: "Balanced and Better, Softer and Moister." In its
pliable foil pouch, it was aromatic and tempting.

"My family was a family of landowners in Georgia. One of the boys
got in a fight with a friend in a barbershop and killed him. And the
judge said to the father, 'Your only chance is to move to one of the

territories.' So they packed up, the whole family, and moved with wagons until they got to this particular area in southwest Mississippi. They might have had a mind of going on further west. But in the morning, when they were starting to move on, they heard a rooster crow. So they knew there were some other settlers there. They went and talked to these people—if the Indians were hostile, and what the land was like, and what the winters were like, and what they grew. And to me the most interesting thing is that where they settled was precisely like where they had come from. If you close your eyes and then open them again you wouldn't know you had left Georgia.

"By the time my parents were grown there was no room for us on the land. My family was rooted there, in that rural community, which made it illogical for some people to say—when I began to work for the civil-rights movement, as a troubleshooter for the National Council of Churches: some people said it was trouble*maker*—that Mr. Lee Campbell's son, who is all mixed up in that nigger mess, is an outsider. Which in a sense made it more dangerous. I'm not trying to romanticize this—it didn't take much to make you a radical in those days. The only thing worse than an outsider is a traitor, and I was seen as a traitor—to the Campbell-Webb-Parker-McMillan family. My grandmother's family were Webbs. It was the Webb family who came and homesteaded there.

"My grandmother, on the trek from Georgia to the Mississippi territory, remembered—when money ran out—seeing her father identify himself to a settler in Alabama as a Mason. They gave the secret Masonic grip, the secret Masonic passwords; and the settler gave some money. Ten dollars. Worth perhaps a thousand dollars today. My grandmother remembered that all her life."

It was a beautiful and touching picture. I said so to Will Campbell.

He said: "This oral tradition had an effect on the tenacity with which they hung on to all the old ways of doing things—and this meant segregation, among other things. 'Will, you weren't raised this way.' Which again makes you a traitor. To them segregation was a Christian way. God created races. And I couldn't explain to them that it wasn't God who created races. But God created people, and some of them would go to the Northern countries and lose the pigmentation of the skin, and some would go to the hot countries and develop the heavy pigmentation. To them God created white people—and Adam and Eve were white. And when he put the curse on Ham, the curse was to be black. But they were and are deeply religious people, and it was important to have a religious sanction for everything.

"Let me say something which appears to negate what I've been saying. When I've been saying 'they' I am referring to the community at large. My immediate family had no vested interest in a segregated society, because they were not slaveholders. They were yeoman farmers. The further historical truth is that 'my people' also came to this country as indentured servants. An awful lot of the yeoman farmers came as indentured servants. And later we had black slaves.

"I'm not denying that I had, and grew up with, racial prejudices. It wasn't something you discussed—black people didn't marry or date white people. They worked with them on farms. In the fields there was equality. We were even playmates. When we were small we played with black children. But at a certain point you knew that they were black—the time you started school. You accepted that."

He said he had written a song about that. He took the guitar that was near and began to sing. I wasn't prepared for this. It took me by surprise; and the effect of the singing and the guitar, filling the small cabin, was hypnotic. I surrendered to the emotion of the singer and his absorption in his song.

The song was long, a ballad, with much recitative. It was about a black boy and a white boy growing up together on a farm in the South, until they were separated according to the racial customs of the place. The black boy's father worked for the white boy's family. The black family lived in the smokehouse; the white family lived in the main house, which was not much bigger. When the Depression came the black worker was laid off, and he and his family went to Memphis. Then the white family lost the farm and they too had to go to Memphis. There one day the white boy, now a man, met the black boy, also a man, and they became friends again.

Parts of the song were true, Will Campbell said; and parts were made up. His family didn't lose their farm; and they didn't migrate to Memphis. So what was sentimental about the song, what made it a fable, gave it a moral, was the made-up part.

"The male members of my family were not bigots. Prejudiced, but not bigots. I remember one day in Campbelltown—all the Campbells lived in one place, within a mile of one another—and this thing happened. An elderly black man, John Walker—he lived in the neighborhood; he had recently been released from the state penitentiary for stealing some corn from his landlord—he came walking down the dirt road. And we were playing in the 'stomp.' Not the lawn. There would be the house, the yard, the picket fence; and beyond the picket fence would be a grassy area, like a meadow, and that was called the 'stomp.' It wasn't where crops were planted, or even pasture; it was more like a playground. Inside the yard there would be no grass. That would be swept down with a dogwood broom. If you had grass in your yard that was a trashy thing to do. And we were in the stomp, and this black man walked down the dirt road, and we taunted him: 'Hi, nigger! Hi, nigger!' To which he never responded. The local mores would not permit him to respond to white children.

"And afterwards my grandfather called us all round him. And he was sitting there on this tree stump. He called us all 'hon.' And he said, 'Hon, there's not any niggers in the world.' And we said, 'Yes, Grandpa. John Walker is a nigger.' We could still see him disappearing down the dusty road. And he said, 'No, all the niggers are dead. Now there's only colored people.' And that was his way of explaining to us that the Civil War was over."

(In *Brother to a Dragonfly* there was another version of that story. The corn John Walker had stolen was "a sack of roasting ear corn." And he hadn't been to jail for stealing the corn. He had been beaten by some men, and he had told about the beating in a humorous way— which had partly encouraged the taunting from the younger boys. "Yessuh. Dey got me nekked as a jaybird. Took a gin belt to me. Whipped me till I almost shat." The story Will Campbell had told me in his cabin—with the black man silent and enduring—was more in line with contemporary sensibility. The version in the book, with the black man making a joke about the beating, and perhaps also about the theft, felt truer.)

Will Campbell said: "My grandfather was a man only with a second-grade education. He could write his name and I suppose could read. But his use of the language! I always hoped that the preacher would call on him to lead us in prayer. We were Baptists. I remember the old man concluding one prayer, 'And when at last we kneel to drink from the bitter spring of life . . . ' And by that, 'the bitter spring of life,' he meant death. . . .

"So these were and are the dominant influences in the life of rural white Southerners—this sense of place, coming out of displacement, indentured servants, migrations, and the finding of this sense of place in the farms, the homesteads, the community. And this sense of place became sacred.

"There was a threat to that sense of place by the racial changes that were taking place. And it *was* a threat. To know suddenly that things you thought were stationary and would last forever would never again be the same.

"And I used to try to explain to my colleagues—non-Southerners in the movement—that, when white people said that to desegregate the schools was to wreck the schools as they knew them, they were saying something that was fact. I used to use the example of Abraham and Isaac. People would say to me, 'You are asking me to sacrifice my children on the altar of integration built by the Supreme Court.' And my response was, and is, 'I'm only asking you to be faithful to the God you profess. As a Christian there is God beyond the idols we have built: place, community, public education—which indeed we may be sacrificing. Abraham was willing to sacrifice his child. We put our child on the altar of integration, we put the sticks of justice beneath. But the child was not sacrificed—by Abraham. Finally the child was saved.' "

Will Campbell said, "Maybe that analogy breaks down. But it held for me at the time."

He began to talk about his civil-rights work; and it was possible to detect the ways of thought that would later lead him, as a churchman, to resist being used politically.

He said: "Our cue wasn't the Supreme Court decision of May 1954. Our cue was far more basic. Supreme Court justices change. It's already changed in our day. The motto of the liberal movement was law and order. But by the time Mr. Nixon and others discovered Middle America, the term 'law and order' became synonymous with 'nigger.' And then it was the other side that was saying, 'We must have law and order.' So that Martin Luther King, Jr. and others were seen as troublemakers, and consequently a threat to law and order."

He talked of the paradoxes and ambiguities of the success of the movement.

"I think that, the way I grew up, my chances of becoming free and open-minded about race were much greater than when my children grew up. Because when I was a child there were assumptions made that were never discussed. You didn't discuss whether black people would serve on juries or go to school with us or live with us. But every child born after May 1954 has heard black people discussed pejoratively. So now you have a generation of people who are full of hatred and in a position of being able to implement that.

"I do think it is extremely dangerous, because you can never again have the kind of nonviolent resistance that you saw under the leadership of Dr. King and others."

In the old days, he said, if you saw five thousand blacks marching around a courthouse, and you asked them why they were marching, they would say they were marching because they weren't being registered as voters. If you saw black people demonstrating at a lunch counter, they would tell you it was because they weren't allowed to eat at lunch counters. There was no trouble at all about the cause then.

"Today, how would a nonviolent, passive resistance work? The issues are not as clear. Today, if you saw five thousand blacks marching, the only thing they can say is, 'We are marching around the courthouse because we are still niggers to you.'

"I remember a song that was sung in our taverns: 'Move Them Niggers North.'

> Move them niggers north.
> Move them niggers north.
> If they don't like our Southern ways,
> Move them niggers north."

Beginning with simply speaking the words, he was soon yielding to the lilting rhythm, and half singing.

He said at the end, "I remember hearing it once in a recently desegregated roadside café in northern Alabama where I had stopped with a black friend. It was on a jukebox. This song was clearly directed at us. And when we left my friend said—my friend was hurt—'I guess there's no law against playing a jukebox.' And I said, 'Not yet. And I hope there will never be.' "

He repeated the response he had made to his black friend. I missed the point Will Campbell was making here; and it was only later that I learned, from his own article, "The World of the Redneck," that the song was a Klan song. It was in this imprecise way that he introduced the subject of the Klan and redneck deprivation and tragedy, and his years in the "liberal wilderness."

He was sitting on a stool at a high desk or table, with the spittoon at his feet. There was an old barber's chair in a corner of the log cabin, near the air-conditioning unit. There was also a rocking chair; a settee against one wall; a carpet on the floor; and a settee table with a polished or varnished tree-trunk slab as a top. A banjo or ukulele hung on a wall; and there were photographs and drawings and originals of cartoons. On a high ledge was an old tin advertisement: *Say Goo-Goo. A nourishing lunch for five cents. 5c.* Goo-Goo was the name of the candy that was still advertised on the "Grand Ole Opry" radio program. And it was that old tin advertisement that made me start seeing the apparently haphazard assemblage of objects in the log cabin as a collection of things of the people.

Will Campbell said: "I went full circle. I grew up in a fundamentalist background—it wasn't called that then. Everyone was Baptist. In that world view to be a Christian meant don't smoke, don't drink, don't mess around on Saturday night." But he wanted more from religion; and his faith developed with his studies. "I was interested in ethical matters." This led in the South directly to the subject of race, and his civil-rights work. "I am still against wars and segregation and paying workers bad wages. But I began to see that I had traded one legalistic code for another. The liberalism of my middle life served me no better than the fundamentalism of my earlier life. The Christian message is that we are created free, and no one has the right to exact more of us than Jesus did. And Jesus had no creed or particular ideology. I found that the social liberal creed was as doctrinaire as the fundamentalist religious creed had been. Jesus asked us to be mindful of the one near at hand."

And for Will Campbell this person was the—despised, as he saw it —redneck: the man like himself. He hated the word. He thought it should be used only by people like himself.

"The tragedy of the redneck is that he chose the wrong enemy. I know a good song. 'Rednecks, White Socks, and Blue Ribbon Beer.' You want to hear it? I'm not a musician. But I like the songs of the people."

He left the high stool and, taking his guitar, went and sat on the settee. A glossy black dog had come into the cabin. When Will Campbell began to play the guitar and sing, the dog sat up and sat still, fixing glittering eyes on the hand strumming the guitar, and listening to his master's voice.

No, we don't fit in with that white-collar crowd.
We're a little too rowdy and a little too loud.

> But there's no place that I'd rather be than right here,
> With my red neck, white socks, and Blue Ribbon beer.

Will Campbell said, "That's the song of alienation. It says a lot: 'We're a little too rowdy,' 'a little too loud.' "

I asked, "Who wrote it?"

"Bob McDill. If you listen to it selectively you'll learn a lot."

AND YET the history that so exercised Will Campbell could be by-passed, just as in some quarters the old, too-demanding faith had been bypassed.

Twenty-five minutes away from downtown Nashville, in the little town of Smyrna, there was the very big Nissan truck-and-car assembly plant. It was three factories in one, on a site of eight hundred acres. The factory building was flat and straight-lined, gray and almost featureless on the flat land. From the outside it was hardly a disfiguring of the site or the surrounding landscape. But, inside, it was a world of its own: seventy-eight contiguous acres under a roof that seemed higher when you were below it than when you saw it against the sky. It was a plant run on Japanese lines, with the Southern work force, white and black and a few Asians, men and women, broken up into small military-style units, each with its own leader, goals, and loyalties.

Thirty miles south of Nashville, in Spring Hill, an even bigger project was under way: the creation, on eleven hundred acres, of the Saturn plant of General Motors, a manufacturing plant (not an assembly plant like Nissan at Smyrna). It was going to cost $3.6 billion, and was going to be the largest industrial plant ever built in the United States. Even with its automation and robots, Saturn was going to employ some six thousand people. But nothing would show from the road. General Motors was landscaping the ground, banking up a low and not-too-noticeable hill, to hide the big plant. Crops would be grown on General Motors land beside the road. To the person driving by, the land would look like farmland. But Saturn, when it came, would physically and culturally alter the country for many miles around. General Motors thought that the "halo effect" would create fourteen to fifteen thousand new jobs in the middle-Tennessee area: new houses, new facilities, a new kind of working population.

There was at the moment little to see. But the area was on the brink of an upheaval. Land values had risen. I had heard stories in Nashville of the "greed" of some local people, and of the readiness with which old Southern people, faced with the prospect of wealth, had alienated old farms and land and cut themselves off from the past that was, until the other day, so sacred to them.

But Frank Bumstead, a Nashville businessman who knew the area well and drove me around it one morning, was less condemning. Frank was in his early forties, a self-made man, a Texan of Georgian ancestry; he had gone through university on a basketball scholarship. As a man with many business partnerships, he had an immense amount of local knowledge; and he had a precise, analytical mind.

Frank said: "The fact of the matter is that in 1985, and today, an *efficient* family farmer is fortunate if his farming covers his variable costs—seed, feed, fertilizer, chemicals, gasoline, etc., labor. If he has any debt on his land or equipment he is in serious financial trouble. Farmers cannot pay for their land or equipment. They can only hope to cover their variable costs. Why should people not sell?

"A lot of the locals in fact were frozen like a frog who has a light shined in his eye at night. They saw the prices escalating and were scared to death to sell too cheap or too soon. That can be interpreted as greed. It can also be interpreted as someone intensely afraid that he is not going to sell a near and dear asset—to a farmer his land is next only to his wife and God—for enough money. Many of the people who sold had those farms in their families for several generations.

"In many cases the people who sold used the money to pay off debts. I know one farmer who owned a piece of roughly 120 acres. It was not immediately adjacent to the site; it was about three miles away. He sold for $350,000. He paid the bank three hundred thousand. After the lawyers' fees he was probably left with twenty, twenty-five thousand."

He talked of land values. "The Saturn project was announced by General Motors in 1985. Six months before the announcement farmland in Maury County, if you could sell it—and there was almost no market for it—sold for a low of four to five hundred an acre, up to a high of a thousand to fifteen hundred an acre, depending on the type of land, pasture being cheaper than cropland. A month after the Saturn announcement much of the land in northern Maury and southern Williamson, to the north, was selling for a low of twenty-five hundred an acre. Some land changed hands at prices up to ten thousand dollars an acre, 'raw' farmland. Some sales were reported in the twenty-to-twenty-five-thousand area. In other words, it was insanity. A substantial amount of that speculation was done by Texas land-buyers who had experienced the land boom in Dallas and Houston and were in the midst of a downturn in those markets—'depression' is a better word.

"There was a terrific amount of wealth created overnight in that area. I know someone who, having sold his radio station and his interest in a successful cable-TV system, bought three hundred acres less than half a mile south of southern Franklin City, on U.S. Highway 31. Lots of road frontage. He paid an average of three thousand dollars an acre six to nine months before the Saturn announcement. After the Saturn announcement he sold the land for seventeen thousand dollars an acre —and he owned it for less than eighteen months. He recognized that the land was far too valuable to raise horses on. He said he made more money on the farm than on the radio station. And he'd bought the farm to retire to. It just shows that it pays to be lucky rather than just smart."

It was with Frank that on another morning I went to see the Nissan plant at Smyrna, moving from green Tennessee to, at first, office suites of gray and chrome, with noticeably thick, soft carpets. Many people were in uniform, dark-blue trousers, light-blue shirt, with NISSAN machine-embroidered above the left pocket of the shirt, and the person's first name above the other pocket.

The public-relations woman with us said at one stage, in a corridor, "That was the president we just passed." He too had been in the Nissan uniform.

In an open office area we saw a robot mail cart. It ran on a chemical strip laid into the gray carpet. The mail cart made the rounds of offices and halted at certain spots, not moving on again until someone pressed a strip at the top. If a person got in its way the cart beeped.

The three-in-one assembly plant was E-shaped. The spine was more than a mile long: a lane, a road, flat and dead straight, disappearing at either end. Frank had seen places as big, and bigger; I hadn't. We rode about the great distances on an electric car, the public-relations woman driving and talking. There were no Japanese to be seen (there were only eleven among the thirty-five hundred staff); the people who looked Japanese were American Chinese or other American Orientals. In free areas in various parts of the plant there were basketball backboards and table-tennis tables. The table-tennis idea had been brought back by the workers who had trained in Japan before the opening of the plant. At many places there were television screens, giving constant production data and schedules and sometimes important items of national or international news.

A real world, a complete world. But it was a relief to get outside and to see, in the distance, a relic of the old world: a corrugated-iron barn, against trees.

Growing up in Trinidad, I had never wanted to be employed. I had always wanted to be a free man. This was partly the effect of my peasant Indian background and the colonial agricultural society of Trinidad. And though it had not been easy in the beginning, I had remained a free man. I had had as a result almost no experience of the twentieth-century world of work; and had few means of understanding the adjustments people made. Here at this Nissan plant people were treated well and paid well; there was freedom of a sort there, and dignity too. But it seemed to me that, for that, they lived in a very small space.

Some days later I asked Frank, as a businessman and Southerner, to tell me what he thought we had seen.

He said, "The first thing you saw there is the Nissan corporate culture. It's a superior corporate culture, that focuses on the participation of the worker in the process. It also focuses on the well-being of the worker. Their average work force is highly educated, extremely well paid, and nonunionized. The Japanese management idea is for the whole plant to be broken into little work groups, and these work groups have a specific responsibility. Within the group they elect a leader and assign responsibilities, and they are involved constantly in making their work more efficient and productive. Part of the culture is that the worker is encouraged to make the workplace a better, more efficient, safer, and happier place. You saw the table-tennis tables.

"The corporate culture was adopted for several reasons. Wages are attractive. The plant is clean, modern, well cared for, and, as far as manufacturing facilities go, a very pleasant place to work in. Nissan provides many fringe benefits. 'Wellness'—that's one: a new word in our lexicon, a process of becoming and remaining well. And exercise facilities. And there's the team image.

"The president walked by *in his uniform* with his first name above his pocket. The uniforms are optional, but the vast majority were wearing their uniforms. Everyone is made to feel part of the team. And there are substantial incentives built into the Nissan corporate culture for excellent performers. These incentives are fair and evenly distributed across the work force and—more importantly—they are attainable.

"You saw two components of the corporate culture that are worth mentioning. People with no experience of working side by side with robots find themselves working side by side with robots. These are Southerners, people whose roots are in the land and the farms. The second culture clash is that Nissan is a well-organized, very powerful, extremely large business, operating in the midst of a culture that had been largely agrarian, largely unorganized, and largely informal.

"And what Nissan means to me is the cutting edge of a debate that is going to rage in the mid-sized metropolitan areas of the South for the next twenty years—Nashville, Lexington, Kentucky, Raleigh-Durham in North Carolina, Charlotte in North Carolina. This debate has quite simply to do with industrialization. Against the money, you have the sacrifice in life style. We've got a very high quality of life in the South, and even when we industrialize in a sensible way there are sacrifices. Increased traffic and the tensions that go with it; increased population and the tensions that go with that. Crime. And the increasing pressures brought on local governmental organizations to provide for growth.

"Thirty-five percent of the Nissan assembly plant are women. In the South women didn't work. Woman's work was in the home.

"Nissan had no effect on land prices. There was a lot of speculation, and most people lost. Because Nissan is an assembly plant, there was no halo effect. And Nissan had local people, people who were already here. Most of the General Motors workers are going to come from the upper Midwest. They will need homes. They're not Southerners. We know they're going to have an effect. They're unionized. Again, there's going to be a clash: standard of living versus quality of life.

"My impression is that the upper-middle and middle class tend to resist growth and change, particularly if they have adequate jobs, a nice house, good schools. The upper class will profit from growth. The very wealthy support growth, because it's good for business. The poor become pawns in the game."

I T WAS now getting towards the end of July. I went to stay in an estate in northwestern Georgia, seeing that area now differently from the way I had seen it almost at the beginning of my trip.

Then I had traveled up from Atlanta and had seen it as a near-Indian wilderness. Now I came down from Chattanooga, an industrial town partly in decay. Not here the fast-food shops of the highways, with their tall standards and vivid liveries; just pawnshop after pawnshop, palmists and card-readers, little offices offering loans, and mobile-home sale lots sometimes strung with pennants. Outside Chattanooga I saw the mobile homes, tarnished and without bunting, in their home settings. I saw the small houses; the hoarded old-metal litter in some yards: Georgia of the crackers, with occasionally a small, disconcerting black figure in a yard, the figure intended to be what it looked like, an "artificial nigger," a local decorative feature, a reminder of the past.

Fort Oglethorpe was my nearest town; James Oglethorpe was the founder of Georgia. There was a new way to Fort Oglethorpe, over the hills. There was another way, through the town of Lafayette (pronounced locally "Laf'ette") and then through the Chickamauga Battlefield Park—war as monuments and rhetoric and difficult strategy: Chickamauga the last big victory of the South over the North.

My normal way to Fort Oglethorpe was over the hills; it was quicker. Driving on from there one day to Chattanooga, I saw from the slum around the Rossville Boulevard—saw and at first could scarcely believe—the patterns of white headstones in the battlefield cemetery: dotted white arcs, tidy and regular, on the low hills beyond the black and white slums, through which, as I drove, I continued to have glimpses of the cemetery. I didn't know the area; I wasn't expecting to see a cemetery there, and of such size, such patterns of dotted white lines; Chickamauga barely a name to me until I had come here, and now—the second day of that two-day battle perhaps the bloodiest day of the war, as I was to hear later in Memphis from Shelby Foote, the historian of the war—far more shocking than the cemetery at Canton in Mississippi. Important, that war, necessary; yet now it seemed past and dead, a waste.

And seeing poor blacks and poor whites (with their jaunty baseball hats) in the decayed town—"pawns in the game"—I had a momentary vision of the world Will Campbell saw; and saw, again, the history of the place in easily seized layers: Indian land, blacks (artificial ones sometimes), war, industry, slum, with far away to the west, in Nashville, the beginning of a new order leading no one knew where.

7

◪◪◪

Smoke

IT HAD been hot from the beginning, from mid-April, that is, when I had gone south with Howard to see the place he thought of as home; and had been surprised by the colors of the Carolina spring, the new green of trees, the purple flowers in the roadside grass, the yellow-white dogwood blossoms; and had been further surprised by the beauty —in rust, wood-gray, faded green, and Indian red—of abandoned tobacco barns and derelict farmhouses and barns with peaked and spreading corrugated-iron roofs.

The degree of heat or warmth I felt that Easter weekend I did not associate—after more than thirty-five years in England—with spring. And there was a morning in mid-May in South Carolina—still the Southern spring—that I found hard to bear: a steamy, stinging morning, in the ground of a great house on the bank of a muddy river, below a white sky, the air so full of biting spring insects that just to open the car door was to let in dozens.

But then, after Tallahassee and Tuskegee, I had adjusted. Modern air-conditioning systems—not the single-room units, as debilitating by their noise and cold currents as the heat they pumped away—made that adjustment possible. The summer became something one had learned to live with. Until, in northwestern Georgia one day, about a week after I had arrived, there came, quite suddenly, the great heat, with thermometer temperatures of almost a hundred degrees. And that heat stayed in its first spell for three weeks.

I wasn't aware the first day that the heat had come. The air conditioning of house and car and shops had set up an expectation of temperature contrasts. But then the ground heated up and the air heated up. Every exposed object radiated heat. To be in the open was to breathe in hot, humid air that irritated one's lungs.

The house where I was staying was on the side of a hill and was set among fields and woodland. Outside the estate there were many small houses. From the road the area would have appeared to be pure cracker country. But from the estate itself the view—and it was an extensive one—showed no other house, showed nothing mean or disturbing. From the house and the pines around the house the hill sloped down, through rough open meadow, to an artificial pond and the branch-littered bank of a creek or river. Beyond, between massed trees, were glimpses of other fields and meadows; and in the distance were forested hills, blue fading into gray, line beyond line.

There had been very few birds in the wood around the house. Now, in the heat, there appeared to be none. The crickets, though, started up as usual in the late afternoon, before the light changed, the cricket sound steady but with occasional, odd fadings-away. The meadows, the one in front of the house and the ones in the distance, browned after two or three days; the trees, both near and far, showed greener and darker. Then the leaves of some of the big trees around the house yellowed and fluttered down in masses for minutes at a time, as though it were autumn.

The house dogs, importunate before for walks and human company, now became more private in daylight, raising a tail in greeting, letting it drop, and then going hunch-shouldered, head down, tail between legs, to the hollows they had dug themselves in the earth below the floor of the porch. In a pond beside the road on the way to Fort Oglethorpe cattle stood in muddy water up to their bellies—one might have been in India.

The sky darkened in various places far away. But it seemed for many days that only other places were getting the rain. One day, though, it came, with wind. I saw it first on the water of the pool. Away from that, on the concrete edge of the pool, on the sandy ground, and on the wood shingles of the house roof, the rain dried almost as soon as it fell. But just as the first flakes of a snowfall can melt before the snow starts building up, so the rain now slowly soaked the roof shingles, and began to fall too fast on the pool edge to be evaporated away at once. Slowly the wet began to show.

I opened the door to hear the rain and to smell it. There was the baked-earth smell—the first-rain smell that in India is re-created by some perfumers, using a kind of clay on a sandalwood-oil base, to make a monsoon scent. To this there was added a deep smell of pine, from the wet and cooling pine logs of the house.

After the rain the dogs were everywhere active, running about the littered yards or ornamented gardens of small houses and mobile homes, or trotting intently at the sides of the road, as though they needed to be up and about in the cooler weather, after their long confinement, and as though they had been called out everywhere by the earth smells the rain had released. For a long time after the rain had fallen, the asphalted roads steamed.

The thermometer fell twenty degrees in a few hours. But it was the merest remission in the heat, which soon returned: as imprisoning, while it lasted, as any spell of severe winter weather in the far North. It was hard to understand how people had made out here before air conditioning and screens. In the days before travel was easy, this kind of heat would have thrown people into themselves, as much as the winters of the Far North are said to throw Scandinavians into themselves. And perhaps this six-month summer weather, hot rising to hotter, was a factor in the still-visible degeneracy of a section of the local white population (the pinelanders whom Fanny Kemble observed would have left issue); and a factor as well in the almost Indian obsession of the South with religion, the idea of a life beyond the senses.

To THE west was Nashville or the area around it, awaiting the change that was going to come with the Saturn plant. To the east, in North Carolina, was the area known as the Research Triangle, bounded by the university campuses of Chapel Hill, Raleigh, and Durham, where over a period of almost thirty years a big industrial park of seventy-five hundred acres had been created: thirty thousand new jobs there, poor North Carolina pineland landscaped into the discreetest kind of industrial garden, many modern technological and pharmaceutical names represented by new buildings, long low lines of brick or concrete and glass, giving an impression of spaciousness and order and elegance, the land of rural poverty remade to suit its new function, the South seemingly abolished here, as it had been abolished at the space-research town of Huntsville in Alabama.

At Huntsville the Southern businessman with me had pointed out a field of cotton—more than a crop: something from the past—literally across the road from a high-tech building: cotton, which, the business-man said, tore your hands and broke your back (because the plants were short and you had to bend all day to pick cotton).

In some such way, at the edge of the Research Triangle Park in North Carolina, a small, well-tended field of tobacco was pointed out to me in late August: tobacco the famous old crop of North Carolina, the very names of some towns here more famous now as the names of cigarettes—Winston, Salem.

When I had gone with Howard to his home town at Easter I had seen the tobacco seedlings being planted. I didn't know the plant and, though I must have seen tobacco in many places after that, I didn't know what I was looking at until now, when the bigness of the leaves was noticeable. I had been told that the great heat we had had in late July and the first half of August would have been good for cotton; and I thought that the same heat—which had yellowed the leaves of forest trees—had scorched the edges of the tobacco leaves lower down. But the tobacco leaves were ripening rather than drying. That was the way tobacco leaves ripened, from the bottom up.

Tobacco leaves had to be picked or cropped only when they were ripe, so a row had to be worked many times. The lowest leaves on the plants we were looking at had already been cropped. Tobacco not only called for stoop labor; it had also to be harvested at the time of the greatest heat. The ridges and furrows of this tobacco field were as without weeds and as clean as a swept dirt yard. This little field, which one might have passed by without a second thought, spoke of a slow, detailed labor, as back-breaking as the cotton labor.

The man who made me see all this was James Applewhite. He was from an old tobacco family in eastern North Carolina. He was fifty-two. He was a teacher at Duke University in Durham—the university founded and endowed by a tobacco fortune. He was also a poet. And though he was no longer part of the tobacco culture, and though he spoke of it as physically far away (though in fact it was reasonably close, two hours by car), that tobacco culture of eastern North Carolina was one of the subjects of his poetry, together with all that old semi-rural family life.

I didn't know his poetry when I met him. But I began to be aware of his quality as a man when he stopped to show me the tobacco field: a poet's sensibility and a farmer's dedication, with an academic evenness of manner. He was a slender man, narrow-waisted, concerned about exercise. He took all my inquiries seriously, and spoke from the heart, without affectation, with a farmer's matter-of-factness, offering me at once, as soon as he saw that I was receptive, thoughts he would have spent some time arriving at.

Durham was not his landscape, he said; he had only recently begun to make it the subject of his poetry. There was no landscape like the first that one knew. He elaborated on that, and he couldn't have known how directly he was speaking to me (the scarcely bearable idea of the beginning of things now existing only in my heart, no longer existing physically in the ravaged, repopulated Trinidad of today). I could understand how the past he meditated on, though physically so close and still existing in Wilson County, was in his mind quite far away.

He took me by byways to his house. At a certain stage, after we had seen a man on a sit-down mowing machine in the garden of a house, he talked about the sweeping of the dirt yards in the old days. The soil would have been sandy; it would have been swept with brooms made of dogwood saplings. "And the marks of the sweeping would have been deliberately left in the yard to show that it had been swept and was clean." Would that sweeping have been done by a servant? No. "The mistress of the house did that with pride, as evidence of her good order."

That touched something in me. But at the time all I could think of was the African huts and their clean yellow-brown yards on the banks of the Congo or Zaire River, seen from a river steamer twelve years ago. The yards were scraped like that, I had been told, to keep snakes away. Jim Applewhite thought there might have been something in that, even in the South. And that brought to mind Will Campbell's story about the "stomp" outside his bare, clean, family house yard near McComb, Mississippi.

Something else remained, though. It came to me later: a memory, from some unplaceable time in my childhood, of the marks in dark sand of a *cocoye* broom, a broom made from the hard central stems—rigid at the top, but thin and limber at the bottom—of the blades of a coconut branch or frond. Those marks in a corner of a Trinidad Indian yard that came back to me did stand for order and cleanliness, almost the piety of a house, its adherence to good old ways. There was a ritual about yard-sweeping in Indian or Hindu families like ours in Trinidad when I was a child. It had to be done first thing in the morning; it was part of the purification of a house before prayers. And there was something like a religious interdiction against sweeping after nightfall (no doubt because valuable things might have been swept away and lost). And perhaps, as well, some such idea of religion and piety lay at the back of the Japanese raked garden.

Farmer, child, and poet came together in Jim Applewhite's contemplation of the physical circumstances of his childhood, and in his serious, generous talk.

His house was in the countryside, in a dead end with a few other houses in a patch of woodland. It was a wooden house. The end wall of his sitting room was made up of old wide planks set diagonally. At the back was an unroofed platform looking onto woodland—a style of living that in other countries was open only to a few, but here in the United States was open to many.

He gave me a copy of his new book, *Ode to a Chinaberry Tree,* published in 1986 by Louisiana State University Press. While he got tea ready, I looked at "A Leaf of Tobacco."

Is veined with mulatto hands

Then the veins were seen as streams, "a river system draining a whole basin," collecting all the historical debris of the South. At the same time:

Scented and sweetened with rum and molasses,
Rolled into cigarettes or squared in a thick plug,
Then inhaled or chewed, this history is like syrupy
Moonshine distilled through a car radiator so the salts
Strike you blind. Saliva starts in the body. We die for this leaf.

The crop that required such labor, slave and free, the crop that gave the region a special calendar and culture, was a narcotic, dangerous to men. Commercially it was on the way out: another little disaster for the South. Jim Applewhite didn't smoke, had smoked only for a short while many years before. But the culture was so close to him that, almost in spite of himself, the tobacco product in the poem comes out as tempting. The idea of rum and molasses and tobacco, the sweet and the bitter, made me think of Will Campbell's aromatic, moist, licorice-sweetened Beech Nut chewing tobacco, and made me think of the cellophane or clear-plastic-wrapped squares of tobacco, as dark and rich as fruitcake, at the checkouts of Southern supermarkets.

He liked tobacco as a culture, for the formalities that went with the growing and curing and selling of the crop. And when, later that evening, I read his poetry in my hotel room, I found it enriched by his talk and the sights I had seen, and already half familiar.

In "For W. H. Applewhite" he wrote of his grandfather. (And in my imagination I saw the tobacco field he had shown me at the edge of the Research Triangle Park.)

> He dug grey marl near the swamp, set out
> Tobacco by hand, broke the suckers and tops
> Before they flowered, leaving some for seed.
> Cropped the broad sand lugs, bent double
> In air hot rank in his face from the rained-on
> Soil.

"How to Fix a Pig," a celebration of a "pig-picking" at the end of the tobacco harvest, was also a celebration of the man who "fixed" or barbecued the pig, a man called Dee Grimes, who was—still—the sharecropper or tenant on the old Applewhite farm.

> It comes from down home, from
> When they cured tobacco with wood, and ears of corn
> Roasted in ashes in the flue.
> The pig was the last thing. The party
> At the looping shelter when the crop was all in.
> The fall was in its smell,
> Like red leaves and money.

Agricultural communities are conditioned, given a calendar, by the crops they grow, and the origin or first purpose of the crop becomes unimportant: rice in Java, tobacco in North Carolina, sugarcane in Trinidad in the old days. The talk in that poem of celebration at the end of the crop—the hard crop, originally the slave crop—brought back very faint memories of something called "crop-over" in Trinidad, when the sugarcane had all been cut, and the horns of the black water buffaloes that drew the cane carts were decorated and there was something like music in the main road of the small country town where I lived, at the very edge of the sugarcane fields, acres upon acres, scene of bitter labor: memories like snapshots from very far back, when I was six or seven, memories seemingly spread over a long time, but perhaps in reality the memories of no more than a week or so.

T HE GREAT size of the land, the distance between places—this was one of the things that would have separated Jim Applewhite's comprehension of the world as a child from my own comprehension of things in Trinidad. Was it oppressive or frightening sometimes, in the old days? Did people feel lost? I asked him some days later, when we met at the hotel where I was staying.

He said, "For my grandfather to go a buggy ride to Wilson, the county center and center of tobacco sales, ten miles there and ten miles back, was a day's journey."

And even that was already familiar to me from the poetry:

> His memory held an earlier era: a steamboat
> To the New York fair, when soot spoiled his hat.
> Horse and buggy courting, when ten miles two ways
> Was a day.

"Automobiles began to come into that area in the 1920s, and electric lights. Electrification tended to follow the roads. My wife's mother was reminiscing earlier this year, remembering when electrification got to the country. People did feel lost here. The sense of needing to form a life that had its own regularities, its own formalities—that was a reason that religion had the contour it had. That's why the formalities of tobacco-growing were so important."

I asked him about the tobacco field he had shown me. I had seen that when I had just arrived in the area and was in a geographical haze.

"We were on the boundary between Orange and Durham counties. The old road from Durham to Chapel Hill. There was a little soybean growing too, a little soybean nearby. What is happening in this area is that the rural agrarian economy is being replaced by another economy. Which made that farm unusual. It was five or six miles from Duke University campus."

Then he spoke about the formalities of tobacco-growing.

"Tobacco was associated with an older mode of living. Associated for me with my grandfather, with a kind of ritualized cyclical time order, where the cycle of the seasons was marked by sowing the plant bed, preparing the land in the spring, setting out the plants in early summer, harvesting in midsummer. You'd be finishing up curing and grading in August."

Grading?

"Grading involved separating the leaves from the different levels of cropping. And actually different levels of ripeness. So that the best tobacco was placed together, wrapped together, in these 'hands,' to bring the highest price at auction. There might be three or four tobacco companies, or five maybe—in flush times—bidding for the tobacco whose quality they liked. The buyers would travel to different markets. There would be a kind of marketing sequence. The market would begin south and go up north, following the pattern of tobacco ripening and harvesting, roughly.

"I think that tobacco in its best incarnation was a sort of folk art. An art practiced by people who were extremely good at it but who might not be able to read and write. I remember when other areas, like Canada and Rhodesia, were trying to get into tobacco-growing, they would come to North Carolina to get to these folk experts—who might not be able to sign their own names, but who knew how to harvest, cure, and grade tobacco.

"The artful thing about harvesting is knowing when the tobacco should be cropped. It won't cure properly if it's picked too soon or too late. You can't make a perfect leaf some seasons. That's why tobacco has a vintage, like wine."

"Are you an expert?"

"No, no. I just know what is involved. I saw this around me all my youth. Mostly, I think I was impressed by the aesthetic contour of the tobacco ritual. Planting had to be done at the right time, with hand care, individually. A handcrafted mode of agricultural production. It's much more mechanized now. But this handcrafted aspect of tobacco was predicated upon cheap labor in the South at a time when the South was economically disadvantaged.

"Typically, the land would be owned by landlords who didn't any longer live precisely on the farm. Like my grandfather. People who had left the Civil War farmhouse homeplaces built by their grandparents or great-grandparents and had moved to town, to small hamlets, such as the one I was born in. And in those houses on the farm there would be living a sharecropper, the tenant farmer. He could be black or white. Typically in my experience, they were white. They farmed on shares. The farmer got half the proceeds on the crop. The owner furnished the supplies and the capital. Typically, there might be one or more black families living in smaller houses on the farm, living rent-free. They were not participants in the sharecrop deal, but worked as a kind of distanced retainer. They worked for money, and their large families provided the many hands required for housing tobacco."

"Housing?"

"The whole thing of getting the tobacco from the field into the curing barn and then the packhouse—where it was packed up and stored until brought to market. It was important to have a good tight packhouse that wasn't too humid and above all didn't leak—you couldn't afford to have your tobacco get wet after it had been cured. If it had too much moisture it would 'mold' and lose its value radically.

"This housing involved whole teams of people with different ranks of hierarchical importance and responsibilities. The croppers, those who actually broke the leaves from the stalk, they were in a sense the most important. They had to do two difficult things. Hard physical labor, and they had to make the decision about which leaves to gather. And they had to work very fast. There would be two or three or four of them going through the field, breaking the leaves. It was most difficult when they were breaking the leaves at the bottom of the stalk. Then they would have to work bent double all day long in very hot temperatures.

"Some of them would go along the row walking on their knees, to avoid bending over. But that is hard too. Following the croppers would be a mule-drawn or a tractor-drawn 'tobacco truck.' These tobacco trucks were really small wooden wagons with wooden wheels. They had stakes at the corners and burlap sides to hold the leaves in."

I told him what Howard had said about the tobacco tar on his hands, and what Howard's mother, Hetty, had said about the tobacco smell making her sick.

"Most of the workers complained about the way the gum got on their hands and arms. It usually wouldn't make anyone ill from the nicotine unless it was wet."

Hetty had said the opposite. She had said that to avoid the smell she and her husband had gone to work in the tobacco fields in the early morning, when the dew was still on the leaves.

"The other persons of most importance were the 'loopers.' They worked in the barns. They tied the tobacco leaves with cotton twine on to the sticks, which were then laid horizontally on racks in the barns, with the leaves hanging down from the sticks, stem ends up. Again, this had to be done rapidly. The loopers were always women—they might be the wife of the tenant farmer. And there would be 'handers.' They would hand the tobacco leaves from the tobacco trucks to the loopers.

"Some people nowadays have even taken the whole tobacco truck with the wheels and made coffee tables out of them. An old-fashioned tobacco truck was only half again as large as a coffee table. They were made small to go down the rows. And possibly one truck packed up with about five feet of tobacco leaves was very heavy, enough for one person to manage. Tobacco, before it was cured, was heavy.

"The looper would receive five or six tobacco leaves, stem end towards her, in her left hand, and with a few swift motions wrap and secure the stem ends together. And then she would flip the bundle"— he made a gesture, but the thing he was describing was not easy to follow—"so that it straddled the tobacco stick and hung there. It was very important that the leaves not fall off the stick, because if several leaves fell and landed on the galvanized steel flue beneath them they could start a fire, and the whole barn could be consumed in fifteen or twenty minutes."

"Did that happen a lot?"

"It was not unusual for a tobacco barn to burn. You would expect one or two barns to burn down in a growing season."

He went back to talking of the various jobs in tobacco. Then he said, "A certain social stratification resulted. The sons and daughters of the owners became the town boys and girls. The sons and daughters of the tenant farmers were the country boys and girls. We went to school together. I really admired these country boys and girls, because they worked harder than I did."

I asked about the effects of mechanization. His reply was unexpected.

"The technological innovations that did away with much of the hard labor also did away with some of the quality of the tobacco. No 'hands' are tied now. Leaves are clamped together in bulk barns and cured." He spelled out the word "bulk" for me, as though the word itself contained some of the grossness of the new method. "Tobacco is no longer graded. The leaf is placed in canvas sheets and sold."

A lot of the ambiguities of his attitude to tobacco came out in that expression of distaste for the new methods, which spared men but were bad for the tobacco. I put that to him. He didn't reject it.

He said: "It's a mystery and a paradox. For me it has a certain resonance, the whole tobacco business, and it is close to the paradox of civilization itself. That this essentially poisonous substance formed the basis of a way of life that had so many attractive aspects—a formalized, seasonal cycle to it, which left the land combed into its even furrows after the stalks had been cut in the autumn. Which had the spectacle of the tobacco market, with the golden piles of aromatic leaf being sold for what were really considerable sums of money."

Jim Applewhite's wife came from a tobacco family as well. They had been talking recently about tobacco, he said, and his wife had said that in the old days it was possible to tell, just from looking at a hand of tobacco leaves, who had tied the hand—so individual were the loopers' tying styles.

"Tobacco was a product which allowed the South at a time of pretty serious economic disadvantage to bring in cash money from the whole country and even from abroad. No other crop brought in so much money per acre, and was so lucrative in return for effort expended. In a sense, as a poet who didn't know he was going to be a poet, the fact that the product was a folk art and nonutilitarian must have appealed to me. The final use of tobacco was as a social gesture. From production to consumption, it was a style-bearing medium. The life style has changed. I don't think the South absolutely needs to produce this poisonous substance any more.

"I think of tobacco as an Old Testamentish aspect of a past way of life, a kind of traditional, conservative, fallen world, a world marked by original sin, of which tobacco was a kind of symbol."

I asked whether members of his family smoked.

"Father smoked a little. Not much. That's part of the paradox. The workers mostly smoked. Two of the sharecroppers who worked on the family farm during my teenage and adult years died of lung cancer."

Those deaths worried him. He had spoken of them with feeling at our first meeting, almost while he was showing me the ripening tobacco field on the old road to Chapel Hill. But, as always in his talk, there was another side to the poison.

"One can argue that any successful agrarian economy has most of the aspects of tobacco-farming. What it doesn't have is the handcrafted, graded, aromatic, sold-by-auction quality that tobacco has. The issue of quality, as determined by color, scent, and flavor, was central to tobacco. There's a region specificity to wine, and tobacco is in a sense analogous: there's a region specificity to tobacco as well."

He said that there was something he had wanted to show me in his house, but he had forgotten. "The wallboards of a tobacco barn from my family farm are in my sitting room. And the ceiling beams were posts in the barn."

But I had noticed the planks on the end wall, broad planks, set diagonally.

He said they were of pinewood, and had been made so hard from the years of heat of the curing process that he had had to use an electric drill to get nails into them.

"The industry changed in its desires when the filter tip came in. The classic cigarette was the unfiltered Lucky Strike or Chesterfield or Old Gold. That's the kind of cigarette the companies wanted the most beautiful tobacco for, the most beautiful, lemon-yellow, 'bright-leaf' tobacco. When the filter came in they wanted a heavier kind of tobacco, less bright, not as good a quality. So the premium for growing the most golden bright leaf lessened. The whole mode of production has been degraded by different kinds of demand and, most flagrantly, by altered growing practices. Chemicals are used to inhibit sucker growth and to artificially increase the bulk, the weight of the leaf. It's called MH 30. It was developed in North Carolina. And of course tobacco doesn't support as many people in its mechanized aspect. Formerly tobacco-growing would support whole countrysides of people. It was the chief cash source for the rural descendants of slaves, white Southern farmers who owned no land of their own, as well as for the landowners. Today there's simply so much more money, and the importance of tobacco is less."

His past had been more or less abolished. But it was this past that gave him eyes for the landscape he now lived in—though there could be no landscape like the first.

"I am now able to write about the landscape of Durham County.

But I realize that that is in part the case because the landscape has been historicized for my imagination by the evidences I can still see there of an older agrarian economy, before the land was covered again with trees.

"A Southern field, if you leave it alone, will grow up in broom sedge, and in a few years young pines will be bristling up, scattered through the broom sedge. After twenty or thirty years it's woodland again." Hardwood trees then grew up in the shelter of the pines; and then the hardwoods killed the pines. He lived in a landscape of second-growth timber, eighty to a hundred years old. "But in places the old farm rows are still there, like small waves in a bay frozen by time. They were the rows of the last crop planted by some farmer, in the last century perhaps, or the early part of this. And deep in the trees you see fallen chimneys, areas where in spring jonquils still come back where there had been family gardens. A few old tombstones in places. Some beech trees with names and dates still legible from being cut into the bark, in 1908 or 1911 or 1914. This is about the period when this change we've been talking about began—electrification, roads, motorcars."

Every stage of history marked by small ruins, a landscape of small ruins—this had been my first impression of the South when I had come down at Easter with Howard, to see the place that to him was home, not very far from here.

Jim Applewhite said: "The landscape of eastern North Carolina was always to me a kind of landscape of the past. There was this dichotomy in my own life between my father and my grandfather. My grandfather had been born in that Civil War–era farmhouse, and he was always associated in my mind with the agrarian economy. My father ran a service station and believed in progress and sold electrical appliances for a number of years. He was always in a hurry. My grandfather was never hurried.

"It was in my grandfather's house—just across the road from our house—that we went for the ritual occasions that marked the farmer's year. My grandfather represented a kind of permanence for me. He had a packhouse—that's where they packed the meat. That's where they cured hams and shoulders. And they did lovely things like rendering lard, making sausages. Very hard work. But formalized, because people were in direct contact with the necessity that constrained them to do what they did. The hogs had to be killed on a very cold day in winter. Otherwise the meat would spoil. Corns and beans had to be canned when they were ripe, or they wouldn't last."

Canning

In kitchens with pots large as vats
Wrinkled aprons and skin with the steam.
Pigs were strung up from timbers in December.
Their blood steamed like ghosts in the cold.

"One has this romanticism, but when one goes and looks at it, it's not a fiction. It does exist. A quarter of a mile away from this farmhouse of my grandfather's is a graveyard, and there my grandfather's parents are buried with some other people."

THE WORD "tobacco" is thought to have come from Tobago, the dependency or sister island of Trinidad. And before "Virginia" became the word in England for tobacco, tobacco was sometimes called "Trinidado," after the island of Trinidad, part of the Spanish Empire since its discovery by Columbus in 1498. Tobacco was a native Indian crop. But after the discovery and plunder of Mexico in 1519–20 and Peru fifteen years later, the Spaniards were interested only in gold and silver; they were not interested in tobacco. It was the English and the Dutch and the French who went to Trinidad to load up with tobacco. There were hardly ever more than fifty Spaniards at a time in Trinidad in the sixteenth and seventeenth centuries.

The Gulf of Paria, between Trinidad and Venezuela, a vast safe harbor, was nearly always full of foreign ships. An English explorer and diplomatist, Sir Thomas Roe (who later went to the Mogul court at Agra in India as the representative of King James), came to the Gulf of Paria one year and saw fifteen English, French, and Dutch ships "freighting smoke." Another English official reported that the tobacco trade might in time be worth more than all the Spanish gold and silver from the Americas.

The trade was illegal, however—even though crops were grown in Trinidad with the complicity of the Spanish governor. Under Spanish law only Spain could trade with a Spanish colony. Occasional sweeps were made by the Spanish navy against foreign interlopers in the Gulf of Paria; and foreign sea captains and sailors who were caught could be hanged on the spot. And the Indian tobacco fields—tobacco a crop requiring such great care, as I was to see in North Carolina—were flattened: part of the process by which in three hundred years both the native Indian population and tobacco were to be rooted out from Trinidad.

The island that the British captured (without a shot) in 1797 was a sugarcane slave colony. And it was to work in the sugarcane estates that, thirty years or so after the abolition of slavery in the British Empire in 1834, Indians were brought over from India on indenture. It was sugarcane that gave a rhythm to the life of rural Indian communities. Tobacco was no longer a local crop.

I would have been disbelieving, and delighted, to be told as a child that Trinidad had once been known for its tobacco. To me tobacco was glamorous, remote, from England (in absurdly luxurious airtight tins), or American (in soft, aromatic, cellophane-wrapped packets), something from an advertisement in *Life*.

S HE HAD a name tag on her blouse: *Paula* in white on black plastic, drawing attention to itself, and making you see that she was almost flat-chested. She was a waitress in a newish salad-and-quiche "gourmet" bar in one of the rich towns of the Research Triangle.

She said, "Would you like a cocktail or a drink before your lunch?" It was a formality. As spoken by her, it held no invitation at all. There seemed to be as little zest in her for these restaurant refinements as there was in me, after months of restaurants and hotels. "Now, let me tell you about our specials." Mechanically, she recited the specials.

At first on this trip, for the first month or so, during these recitals in restaurants, I used to smile: the recitals seemed ironic, to be a kind of joke between the waiter and the customer. But the recitals were always perfectly serious; the waiters were doing, often doggedly, what they had been told to do.

Paula got through to the end of what she had to say. It was then, unexpectedly, that life came to her voice. She said, "I'm leaving today."

"Leaving the restaurant?"

"After this serving. Leaving here. Leaving the town. Going to Wilmington. Tomorrow."

"Have you packed? You don't have much time now."

"I'll just throw it all in the Chevy. One of those little subcompacts. Like a Pinto."

"You won't take a U-Haul?"

"I've been throwing away things for like a month. You throw away and throw away and then you find you still have things you want to throw away."

"You really think it will all go in the Chevy?" It had become one of my own little anxieties about traveling and the hotel life: telephoning for the bellman, emptying the safe-deposit box, loading up, wondering whether it was all in, whether there was going to be a doorman at the other end, to help with the many bits and pieces: so many books and papers and files and notebooks now, so many little bags and sacks.

She said, "Well, you see. My husband and I had like a fight about a month ago. And he took half the stuff, and I had, like, well, the other half. But God gave me the strength to see that through."

"What are you going to do in Wilmington?"

"Peter's there. I'm going to ᴅᴇ with him."

"Your husband?"

"God worked the miracle. Let me bring you your salad."

When she brought the salad I said, "The U-Haul people have a depot here. I saw it yesterday."

"We have a lot of bills. I want to pay those off first. It'll all go in the Chevy."

"Bills. I know."

"It was one of the things we used to fight about. He'd pay some. And some he'd outright refuse to pay."

"Why did he do that?"

"Exactly. He said he was saved. Like me."

"Are you saved?"

Her voice trembled. "Oh yes. But he didn't, like, grow. Grow in Jesus, as they say." The last phrase, and its tone, suggested that she was slightly mocking what she was talking about, or keeping at a certain distance from it. But, as with the specials, she was speaking seriously.

She wore cheap jeans, of a vivid, factory-fresh blue. The body below the heavy blue cloth was thin. There was a lot of Southern makeup on her face: rosy cheeks below big tinted glasses and above a thin white neck. A small, worn-away woman with a rustic accent: all the weakness and the fight, all the will to survive, contained in that little body.

She brought the quiche, stale, soggy, dead-looking from its long exposure.

She said, "We were always quarreling. Fighting every day. We would fight and he would want to go away, and then I would beg him not to leave."

"Had you been married long?"

"Three years."

"You didn't think you would get someone else?"

"I was frightened of being alone. But God gave me the strength this time. I didn't ask him to stay. I let him go. And then God worked the miracle in both our hearts."

"How were you saved?"

"I just got saved."

"Did you have a pastor? Was there some preacher you were following?"

"Nothing like that. I was feeling for some years that I had to do something. Feeling that if I didn't do something—"

"You would be unhappy with yourself?"

"Unhappi-*er*. But I felt that the God of the earth or the universe or whatever couldn't be interested in someone as unimportant as me. And I did nothing."

"No one was advising you?" Many of the words she was using seemed to have been put in her mouth by someone who knew about the saving of souls.

"There was a minister." She gave the name of a fundamentalist Protestant church. "And one day I don't know what came over me—I found myself walking to the altar during a service, and I said something, I don't know what, and I knew I was saved. I just felt the love of the Lord in me then. It was after that that I met Peter."

"Was he already saved?"

"He got saved after me. When I told him. But Satan was tempting me with an ex-boyfriend."

"After you were married?"

"After I was married. That was when Peter stopped paying bills and started to make trouble about the tithing. Started to make trouble generally. And we had these fights."

"Did you fall when Satan tempted you?"

"Only in my head."

"Did you meet the ex-boyfriend?"

"No, never. He wasn't interested in me. He never wanted me. That was the trouble."

"What was it about the ex-boyfriend that was so attractive?"

"I can't say. I don't know. It was just there. Satan's temptation."

"I can see how your husband would get unhappy."

"I'm not blaming Peter. But the tithing and the bills, and especially the tithing—that didn't have anything to do with anything. But God gave me the strength last month, when he left. I didn't fall before him and hold his knees and ask him not to leave. I just had the strength. I didn't know what I was going to do, what was going to happen to me. I just felt the strength God gave me. And now it's all right."

"How often do you pray?"

"Every morning. For about twenty minutes."

"Do you speak to God in your head? Do you feel you have to make some physical gesture? Do you kneel?"

"Sometimes I talk to God in my head. Sometimes I talk to him aloud."

"You enjoy it?"

"Most definitely. And the prayers are answered. Like the way Peter and I have come together again. That's prayer. That's God. But he answers prayers only when they're according to his wishes."

"How do you know when they are according to his wishes?"

"I used to pray to get my ex-boyfriend. But that wasn't according to God's wishes."

"When did you pray to get your ex-boyfriend? After you were saved?"

"After I was saved." She smiled at the boldness.

"Do you love your husband now?"

"That's why I'm going to him. I love him. I love him. God worked the miracle in both our hearts."

"And your ex-boyfriend?"

"I've forgiven him."

Or she might have said she had forgotten him.

Satan and God fighting for Paula's soul, Paula herself not responsible for the movements of her passion, helpless, capable only of choosing salvation and asking God to reveal his will: a medieval idea of chaos, and the solitude and helplessness of men, and the necessity for salvation. But this was not set in a medieval world of plague and disease and deprivation, the arbitrariness of the sovereign and the humility of the poor. We were in a town of the Research Triangle; and the theme of this culture was abundance and choice, the paramountcy of the individual (if only as consumer), with beauty and luxury and sensual satisfactions as imminent possibilities for all.

Abundance and choice was the motif even of this little restaurant, where there were very big color photographs on the wall of loaves of bread and ears of wheat and unsmeared glasses of translucent red wine, and where even on her last day Paula dutifully recited the specials.

"How old are you?"

"Thirty-two."

"I thought you were much younger."

And that was true. The orange-colored thread zigzagging down the crotch of the blue jeans had come out less as an erotic device than a beginner's attempt at style, a signal of the inexperienced frailty of the body beneath—the body that was in fact the thirty-two-year-old woman's capital and liability. The big tinted glasses masked her eyes; and below the glasses the thick, flaring Southern makeup concealed the skin of her cheeks. She was like someone in disguise.

She said, in the Southern way, *"Thank* you! Thank you. When I was going through it I looked much older. I looked like nothing."

I had asked Jim Applewhite whether in the old days people in the countryside hadn't felt lost. He had said, "People did feel lost here. The sense of needing to form a life that had its own regularities, its own formalities—that was a reason that religion had the contour it had."

To the east it was a land of small farms, never absolute country, no big towns. The fields of corn (or maize) were tall and brown. The big thick leaves of tobacco, ripening fast now, were lime-yellow; and for me it was as though, having learned a little about the crop, I had learned to see its beauty: lime-yellow, gold, "bright leaf," against the brown and green of other fields: the green of potatoes or soybean, plants low to the ground, dotted with white and purple flowers that Jim Applewhite later told me would have been the flowers of the morning glory.

There were old tobacco barns everywhere, tall, squarish, sealed structures, sometimes with green asphalted felting on the outer walls, the felting (originally intended to keep the barn as tight as possible, and now much torn) held down by closely spaced vertical battens. Battens and tattered felting sometimes suggested, from a distance, an old barn wearing down to its frames. Weeds and small trees grew right up against abandoned houses and farmhouses; vines covered chimneys; crape myrtle marked the site of drives and old gardens.

Small fields, small houses, small ruins, churches, small towns, the freeways of the central part of the state giving way to crowded and dangerous two-lane roads—the land spoke of the nature of the people, independent small farmers, conservative or fundamentalist in religion, and conservative in politics.

I had been told that the politics of the region were "tobacco politics," small-farmer politics, in which a promise of a continued subsidy for tobacco-growers could somehow also be read as containing a promise to keep blacks in their place.

But Reverend James Abrahamson, pastor of the Chapel Hill Bible Church, thought that this ridiculing or underplaying of the conservatism of eastern North Carolina was foolish.

He said, "The fundamentalist political impulse has always been there. From the 1930s it has been repressed, largely because it did not have the support of the universities. Ideologically, the universities pulled up their tent pegs and moved to another side. Ideologically, they moved from a world view which embraced a Christian God to a place where the only reality that was recognized was material, could be measured, scientifically defined. They are reappearing—the fundamentalists—largely because they have seen or felt the pressure of a secular society.

"That eastern–North Carolina conservative side is viewed by many as being redneck and knee-jerk. Irresponsible—fanatical, almost. Unenlightened, lacking what I call the three 'I's—intelligence, information, and integrity. But they've got a stronger argument. They're easy to laugh at, and they'll never be popular. Our culture may self-destruct before they have a chance to articulate clearly the common sense they represent—for a culture that is based on more than self and materialism."

Jim Abrahamson—it was the way he announced himself on the telephone—was from the Midwest. He was a fundamentalist himself, and he felt that his Bible Church was meeting a need in Chapel Hill. He had a number of Ph.D.'s in his congregation; and his church was expanding. Extensive construction work was going on when I went to see him. American society, he said, had been built on a religious base. It couldn't float free. A recent poll had found that one out of every three Americans was a born-again Christian. "That's a lot of people."

But he had his quarrel with the fundamentalists of North Carolina.

"I think there are powerful and legitimate and almost eternal principles that would recur again and again. But the people fighting for those principles are not able to articulate them palatably. The religious right appear not to understand the world view the left or the secular intelligentsia embrace. They tend to dismiss them as God-haters or infidels. And they have a difficulty about knowing how to translate religious ideals into a political policy."

It was the Islamic problem too—since the Islamic state had never been defined by its founder—and it was the prompting to fundamentalism in many countries: how to know the truth and hold on to one's soul at a time of great change.

It was strange that in a left-behind corner of the United States—perhaps the world motor of change—the same issue should come up, the same need for security.

B UT NO one was more secure in his faith and in his politics than Barry McCarty. Politics and faith made with him a whole. He was only thirty-three, but he had already made some impression, and people who followed political affairs in the state saw him as one of the new generation of New Right leaders, someone whose time was going to come in ten or fifteen years.

His training had been in theology and debate. (Like the training of many fundamentalist leaders in Muslim countries: again this curious convergence of two opposed cultures.) He had taken a first degree in Bible at Roanoke Bible College in 1975; had done a master's degree in speech and rhetoric at Abilene Christian University in 1977; and had got his Ph.D. in rhetoric and argumentation at the University of Pittsburgh in 1980. Since 1980 he had been professor of public speaking and debate at his old school.

Roanoke Bible College was a Church of Christ institution. It was in Elizabeth City, a small town far to the east, on the coast, nearly two hundred miles away from Raleigh and the landscaped pinelands of the Research Triangle.

Beyond the Chowan River the land, already without hill or accent, became flat, the land of a delta, with a high sky. Albemarle Sound (unknown to me, even as a name, until that moment) gave a great, continental sense of the North Carolina coast, making me half regret that I hadn't known of it before, and making me want to come again and be for a day in that openness. It was one of those places where it was easy to imagine the excitement of the early explorers, finding themselves in what was truly a new world.

Barry McCarty's office was a small room on the upper floor of a turn-of-the-century wooden building. There were framed and autographed color photographs of President Reagan and Senator Jesse Helms on one wall. Below those photographs, and also framed, were Barry McCarty's various admission tickets as a delegate to the Republican convention in Dallas in 1984. A young politician's treasures. He also drew my attention to a flag laid flat on another wall: a flag with two red bars and a white bar, and seven stars in a circle on a blue field. He asked whether I knew the flag. He said the seven stars gave a clue. I didn't know the flag. He said it was the Stars and Bars, the first flag of the Confederacy.

He was a small, stocky man, cool, self-possessed, pink-faced, with glasses. He looked very clean and neat in his collar and tie, as neat as his office, his bookshelves, his photographs, his files. He looked a middle-class professional man from a small town; not a politician, not a man anxious to stand out.

He idolized Jesse Helms. On the telephone, trying to persuade me to make the two-hundred-mile run to Elizabeth City, he had said (as though it was going to be reward enough for me), "We're Jesse-crats here."

I asked him what a Jesse-crat was.

He said, "It describes a conservative North Carolina Democrat who votes for Jesse Helms and people like Jesse Helms. They represent the conservative values of the Old South. Faith in God. A belief in limited government. A belief in free enterprise. Individual liberty and individual responsibility—two ideas that go together."

And within those principles were contained all his politics, all the conservative program. He showed me the text—typewritten or word-processed in capital letters, with emendations in handwriting—of a speech he had made in praise of Jesse Helms at a dinner for the senator. The speech began, "It is one of the greatest honors of my short life to be asked to present to you one of the greatest living Americans." And very quickly then, while offering praise to the senator and criticizing his enemies, the speech outlined the conservative program on taxes, welfare, government spending, education, communism; and fitted it together with freedom and religion.

There was a story, in the speech, about the senator: "I was with him on one occasion as he checked into a hotel for an overnight stay. The woman behind the desk asked the senator if he had a credit card to charge his room to. He turned to her and said, 'Young lady, I'd just as soon carry a rattlesnake in my pocket.' And paid cash."

Was it still true about the senator and the credit cards?

Barry McCarty smiled. "He has one now. But that's the mind-set of someone prudent with his own finances."

In 1985 the governor of North Carolina appointed Barry McCarty chairman of the state Social Services Commission for a four-year term.

"We've been trying to introduce the 'workfare' idea instead of welfare. The basic idea of workfare is that welfare recipients who are able to work are required to work in order to continue to be able to receive their benefits. It's part of the Southern work ethic.

"You must remember that the majority of the Founding Fathers of this country were Southerners. The first English-speaking colony on these shores were founded in 1584 by Sir Walter Raleigh—not sixty miles from where we are—at Roanoke Island. It is known as 'the lost colony,' because Walter Raleigh established the colony and the next time the provision ship came to find them they were lost."

(But Sir Walter Raleigh also had other projects at that time. He became interested in the idea of El Dorado. In 1595 he raided the island of Trinidad with a large force. He killed the small, half-starved Spanish garrison and captured the Spanish governor, a crazed old soldier who had spent his fortune looking for El Dorado. Raleigh wanted Trinidad to be his base for El Dorado; he wanted the kidnapped Spanish governor to be his guide; and he wanted the Indians of Trinidad and Guiana—in the Orinoco Delta—to be his allies. He took Indians back to England, to prove to people where he had been; and in that same year, 1595, he wrote a book called *The Discovery of the Large, Rich and Beautiful Empire of Guiana,* which suggested that he had discovered El Dorado and its gold mines without actually stating that

he had. He talked of an English-Indian South American empire, Ra-
leana. But nothing happened. He had roused the local Indians against
the Spaniards, but he could do nothing for them; they were ground
down by the Spaniards. In 1617, as crazed now as the Spaniard he had
dispossessed twenty-two years before, he was let out of the Tower of
London to find the Guiana gold mines he had spoken about—which
he had never seen, and which didn't exist. His son died in the fraudu-
lent quest; Raleigh blamed a very old friend for the disaster and drove
that friend to suicide. It is a squalid story. But Raleigh, because he is
known mainly by his own writings, remains a romantic costume figure
—and an exquisite tapestry of him in costume hangs in the Carolina
Inn in Chapel Hill.)

Barry McCarty said: "The country actually began here in the
South. And when you look at the guiding minds of constitutional gov-
ernment in America you find that so many of them were Southerners
—Jefferson, Washington, Patrick Henry, Randolph, the Madisons.

"Slavery was not the real issue in the War Between the States. The
real issue was the power of the federal government over the states. The
same distrust of a central power, the same jealousy over individual
rights that moved the Founding Fathers to demand the Bill of Rights,
that same spirit is really what led the Southern states to resist the North
in the issues that led to the War Between the States."

Was that still of moment today?

"Here is a man—Jesse Helms—who believes that the powers of the
federal government ought to be strictly limited. The most important
government to the individual should be the one closest to him. The
more remote the government becomes, the less it should have to do
with the life of the individual."

"Where did you get your passion about politics? Was it through
your father, your family?"

"The first influence could be religious. The Bible teaches that governments are necessary in order to establish order and justice in human
society."

"Does the Bible teach that?"

"Romans, chapter 13. Where the Apostle Paul teaches that governments have the authority of God."

(Later, in my hotel, I read the chapter in the New International
Version of the Bible. I thought it was full of repetitions and anxiety,

the work of a man who had a very good idea of the power of the Roman Empire and didn't want his little group to be crushed. It was more than "Render unto Caesar the things that are Caesar's"; Paul appeared to be making up a theology to suit his purpose.

"Everyone must submit himself to the governing authorities, for there is no authority except that which God has established. The authorities that exist have been established by God. Consequently, he who rebels against the authority is rebelling against what God has instituted, and those who do so will bring judgment on themselves. For rulers hold no terror for those who do right, but for those who do wrong. Do you want to be free from fear of the one in authority? Then do what is right and he will commend you. For he is God's servant to do you good. But if you do wrong, be afraid, for he does not bear the sword for nothing. He is God's servant, an agent of wrath to bring punishment on the wrongdoer. Therefore, it is necessary to submit to the authorities, not only because of possible punishment but also because of conscience. This is also why you should pay taxes. . . ."

The epistle could be used to defend anything. Barry McCarty's interpretation, which appeared to turn things inside out ["Governments are necessary in order to establish order and justice"], was the interpretation of a believer. Though that injunction about taxes seemed to go against some of his Jesse-crat political beliefs. The whole of that chapter, in fact, could be said to be contrary to his ideas about government. But I did my reading later. I couldn't at the time raise the points with Barry McCarty.)

He said, continuing his thoughts about the 13th chapter of Romans, "That teaching suggests that the first function of government is to establish order, to punish the lawbreaker." He went on: "But nowhere in the Bible are such things as charity enjoined as duties of governments. They are definitely enjoined as the duties of individuals, but never of government. So I have a personal obligation to feed and house and clothe the poor."

"You?"

"Yes. The poor who it is in my power to help. There is another biblical belief that shapes my passion for strict constitutional government. The Bible teaches that we are fallen creatures, that men are by nature sinful. The way that constitutional government provides a remedy for that is that the collective power of men is checked and balanced.

I believe that the basic difference between the liberals and the conservatives is that the liberals believe in the perfectibility of men, and conservatives do not.

"Conservatives believe that human beings are fallen creatures whose collective power must be checked and balanced. Look at social spending in this country. Their belief—the liberals' belief—is that, if you give the right people enough money, they will eliminate poverty. I don't think that will ever happen. What will happen is that those people who have all the power and money become king, and because they are human, in some way sinful creatures, they will find a way to abuse that money and power.

"I question the very morality of the federal welfare system. If you were hungry, and I take you home and feed you, that is benevolence, because I have chosen to show charity towards you. But when the federal government legally plunders me through taxation in order to give to you, I consider that immoral."

He had so far not been interested in answering personal questions. He hadn't given a personal twist to any of his ideas. So I hadn't been granted any human understanding of his political drive. I tried again now. I knew that he had not been born in North Carolina, but had come there from Atlanta. I asked about his background.

He didn't reply directly. He said he had got an up-to-date biographical sketch in his word processor. And, saying with a smile and a shake of the head how strange it was for someone like him to be using a word processor, he sat before the instrument, pressed various keys, and after a while presented me with a printed text. It was formal, an account of his education and his professional experience, his political life, and his career as a Church of Christ minister.

I put the sheet with the other papers he had given, and asked what his father did.

"My father was a fireman. He served in the U.S. Navy in World War II, and for the first eleven years of my life he worked as a firefighter in East Point, Georgia—a suburb of Atlanta. Then, until 1981, the year of his death, he was a safety engineer for an insurance company.

"I was two weeks old the first time I was in church. I grew up in the Church of Christ. I happen to come from the branch of the church that uses music in its worship. Our people don't have the Calvinistic belief that you have to see some sort of miraculous sign to become a Christian. Our approach is more rational."

"Did you have the weekend camps?"

"I attended Christian-service camps as a boy."

"Someone told me that he found those camps boring."

"Some of my fondest memories and friendships of childhood come from my experiences in Christian camps."

He came to Roanoke Bible College from Atlanta when he was eighteen. He was the first person in the history of his family to have a college education; and the course of study he had then started on was like an extension of his family faith. He was proud of his doctor's degree from the University of Pittsburgh. When I asked about the subjects he had taken for that degree—rhetoric and argumentation—he said, "I found I was attracted to the basic skills of thinking and speaking. These are two keys to just about any field of endeavor in life."

I told him about what I had seen of the Church of Christ in Nashville. Had he had doubts, like two of the people I had met?

"I have found that whenever I have questioned my faith I have always been able to find that evidence confirmed rather than denied my beliefs. I don't think I ever came to a place where I had any crisis. It has been a lifelong growing process. As I learned more and more about science I found the world to be a more and more complex and intricate phenomenon, which confirms my faith."

Did he feel that the church made too many demands on people?

"We live in a secular society, and a real commitment to Christianity becomes harder and harder. However, I don't think that that observation can be used to determine whether Christianity is true."

I asked about the strength of the Church of Christ in the region.

"The movement began in the early nineteenth century, through the efforts of a Scottish Presbyterian preacher, Alexander Campbell. Campbell said he wanted to be just a Christian. Campbell lived in West Virginia. From there the movement moved west and south." So it was fairly new in eastern North Carolina. The Church of Christ college had been founded in Elizabeth City in 1948. "To provide ministers and Christian leaders on the Eastern seaboard."

It was an impressive set of buildings, occupying two residential blocks in what Barry McCarty said was the nicest part of the town. Most of the buildings were turn-of-the-century frame houses. The college had also bought eighteen acres across the road, beside the Pasquotank River. That was an Indian word, Barry McCarty said, meaning "where the current divides." The way he said that made me feel that he had some romantic feeling for the Indian past on this grand coast. But that wasn't so; he had got that fact about Pasquotank from *The North Carolina Manual*. Two dormitories, in brick, had recently been put up on the Pasquotank land. There were now 160 students at the college. In five years the college was hoping to have two hundred.

All his professional life had been spent with religion and related matters, and he hadn't found it dull.

"I find the Christian life an adventure. To know God and to share in making him known to others is the greatest quest upon which any human could set himself. I would say that my views are stricter than most. I will admit that."

I asked him to describe the people of the region.

"Most of the people here are very traditional and very conservative. They would be of basic European stock."

"Scottish, mainly? That was what I was told."

"Not Scottish. Most people can't remember that far back. They are very American. Southern. One of the phrases you might hear, or see on a bumper sticker, is, 'American by birth, Southern by the grace of God.' The people of this region are proud to be Americans and Southerners. They are small farmers, many of them with one or two hundred acres. Some of them are fishermen. Some work in the tourist trade. There isn't a lot of heavy industry. People are more tied to the land here than in Raleigh or Charlotte. I like the small-town atmosphere. The suburb where I grew up had very much of a small-town flavor, where you knew your neighbors and they knew you."

"What do you feel is the difference between people here and people in towns?"

"I probably qualify for membership in the yuppie society, as someone with a doctor-of-philosophy degree from a major American university. But I have a respect for the old values of Southern culture. Earning money is not the most important thing in my life. The people here have a devotion to principle over a love of profit. The basic difference from the towns is materialism. People in the towns are more devoted to things than ideas. The people here admire a statesman, a man of principle."

"But they like people to look after their economic interests?"

"Helms is interested in the right of the individual back home to earn a living for himself. The small farmer, the small entrepreneur."

But how could the small farms last? Tobacco was on the way out.

He agreed. He didn't himself like the idea of the tobacco subsidy, and he thought that most of the farmers accepted that tobacco was on the way out. "I know many people here in North Carolina who do not earn their sole livelihood through farming. You will find people who will be farmers and carpenters, farmers and mechanics, or farmers and other things. Or they will farm and log. I do not own a wood stove now. Before, I would buy firewood from a man who farmed in the summer and logged in the winter. The average person in eastern North Carolina—the colloquial phrase would be 'down east'—is not wealthy. They are working-class people."

And the future for them?

"I'm not in a position to predict the future of the small farm. But I would make two observations. One would be that simple, decent people have been working and making ends meet for centuries on this continent, here in the Americas. I see most of the folk of eastern North Carolina as being sons of pioneers. The people who carved this country out of the wilderness did so by simple, honest labor, and there wasn't a gigantic federal system to take care of everybody—the people on Roanoke Island and later at Jamestown.

"The second observation is that these simple, honest people who are laboring down here are not so far behind the times as they appear. They watch the same TV programs as people in Chicago or New York or Atlanta. And many of them send their children to school in Chapel Hill or Vanderbilt or Raleigh. What I'm saying is that the conservatism and values that are held are held by choice, and not through ignorance of what the modern world has to offer. They are timeless values, enduring values.

"And here in eastern North Carolina, when you talk of the future, you talk of something that only God knows for sure. And these folks know God pretty well."

"How would you describe your opponents?"

"People who believe that government has all the solutions."

"And locally?"

"It's hard to find any flaming liberals down here."

"Describe the region."

"It is one of the places where old Southern values still reign. It is a beautiful land, green, with much water. It is a place where people live close to the land, even those who don't live on farms. And you have many people who enjoy the water. There's fishing, hunting. The land is good here."

The beauty of the land, the outdoor life—I had heard it before, from many kinds of people.

Barry McCarty himself was a hunter. He hunted duck; he was looking forward to the opening of the dove-hunting season. And without any prompting from me, he spoke of his resentment of the federal regulations about guns. He possessed the conservative ideology complete, even down to this, its most puzzling aspect: the right to have guns.

He said, "For the first time since talking to you, I find myself almost concerned how I present this attitude about guns." I liked that "almost concerned": it might have come from his training in speech or rhetoric. He went on: "Often Southerners are portrayed as gun-toting rednecks, racist, and it is said that a Southerner who really cares about his right to own a gun is really a member of the Ku Klux Klan. This connects with our discussion earlier about the Bill of Rights. Under Article 2 the right of the people to bear arms shall not be infringed. I think you will find among Southerners that since they are jealous of all their constitutional rights they are also jealous of their right to keep and bear arms.

"I will live at peace with my neighbors. But I will not hesitate to protect myself and my wife and family against an intruder. A gun in such circumstances is the civilized man's last line of defense against an uncivilized man."

I said I had been told in Mississippi that the hunting grounds of the common man were shrinking. Was the same thing happening here?

"Not yet. The world constantly changes. We have to adapt. You have to be ready to defend your way of life. There are some values that never change."

"But the physical world changes."

"Yes. I used to write with a pen. Now I use a word processor and computer."

How was he defending his way of life?

He was going to pay for his children's education at a private Christian academy. It was going to cost $100 per boy a month. It was going to be expensive for three boys. "But we'll do it." And this led to his other point. "Excessive taxation is a threat to my way of life."

I was moved by his passion and directness, and I read out to him what Jim Abrahamson of the Chapel Hill Bible Church had said to me about the Religious Right. They were people, he had said, who were easy to ridicule; but they represented a necessary common sense.

Barry McCarty's eyes softened behind his glasses. He was surprised and pleased by what I had read out; he hadn't been expecting this degree of understanding. He became philosophical.

"Up until the seventeenth century Western civilization basically was Christian. Within that world view the universe and everything in it, including human beings, had meaning and purpose. In the modern view the world is just one damned thing after another. A *horrible* world view. Ultimately a world view human beings cannot live with. It cannot last. It will destroy itself.

"When you look at the paintings of the Dutch masters and other artists whose work was informed by the Reformation in Northern Europe, the world view is of a world God made and God is in control of. A world in which individual people possessed freedom and dignity because they had been made in the image of God. That's why Rembrandt would bother to paint a picture of a woman cleaning a fish or slicing a loaf of bread. Because that woman had infinite value to God —she was made in the image of God."

Easy to ridicule, conservatives like himself? But he had been to a major university, he said; he had studied philosophy; he knew the modern world. People knew that about him.

He said, "That is why they feel that that man, the man who has looked at the new world and dismissed it, is to be feared."

The eyes that a minute before had been soft grew hard. And I felt —quite suddenly—that within him, within the correctness of dress and manner, was a fire.

When we had talked on the telephone to arrange our meeting, I had asked him to think of some educative or illuminating thing he might show me in Elizabeth City. He hadn't forgotten. At the end of our meeting he took me to see the Confederate Memorial in the Court Square. It had been put up in 1911 by the local chapter of the Daughters of the Confederacy, a chapter that, he said, perhaps no longer existed. He showed the memorial: the pillar (suggesting mass manufacture), the soldier at the top. He said nothing more about it; he said nothing while I looked. And then it was time to drive him back to the Bible College.

I asked him about the blacks of Elizabeth City. He spoke with puzzlement and sorrow about them. Most of them had the Southern work ethic, he said; most of them, in their values and day-to-day life, were conservatives. But they didn't vote conservative; they voted for black candidates.

It had been a long day, and it was a long drive back. About fifty miles from Elizabeth City, on the narrow, crowded road, there was a nasty-looking accident: one car smashed in, another overturned, people running to the spot, and then the sound of an approaching ambulance.

My thoughts remained there for a while. And it was only a day or so later that I saw that Barry McCarty had opened our meeting by showing me the Stars and Bars in his office; and had closed it by showing me the Confederate Memorial.

The past transformed, lifted above the actual history, and given an almost religious symbolism: political faith and religious faith running into one. I had been told that the conservatives of North Carolina spoke in code. The code could sometimes be transparent: "Tobacco Is a Way of Life" being the small farmer's plea for government money. But in this flat land of small fields and small ruins there were also certain emotions that were too deep for words.

J IM APPLEWHITE took me one day to see his family farm in Wilson County, in what he said was the heart of the eastern–North Carolina tobacco country. We went first to Wilson, the main town of the county. It was ten miles from the farm—I knew that distance from the poems and from Jim's talk.

Wilson was a more substantial town than I had expected. The residential part through which we drove looked rich and settled, with big houses set back in wooded gardens. In the old days money in Wilson came principally from the tobacco market. On the other, industrial side of the town (we drove through that side on the way back in the afternoon) there were the tobacco warehouses.

We stopped at a supermarket to buy nuts and fruit for lunch. Ahead of me in the checkout lane was a drunken young black man with cans of beer. His speech, already Southern-slow, was made slower by drink, and he seemed to be making private sounds rather than words. The cashier, a white girl, was correct, appearing to notice nothing, speaking the supermarket's formula of thanks after she had taken money and given change. The forecourt, when we went out to it, looked less attractive: supermarket carts, litter, some lounging blacks. It wasn't a place to have a car snack in.

Jim said, "We'll go to the farm."

We crossed the railroad track. It had once divided the white town from the black. There was still an Amtrak station; and, on what would have been the white side of town, the old hotel. Like an arrangement of properties in a simple film set: station, rails, the small hotel.

"Traveling salesmen would have stayed here," Jim said.

"What a life."

"Some of them would have liked it."

Beyond the rails, and in what was still the black town, there were shotgun houses, as narrow as mobile homes, and set close together side by side. Already the Wilson of the big houses seemed far away.

The ten miles to the farm went very quickly. There were old tobacco barns everywhere, three or four together sometimes in a field. And, before I was ready for the farm, we had turned off the road and parked in a clear space between an old two-story frame house and many galvanized-iron farm buildings. There were two oldish cars in the yard: part of the yard's metallic aspect. Across the road were fields connected with the farm.

I had been told by Jim about the family house and farm, about the family move to the nearby small town of Stantonsburg, about the sharecropping family and the black hired hands. But I hadn't taken it all in. I was confused by all the things I had been told; and when we stopped in the yard I didn't absolutely know where I was. I thought that there would have been Jim's family in the old frame house; I thought of the sharecropper as a kind of employee.

When Jim got out and went into the house, I opened my can of nuts and poured orange juice into a paper cup. Nuts in one hand, orange juice in another, with an elbow keeping the supermarket orange-juice carton upright beside me—that was how I was when a heavy pink-and-white man in his late forties, in dark-blue trousers and a check shirt, and with glasses, came out to the car, smiling.

He said, with a certain confidence, "I'm Dee Grimes."

I knew the name well. He was the man celebrated in the poem

"How to Fix a Pig." His speech, his life in tobacco, had been turned into poetry.

He waited for me to make a move out of the car—he had been told that I was coming. But I was encumbered. I couldn't open the car door just then, and couldn't find words to explain. He became abashed, said something I couldn't follow about "Mr. Jim," and took a step back.

I said at last that I had read the poem about him.

This pleased him. He said that someone else who had read the poem had wanted him to do some cooking.

And it was only after some time that I understood—what in fact I had been told before—that Dee Grimes, the sharecropper, lived in the old Applewhite family house—one of Jim's sacred places.

> It stands today, upstairs porch railed in
> Before narrow windows, their antique glass
> Upright and open toward the cleanly furrows.
> Their hand-blown panes show lines imperfectly,
> As if miraging heat since the Civil War
> Had imprinted ripples.

Between the main house and the kitchen, which was a separate building, there was a wide, covered passage, a "breezeway," with open screen walls. (There would have been no screens in the old days, Jim said.) It was there that we eventually sat, though Dee Grimes would have liked us to go inside to enjoy the air conditioning.

His talk—not easy for me to follow: he sat on the other side of a table and at some distance from it—was about the drought. There had been no rain and no rain. He had tried to dig a well, but he had found no water. Some of his talk was also about Dan, a neighbor. Dan had an irrigation system; Dan had watered three times this summer. Dan also had a mechanical tobacco-cropper; it had cost him $35,000 some years ago. Dan was that very day "putting in" tobacco, using the mechanical cropper to pick the ripe leaf, and then getting his people to "put in" the leaf in the curing barns.

He talked about the house; he had been told that I might be wanting to see that as well. He said that one of the most notable things about the house was that so much of it had been put together with wooden pegs, even the rafters of the breezeway. He took us inside. The house was more spacious than one would have thought from the outside. There was a solid feeling to the floor, no hollow sound in the wooden house, no resonance. The front rooms were of beautiful proportions, almost square, seventeen feet by eighteen, and high. When we were outside again, we considered the brick chimneys at the sides of the house, and the two railed porches facing the road and the fields across the road.

Jim said: "It's a lovely old house. A noble house, in its plain vernacular fashion. I especially like the tall windows. Although I have never actually looked out across fields from the upper porch, it seems to me a vantage point."

The bulk barns for curing tobacco were at the other side of the open yard. Three or four stood side by side and were like little mobile homes. The heat inside was electrically generated, and the air around the barns smelled of hot green leaf. When Dee opened the door of one barn the air that came out was very hot and the smell was a little cloying. The outer leaves on the racks, leaves already brown, were ragged. Dee said this was from the colder air striking them every time he opened the door to have a look; the leaves farther in would be better.

In the packhouse—where the cured tobacco was stored, after it had been "ordered" (given moisture, that is) to prevent the cured leaves from going brittle and shredding away—we saw the poor crop of the year. In the large space there were just a few bundles of golden leaf in sacking. There was a warm, rich smell here, and the floorboards had a sheen from the resin of years. Without being asked, Dee prepared a couple of old-fashioned "hands": taking six leaves or so, holding them stem up, and then tying them tightly at the stem (on the principle first of the cummerbund and then of the loincloth) with a good-quality leaf folded two or three times.

Dee's wife—she had been out somewhere, and had just got back—came into the packhouse. She stood silently with us, watching Dee tie the hands.

The old mule barn was still whole, another of the metallic structures of the yard: a reminder of another labor of the past. There were no mules to look after now, but there were reminders of mules that had been there: the top boards of the stalls had been gnawed away in a wavy pattern.

At the end of the yard was an amazing contraption. It was a tobacco-leaf harvester, with a canopy. There were low metal seats for four croppers, and the idea was that as the harvester was pulled along by a tractor the seated croppers would break off the ripe leaves from the tobacco stalks, without the strain of bending or walking on their knees. But, with the "handers" and others needed to transfer the picked leaf to the clamps, it took eleven people to keep the harvester going. Labor, labor in midsummer—and a little distance away, just the roof and upper walls visible, was the small one-story house where the black hired hands would have lived.

Farmhouse, barns old and new, the house for the hired help at the back—there was as great a simplicity about this layout as about the railroad station, the railway track, and the small hotel at Wilson. But a poet had looked long at this yard; and everything in it was shot through with radiance for him. As I saw when, just before we left, Dee and his wife began to talk about the danger of branches falling off the oaks near the farmhouse.

Dee and his wife wanted the trees to be lopped. Jim was concerned; he didn't want the trees to be lopped too hard, to lose their appearance. And for a while they talked, each side with its own interest.

We left at last to go on to the small town of Stantonsburg. This was where Jim Applewhite's grandfather had moved after he had left the family farmhouse. It was there that Jim had been born. It wasn't far away.

Jim said: "The Applewhites came from England, from Suffolk, and seem to have landed in Barbados. There are Applewhite or Applethwaite records in Barbados. The next records are in Virginia in the eighteenth century, and then in North Carolina. They were probably in Stantonsburg before the town was incorporated in 1818.

"I've been told that at one time the Applewhites owned the land on both sides of the road between Stantonsburg and Saratoga, the next small town."

There it was again, the recurring Southern story of great wealth in the past (the whole of the island of Trinidad, a third of an English county, a chest of gold that sent up a cloud of gold dust when it was emptied on to a floor). But there would have been some substance to this story: the Applewhites owned the Stantonsburg general store as well as a sawmill.

The town was like Wilson in miniature. There was even a railroad track dividing the black town from the white, the side-by-side black shotgun houses from the frame houses and the lawns.

We passed what had been the Applewhite store. It was a low white frame building with a shelter over the sidewalk. It now looked empty.

Jim said: "It held everything you'd need to house a crop or carry on your life. In the old days these stores were essentially a company store. In other words, the farmer would get everything they needed on credit, paying back when they sold their crop. And when my grandfather owned a lot of land the tenant farmers would get their things there and pay him back."

And it occurred to me just then, driving past the now empty store, that—without my having intended it—my journey was ending almost as it had begun. I had gone to the town of Bowen at Easter with Howard and seen his home district from the other side of the tracks, as it were. (I had such a clear memory still of the oddity I had felt on the Sunday morning when, as we were walking to the black church, three white men had stopped in a car to ask the way to the country club.) This town was like Bowen in its size and appearance; and the Applewhites (as I was to learn, but not from Jim) owned slaves, at one time forty. (And how odd it was that, as soon as you began to live with the idea of slaves, you developed this other way of reckoning wealth—in slaves.)

Hetty, the daughter of a black sharecropper, had taken me to see Mr. Bowen, to pay my respects. She had then taken me to the black cemetery, where her father was buried. She had shown me the farmhouse, now in ruin, with small trees and vines growing right up against it, where her father had lived as a sharecropper. She had her special way of looking: her chant, as we had driven through the countryside, had been, "Black people, black people, white people, black people. All this side white people, all that side black people." She had said, but quite late, unwilling to go into the gloom of the past, that tobacco (which she had grown both with her father and her husband) had made her cry.

At Bowen in the spring the flowers in the roadside grass had been purple. Now, in Stantonsburg, almost at the end of the summer, the flowers were yellow, little all-yellow daisies. And now, with Jim Applewhite, I was considering another kind of past: a past where the child had seen completeness, even in the stock—for tenants—of his grandfather's general store: mule collars, tobacco twine, ten-penny nails ("Probably they were ten for a penny"), bonnets, shoes for children.

"I did feel there was a kind of complete world contained there. Partly because the houses here were built without architects, without trained builders, and I grew to feel that the capability of building those houses was contained in those objects in the store."

The Applewhite house was in a residential street with two or three churches. Outside the Baptist church some black men and a white man were working. The street was full of children, many of them black, and for some reason they all had large ice-cream cones.

Old Mr. Applewhite was in the sitting room watching football on a big television set. He was eighty, and a little proud of his age. He was much shorter than his son, and stouter, his physique suggesting a man who had been very strong. He explained about the children and the ice cream. A local shop was celebrating its seventy-fifth anniversary and selling ice creams for 5¢—which was what the shop had charged for an ice cream in 1912.

On the table in the dining room was food for our visit. And the old man had got out a magazine for me, *The Flue Cured Tobacco Farmer*, together with a booklet for tobacco farmers, *How to Grow It Ripe*.

Jim ate. I talked to his father.

He said, "Did my tenant show you some good stuff? This has been the sorriest tobacco crop for thirty-five years. There's been no rain for thirteen weeks."

He told me that the farm was between 150 and 175 years old, and he showed me a framed certificate that said that the farmhouse was on the Register of Historical Places. He thought that Dee should have persevered with his well and gone down a further twenty feet; someone he knew had found water at 150 feet.

Then he grew philosophical, religious. "We can't complain. The farm has done very well, up until this year. If you do right by your fellow man it will be all right. My father was in the best financial shape of anybody around. And he did like kind of what Social Security does now. He was blessed."

Later, in a back room, with a view through a screen door of the shaded lawn and the neighboring house, Jim and I sat and talked and I took down his words.

He had from the start spoken as though he had cut himself off from his past, made a far journey. But that past was here still, a couple of hours away from Durham—or as much of the past as a man of fifty-two might reasonably expect still to find. But a journey had been made; there had been a break.

"I was put to bed when I was six with what was then said to be rheumatic fever. My mother read me the whole of *Huckleberry Finn*. I stayed in bed for a year. I was protected more than my fellow students for a few years. It set me apart. Something like that always happens to the person who is going to be a writer.

"I think I'm always conscious of the fact that I'm not truly of the world I've been showing you. I've not worked in tobacco. Dee Grimes is truly of that world. A real tobacco man, if you want to be colloquial. Educated in the school of hard knocks, educated by experience. I feel a kind of kinship and a kind of separation when I am with him."

"Separation?"

"Presumably it began with that separation when I was a child, when I was set apart from those who were unselfconsciously playing their part in this eastern–North Carolina world, which is a world of action, not of thinking."

Separation, and kinship. The Applewhite name was no longer in the windows of the store. But for Jim the letters on the glass— they had been in gold, and set in an arc—still existed, "in a ghostly way."

"I do remember occasions of visiting back during my early years of college and once again experiencing what I have now almost forgotten —and that is a sensation of being so utterly at home in, and a part of, a place, that one feels somehow coextensive with the place.

"On the other hand, there is a sense of separateness in being in part of myself an observing stranger in my own native land. To the extent that at times I was fascinated by the idea of the pre-existence of the soul. Fascinated especially by the original Edgar Rice Burroughs book, *Tarzan of the Apes,* the first and best of the Tarzan books. Because in that book the Tarzan-to-be was landed in the jungle by the crash of his parents' plane. There was something in that idea—of a person from another culture being deposited from the sky in a tropical environment —that was fascinating to me."

It was extraordinary. Not only (as had happened more than once) did I find Jim Applewhite talking for me, expressing things I had felt as a child and an adolescent in Trinidad. He was also—though he was from the other side of the tracks—talking like Howard, Hetty's son. In New York, at the airport, Howard had said, of the place that was his home, "I hated the place when I was young, for the continuity." I had puzzled over that word "continuity." It had meant old things, old buildings (like tobacco barns and farmhouses) still standing, keeping a place physically dull. It had also meant, as came out later, old ways persisting. When we had returned to New York after our Southern weekend, Howard had said, "I'm different. I felt different at the high school. It's what you think and what you feel that makes you different. I always felt different. Which leads me to believe I was born in the wrong town. Like many people."

Jim Applewhite said: "My feeling of duality at that time was being physically in the world I identified with, but which on the other hand completely left out a whole other side of my psyche or my soul. There was still a cultural transmission here—from something quite other— through the churches, the hymns, the words and the music, the poetry of the Psalms in the King James Bible, and through books. My uncle would stay with us in the summer. He was a bachelor. He was probably my first literary influence. When I was six years old he told me stories which I later realized were from the *Odyssey*.

"There was a duality of worlds as a child and a young man that is probably not at all unique for a person of artistic inclinations, but which was given an exceptional tension by the intensity with which so many in this small-town world defied or opposed those values which were foreign to it—those cultural values that were transmitted from afar. There is a sense of self-subsistence about the South—that it is itself, knows itself, and needs nothing else. Because of this sense of beleaguered self-sufficiency it can be extremely pigheaded. It can cherish ignorance. It can cherish the unreasonable, the unreasoning.

"And I was hungry to have things explained. I remember looking up at the constellations and not knowing the names of the constellations. Or not knowing the names of trees. I have my telescope now, which I didn't have then.

"Finally, one wanted consciousness, the right to be aware, or to name in language, in harmonious language, or in music—to name things, or else simply to name. Art is a sort of divine uselessness. That's one of the reasons I'm also attracted to tobacco. It's not practical. It's not for any use that's good for anything."

WE HAD heard much, from Dee Grimes and from Jim Applewhite's father, of Dan the neighbor, the lucky man with the irrigation system and the mechanical harvester, who was that day "putting in" tobacco. And when we left Stantonsburg we went to see Dan.

He was a friendly, well-exercised middle-aged man with glasses, in pale-brown clothes and with a dark-brown baseball cap ("Pride in Tobacco")—through he himself didn't smoke. His hands were black with grease and also with tobacco tar, from the leaf he was "putting in"— the green-leaf tobacco tar I had first heard about from Howard.

His harvester—with a black man at the controls—was at work, straddling many rows. It was fascinating to watch this large, awkward-looking, but delicate machine, which had done away with the brute labor of tobacco-cropping. The wheels of the harvester, and the driver's seat, moved along furrows; on either side two long rubber rollers with a little space between them caught the tobacco stalks and rolled off the leaves up to a certain height. The rolled-off leaves fell into bins and were taken up fast-moving bands to the leaf basket. The tobacco stalks with the uncropped upper leaves snapped back into their upright position; and at the end only an occasional yellow-green leaf remained on the ground to show that the harvester had just passed.

In the shed outside Dan's bulk barns four black people, two men and two women (casual workers, to judge by their goodish clothes: no overalls), unpacked the leaves, fixed them into metal clamps, and slid the clamps along the racks in the bulk barns. To "put in" in a bulk barn was easier than in the tall old barns, where a man had to climb on a ladder to hang the sticks on the upper racks. Some years ago, Jim said, Dee Grimes had fallen off a top rack and fractured his hand. The racked leaves in the bulk barns looked like gigantic green salads.

It was easier with the bulk barns. But some of the ritual of the old days that the boy had studied on the Applewhite farm had also gone— the many black women looping tobacco leaves on sticks, the heated barns tended all night, the sweet corn roasting in coals, the pig being barbecued.

The field with the old Applewhite family graveyard no longer belonged to the family. But there is always a right of way to a graveyard, and a grass track led to it from the road. It was a small enclosure, about thirty feet by twenty. The iron rails were overgrown with weeds and orange trumpet vines. The oldest stone, very nearly indecipherable, had been put up in 1849. Small stones marked children's graves. There were two wooden markers.

Jim said, "Probably heart of pine. What they call 'fat lightwood.' Possibly a slave. Sometimes slaves were buried with wooden markers."

These markers looked scorched. I thought it might have been from age, but Jim said there might have been a fire in the field. The softer wood had worn away around the ridges of the harder grain.

Across the grass track from the graveyard there was a field of tobacco, the veined, resilient, umbrellalike leaves drooping a little after the weeks of drought. These small fields and rusting old tobacco barns —picturesque when I had first seen them—spoke now of great, detailed labor. And in the graveyard in the center of the field it was easy to imagine how confining it would have been in the old days, before roads and motorcars and electricity, and how the country town of Wilson, ten miles away, made a day's journey.

> . . . Closed in by miles
> Which sandy roads, pine barrens, swamps, made
> A limit to curiosity. The stars' light,
> The King James Bible and Wesley's hymns,
> Traveled equivalent distances, unquestioned.

But now there was an easy road to Durham.

OUT OF his intense contemplation of the physical world of his childhood—an act that made me feel close to him, though his world had not been at all like mine—and out of his separation from that first world of his, Jim Applewhite had gone beyond the religious faith of his father and grandfather and arrived at a feeling for "the sanctity of the smallest gestures."

It was an imaginative, poetic resolution, quite different in its calm, its positiveness, and its import from Barry McCarty's feeling, as a politician and a Church of Christ minister, for the beauty of the simple life—which, with him, seemed also linked to the idea of a world threatening to get out of control.

Such different men; yet they had certain important things in common. They had been made by the same history. And it was that sense of a special past, the past as a wound, that I missed almost as soon as I went north to Virginia, to Charlottesville.

There was history there in quantity—Jefferson, Monticello, the University of Virginia. But that was history as celebration, the history of the resort, the history that was causing the subdivisions (or housing developments) to multiply in Virginia, and was even threatening the fox hunt (where already the hounds were trained to hunt foxes and foxes alone in special rented fox-compounds with deep-buried fences; and where the huntsman knew where all the foxes were in his "country" and inoculated all the cubs against rabies).

I had been living until then—and this perhaps had made the people of the South or Southeast so congenial to me—with people coming to terms with a more desperate kind of New World history, and a poorer land reflecting this history—the history that, in his poem "Southern Voices," Jim Applewhite writes of as *"defeat,"* putting the word in italics, the defeat that he hears in Southern speech:

> This colorless tone, like flour
> Patted onto the cheeks, is poor-white powder
> To disguise the minstrel syllables lower
> In our register, from a brownface river.

picador.com

blog
videos
interviews
extracts